The Strange Death

of

Moral Britain

The
Strange Death
of
Moral Britain

Christie Davies

Transaction Publishers
New Brunswick (U.S.A.) and London (U.K.)

Library of Congress Catalog Number: 2003067189
ISBN: 0-7658-0223-6
Printed in the United States of America

Library of Congress Cataloging-in-Publication Data

Davies, Christie.
　The strange death of moral Britain / Christie Davies.
　　　p. cm.
　Includes bibliographical references and index.
　ISBN: 0-7658-0223-6 (cloth : alk. paper)
　　1. Great Britain—Moral conditions.　2. Great Britain—Social conditions–1945-　I. Title.

HN400.M6D375 2004
306'.0941—dc22　　　　　　　　　　　　　　　　　2003067189

For Janetta and in memory of my father Christy Davies

Contents

Acknowledgements

A book such as this, drawing on a great variety of sources and employing a number of linked themes, of necessity requires the use of many libraries and archives and discussions with and advice from numerous colleagues. I would like to thank the staff of the libraries at Lambeth Palace and those of the special collections at the University of Birmingham for granting me access to the private papers of a number of leading churchmen, and similarly the staff of the Lord's Day Observance Society. I must also thank the librarians and staff of the British Library, the National Police Library at Bramshill, the Public Record Office, and the libraries of the University of Cambridge , the London School of Economics, and the League of Nations in Geneva. I owe a particular debt to the library of the University of Reading and especially to its inter-library loan staff. Many colleagues have provided helpful advice, particularly with regard to sources, and I would like to thank Digby Anderson, Paul Badham, Chris Blundell, Callum Brown, Philip Davies, Bill Durodie, Frank Furedi, Sandy Ghandhi, David Green, Simon Green, Arnold Harvey, Ian Hindmarch, Brad Hooker, Steve Hunt, Ellie Lee, John Marks, David Martin, George Moyser, Mark Neal, Ulrich Nembach, John O'Sullivan, David Oderberg, Ludek Rychetník, Eugene Trivizas, David Warburton, Martin Wiener, Bryan Wilson, and Roy Wolfe for their comments and suggestions. Any errors and misinterpretations are mine alone. Much of the manuscript of *The Strange Death of Moral Britain*, as with my previous work, was first entered into the word processor by Helen Davis, on whose speed, accuracy, and good nature I have once again depended. I owe a further debt to my colleague Dawn Clarke for her help with the checking and amending of the manuscript that emerged.This volume is the product of many years of research, thinking, and planning, but its publication is due to the consistent encouragement I have received from Irving Louis Horowitz. He made it possible. I would like to thank him and his many colleagues at Transaction, particularly Mary Curtis, president, and Anne Schneider, editor, for their kindness as well as hard work in seeing it through to publication.Janetta as always provided the support that enabled me to complete the work and it is to her that the book is dedicated.

Introduction

The Strange Death of Moral Britain is a story about surprises, about radical changes in selected moral aspects of Britain during the course of the twentieth century, which would not have been envisaged by most of the people living in that country at the beginning of that century. It is also likely that if these changes had been suggested to them at the time they would have viewed them with outrage and indignation. This volume is about the strange death of *their* moral Britain, a world with a low and declining incidence of crime and illegitimacy and falling drug and alcohol abuse in which respectability ruled, a world in which the value of duty, religion, and patriotism was taken for granted, even though their requirements might be evaded. It was a world that assumed that individuals were autonomous moral agents responsible for their own behavior, that the innocent ought to be protected, the virtuous rewarded, and the guilty punished. That moral world is now dead, and it is the task of this book to explain how and, rather more tentatively, why it died.

It is up to the individual reader in our much more morally fragmented twenty-first century to decide on balance how much was lost, or indeed gained, by its death. The British people at the beginning of the twentieth century lived in a world of shared virtues, even though they were strongly divided over politics, and they would have been shocked at the thought of the death of their moral Britain. Those looking backwards from the twenty-first century will be in disagreement, though most will have mixed feelings, seeing both losses and gains and also appreciating the curious ways in which particular losses and particular gains may well be inexorably tied together. On any particular issue the reader may well be able to discern my own evaluations or, indeed, ambivalence. I have not sought to banish these or hide them out of sight but I have tried to prevent them from damaging my analysis and, indeed, I have often changed my mind as a result of carrying out the work on which this book is based. What remains is neither a nostalgic account of moral Britain nor a rejection of it, and I am using the phrase "moral Britain" neither to shout "hurrah," nor ironically. No doubt some will feel that I should have used the contested word "moral" in some other way, but the way it is used here, though contestable, is both reasonable and consistent and I make no apology for employing it.

Were imaginary beings from 1900 suddenly able to look forward and observe the material progress evident in twenty-first-century Britain they would be surprised *only* by the scale and the detail of the changes that have taken place, not by the fact of the changes themselves. The British people are far more prosperous than they were in 1900 and live longer than they did then, but in 1900 they were more prosperous and longer living than they had been in 1850; thus, they were confident that these improvements would continue. Likewise the people of 1900 already had experienced rapid scientific and technical change and knew that further change was both possible and likely. They knew with certainty—not absolute certainty, but as good a certainty as anyone is ever going to get—that their scientific knowledge and technical capacities were vastly improved over those of 1850 and would *not* have been surprised at further change in the same direction. It is impossible to predict any particular scientific discovery or new invention and for this reason futile to attempt to predict future changes over more than a very short period of time. However, we can be certain, and long have been certain, that there will be further major advances. This is the key, indeed the only, defining characteristic of modernity, the one sense in which we know today is more "modern" than yesterday (Davies 1999). Where our ability to understand and manipulate the material world is concerned, there is no late modernity and no post-modernity for there is nothing to be "post" to and late implies an approaching terminus for which there is no evidence. Contemporary Britain is more "modern" in its scientific knowledge and techniques than the Britain with which the twentieth century began, but both times are equally modern in that people knew at either time and throughout the intervening period that further unknown and unknowable changes were inevitable. Those who have experienced scientific and technical progress over a long period of time are unlikely to be greatly shocked when it continues.

It is doubtful, though, whether anyone other than a few prophetic figures or speculative minds see morality in this same way. I will argue in this study that the origin of one of the changes described here as the death of moral Britain, namely the death of a moralist Britain based on an image of autonomous individuals making moral choices and receiving their desserts, is discernible in the last years of the nineteenth century and the early years of the twentieth and that this period constitutes a turning point. Those whose business it was to think about the changes taking place within the moral order were often aware that such a point had been reached, but even they would not have foreseen the death of moral Britain in the last half of the twentieth century. Most people expect future social changes to be a projection forward of changes that have already happened. They expect tomorrow to be a continuation of what they have experienced since yesterday. In 1900, crime, illegitimacy, and drug and alcohol abuse had been falling, so why should they not continue to fall in a world where improving social conditions were conducive to yet further increments of respectability? Those who could look back to the birth of respectable Britain and lived in its high maturity were unlikely to envisage its death. As we shall see in detail in chapter 1 the people of 1900, or indeed 1925 or 1955, were living at the bottom of a U-curve of deviant behavior and it is this reversal of what must have seemed to be an established and beneficial social trend that would have made the strange death of moral Britain both unpredictable and morally shocking to our imaginary traveler in time. From the standpoint of the twenty-first century it also necessitates taking a longer view of that aspect of the death of *moral* Britain that I have called the strange death of *respectable* Britain. It is impossible to understand the death of respectable Britain in the last half of the twentieth century without considering the experience of, the context of, and the forces that shaped the creation of respectable Britain in the last half of the nineteenth century and allowed its continued, if uneasy, strength into the first half of the twentieth. It is to be hoped that the patterns observed will be of value to scholars in other Western countries with a history similar to Britain, but it is beyond the scope of this book to extend the detailed account of respectable Britain's rise and fall to other countries. The strength of the argument depends rather on the weight of the highly diverse forms of evidence assembled for Britain itself; indeed, this is the first time that long-range patterns of crime, illegitimacy, drug and alcohol abuse, and the evolution of religious and economic institutions over a long period of time in Britain have been considered in conjunction with one another.

As we shall see in chapter 2, the strange death of moralist Britain is linked to the strange death of respectable Britain, but it should be stressed that the changes occur at quite different levels in that society. The account given here of respectable Britain concerns changes in the behavior of the great mass of the population; it is the story of the birth and death not of a planned but of a spontaneous moral order in which the state was only peripherally involved. The analysis of the death of moralist Britain concerns rather the way in which the members of the British legislature changed the laws relating to abortion, capital punishment, divorce, and male homosexual behavior so as to replace the moralist principle that rewards and punishments should be allocated according to individual dessert with the causalist principle that the purpose of legislation is to minimize harm in the aggregate regardless of moral status. The nature of causalism will be made clear in chapter 2; however, since it is a word I have invented (Davies 1980: 13-14), it is necessary to explain at this earlier stage exactly what I mean by it. The causalists are clearly consequentialists and, indeed, utilitarians, but of a distinctive kind. First, they are only concerned with the minimizing of pain, harm, and suffering and not with the promotion of happiness or pleasure. They seem to assume that we all have a common and equal capacity for suffering, whereas each individual wishes to be happy in his or her own way since tastes vary. Second, causalists are concerned only with the short-term, with the immediate effects of legislation in removing a particular group of individuals from harm or the threat of harm and not with the long-term or indirect consequences of such a measure. Third (which to some extent follows from the second point), causalists place greater importance on the visible harm experienced by particular persons than on that inflicted on mere "statistical" persons. In a sense, the contrast between the virtuous and the wicked individual has been replaced by a distinction between the known and unknown individual. Whereas the moralists assume that individuals are autonomous persons making free choices, the causalist sees their actions, to a substantial extent, as "caused" by external pressures. Causalism is not a coherent, consistent, and systematic framework for making moral decisions. It contains contradictions and it is not the explicit philosophical position of a particular group. Causalism, as the term is used here, is an ideal type constructed from empirical observations of the nature of the moral arguments used by those seeking changes in the law in the last half of the twentieth century. It is, however, one that can be usefully applied to other periods. Causalism is important not only because it replaced moralism, but because it was invoked in Britain under circumstances where in other countries arguments about rights might have been employed. Arguments based on, say, a right to privacy or to equal justice were noticeably absent from moral debates in Britain. In the later decades of the twentieth century, laws justified in terms of rights were imposed on Britain (and on Ireland) from the outside by the European Court of Human Rights and these laws represent another aspect of the strange death of moral Britain, the loss of power by the British people and their elected representatives to make independent decisions about law and morality that would reflect their own moral priorities and perceptions.

Prior to this time, the British constitutional doctrine of parliamentary supremacy had not been challenged and the dominance of causalist arguments in Britain was a reflection of where power lay, for such arguments are appropriate to a body that spends most of its time deliberating the relationships between large, impersonal institutions. Yet causalism was also a distinctly British way of approaching moral questions; it was part of a tradition that avoided the fiction of essential rights that was so central to the making of other countries' constitutions. Ironically, parliamentary supremacy was established by the British Bill of Rights of 1688, a document more concerned with protecting Parliament from the acts of a would-be oppressive monarch than protecting the individual from the power of Parliament; the role of the courts was only to ensure that individual cases were considered fairly and independently of outside interference and not to obstruct legislation approved by the British Parliament.[1]

The British Parliament consisted of two houses: the House of Commons, which for most of the period considered here, was elected by universal suffrage; and the House of Lords, a body consisting of hereditary peers and later, life peers, the Anglican Archbishops of Canterbury and York, together with the bishops either of certain important dioceses or of greatest seniority, and the senior judges, the Law Lords. The latter also acted in a judicial capacity as the highest court in England, the House of Lords. The party that won an election and held a majority of the seats in the House of Commons would form a government. As a result of two twentieth-century constitutional changes such a government could enact its legislation, even if a majority of the members of the House of Lords voted against it. The moral questions discussed in this volume were, however, by convention placed outside party and electoral politics and decided by a free vote of individual Members of Parliament (MPs) in the House of Commons and members of the House of Lords. Governments rarely intervened, except that they might be helpful or unhelpful in the way they allocated parliamentary time to reformers faced with filibustering opposition, and the parties did not instruct their MPs or individual adherents in the House of Lords on how to vote.

The strange death of moralist Britain, like that of respectable Britain, will be discussed in terms of a sequence of events and trends within Britain itself. The discussion of the fall of moralist Britain in chapter 2 relates mainly to the last half of the twentieth century, although there is a detailed discussion of the earlier history of the law relating to capital punishment and abortion in chapters 3 and 5. It should be stressed, however, that the decline of moralism did not suddenly begin in the middle of the twentieth century, but was already apparent in the last years of the nineteenth century. The death of respectable Britain could not have been predicted at the beginning of the twentieth century because it was a reversal of previous trends; by contrast, the death of moralist Britain and the victory of causalism in the last half of the twentieth century can be seen as a marked acceleration of what had gone before. As with the death of respectable Britain there are reasonably distinct turning points in the death of moralist Britain, but they are turning points of a different kind, points at which the pace of change quickens rather than reverses direction. In each case it is reasonable to treat these broad changes as self-contained aspects of British society that make sense in their own terms.

However, in the case of laws penalizing male homosexual behavior and constraining homosexuals generally, an additional and stronger mode of argument has been employed, that of comparison with other societies as well as with earlier times. The reason for doing so is that the strongly negative view taken of male homosexuals and their activities, not only in the first half of twentieth-century Britain but for centuries before, is a puzzle, not only because this antipathy has been decisively challenged in the last decades of the twentieth century but also because it has not necessarily characterized other societies at other times. It is fairly easy to see why the population as a whole should fear murder or burglary or drunken violence, or disapprove of fatherlessness and want action taken against their perpetrators, but it can hardly be said that the activities of a tiny sexual minority, constituting 1 to 2 percent of the population (Wellings et al. 1994), impinged on, let alone threatened, the heterosexual majority. Why should such severe penalties ever have been inflicted on those found guilty of homosexual acts? Why did the framers of the law bother to jail and even execute sodomites, or, come to that, lonely rustics having congress with sheep? Gay readers and indeed shepherds may find this linkage offensive, but they should now read on eagerly to find out why it is made; they will discover that it is one derived from the mind set of their persecutors and that it has an important explanatory value. No one gained any material benefit from the exercise of such persecution and from a utilitarian point of view it is preposterous. Even if the answer lies (as it does) in the religious traditions of Britain as a Christian country, it still needs to be explained how and why such prohibitions were part of those traditions and also why they were sustained when other forms of behavior forbidden by scripture such as usury were tolerated or, at the very least, the prohibition was not enforced by law; incest was not a criminal offense in England and Wales until 1908. The moral condemnation of homosexuality had nothing to do with family life or with the workings of a capitalist market economy; it was related to the defense of the boundaries and identity of the nation, which, in turn, were closely tied to Christian tradition. When in the course of an increasingly secular twentieth century the fervent sense of a special and particular British and Christian identity faded, so, too, did the prohibitions of and prejudice against homosexual behavior.

The various religious denominations were probably in agreement on the abominableness of homosexuality for there is little evidence of marked disagreement either within or between them during the nineteenth or the first half of the twentieth centuries. For the Church of Scotland and also the Nonconformist Protestants, the indisputable condemnation of homosexual practices in the Scriptures (which was not questioned at that time) would have been sufficient; this condemnation would have been reinforced by the hierarchical nature of the Church of England and the Roman Catholic Church. All-male hierarchies, notably those that characterized these churches and, indeed, the armed forces, particularly when accompanied by celibacy or by an incidental or even temporary absence of women, tend to be particularly hostile to male homosexual activities. Such activities are seen as a threat to their central structures and as the very essence of the disorder against which they define their own orderliness. Homosexual ties are seen as a threat to the boundaries of the organization and its structure of ranks and to the cohesion of the smaller groups of closely cooperating men on whom it depends. There is no evidence that hostility to homosexuality is stronger in those societies that place the greatest reliance on family or kinship, but it is clear that when all-male hierarchies become more tightly organized and disciplined from the center, it leads to an enhanced persecution of homosexuals. Paradoxically, such institutions are very likely to contain a greater proportion of male homosexuals in their ranks than there are in the general population and just as important is the possibility that prolonged separation from women may tempt some men to commit homosexual acts as a temporary substitute. This fuels the suspicion and hostility of the leadership even further. In Britain, it was the senior members of the Church of England and of the armed forces who led the opposition to any liberalization of the laws regarding homosexual behavior. In the late twentieth century, the Church of England was badly divided on and, indeed, obsessed with the question of homosexuality, and the armed services remained resolutely hostile. Given that these institutions were the key bearers of English identity it reinforces the point that it was the declining power and importance of that identity that led to the diminishing hostility toward homosexuality within the society. The same link between nation, church, and identity, on the one hand, and moral disapproval of homosexual behavior to the point of wanting to punish it by law can be seen in the case of Ireland, where the relevant laws were struck down from the outside by the European Court of Human Rights. Moral Britain jumped to its own death; moral Ireland was pushed.

Attitudes towards "hierarchy" were a key source of political division within the United Kingdom in the nineteenth and twentieth centuries. The divisions between the Conservatives, the party of the English hierarchies, the anti-Conservatives, who opposed hierarchies, and the Irish persisted throughout the entire period; when other political disputes based on social class or the management of the economy became important they were superimposed on this older set of categories. These older, almost primordial, divisions were the basis of strong disagreements about capital punishment and about abortion that were to be found in Britain from the 1920s to the 1980s. These were not disagreements that could be related in any simple sense to the clashes about economic governance and welfare matters that came to lie at the center of British electoral politics in the twentieth century, and by convention they were discussed and resolved outside the framework of party politics.

As with the case of homosexuality and divorce, these "moral issues" were decided on a free vote by the individual members of the two Houses of Parliament. Nonetheless, it is clear that the supporters of capital punishment within the legislature (but by no means among the electorate) were drawn from the Conservatives and the opponents from the anti-Conservatives, a major rift in British politics. The Conservatives were the party of hierarchy, the party of the armed forces and the British Empire and of the established Church of England. Although England had an established church it also had other influential Protestant denominations, the Presbyterians, Methodists, Baptists and Congregationalists, the Free churches who, to a greater or lesser extent, aligned themselves in opposition to the established church and in opposition to the official hierarchies. In Wales, they were also the bearers of a distinctive Welsh identity that set Wales apart from England and in 1922 they succeeded in getting the Church of England disestablished in Wales, a mark of their predominance in the principality. By the end of the nineteenth century the Nonconformists were a crucial force within the Liberal Party, the key anti-Conservative party, the party opposed to hierarchy and establishment. It was a clash that saved Britain from the anti-clericalism of many continental countries and indeed invigorated the people's adherence to religion because the key political conflict lay between an established hierarchical church and the excluded anti-hierarchical Christian denominations and not between a Christian establishment and the bitterly alienated non-believers. At the beginning of the twentieth century, denominational loyalty or affiliation was probably the best predictor of how an individual would vote. When the Labour Party appeared as the representative of the unionized workers in the early twentieth century, it attached itself to the anti-hierarchical wing of British politics. Many of its early leaders and members were Protestant Nonconformists. There was continuity between Labour and its Liberal predecessor. Both were the parties of those who stood outside the traditional hierarchies and were opposed to them, the parties of those who were outsiders because of their class, their religion, or their possession of a peripheral, regional or, in the case of Wales and Scotland,[2] national identity. Capital punishment became one of the issues that divided Conservatives from Labour and Liberal politicians and Anglicans from Nonconformists. It is for this reason that the abolition of capital punishment has been given a chapter of its own, for it represents the strange death of the moral outlook of hierarchical and Conservative Britain, a particular facet of moral Britain. Whereas the death of respectable Britain and of moralist Britain can be treated without great difficulty as part of a set of general processes that affected the entire society, in the case of the abolition of capital punishment we can also see the working out of a very old and deeply rooted political conflict.

The original enacting of England's laws against abortion had nothing to do with Roman Catholicism, but in the twentieth century opposition to their relaxation was a Roman Catholic issue and it is, perhaps, significant that the liberal reforms of 1967 were never extended to Northern Ireland where there is a large Roman Catholic minority. In mainland Britain itself, perhaps 10 percent of the population is Roman Catholic, most of whom are descendants of Irish immigrants who had come to Britain when Ireland was part of the United Kingdom or after the Irish Free State (later the Republic of Ireland) seceded in 1922. It is likely that if the whole of Ireland had remained within the United Kingdom it would have been impossible to reform the law relating to abortion in 1967. The separation of the two countries, however, created two quite different sets of Roman Catholic politics of abortion, which make sense, however, only if studied together. Within Britain the substantial Roman Catholic minority of Irish descent occupied a curious position. Its members were ethnic outsiders whose ancestors had often been in conflict with the British state. They belonged to a church that was far more fiercely hierarchical than the Episcopal Church of England, yet it was also an alien church, the church against which the essentially Protestant British nation had defined itself and the church at the center of an Irish national identity defined in opposition to that of Britain. Furthermore, the Irish in Britain lived for many generations in relatively enclosed working-class, immigrant enclaves, notably in Lancashire in England and in and around Glasgow in Scotland. Almost by definition they could not support the Conservative and Unionist Party of hierarchical Britain and so found themselves supporting first the Liberal Party that favored Irish Home Rule and later the Labour Party that represented their class interests. Yet they were in a paradoxical position, being members of the Roman Catholic Church, an institution dominated by a rigidly centralized, all-male celibate hierarchy and yet also supporters of political parties whose anti-hierarchical stance was linked to the traditions of the more individualistic forms of Protestantism. It involved them in a bitter conflict over abortion, which they lost decisively and which led to the strange death of Roman Catholic Labourism, which had been an important, if in some respects aberrant, section of moral Britain. At the time when their cousins in Britain were going down to defeat over abortion, in Ireland itself where national and religious identity were strong and fused together, the law on abortion was strengthened and built into the very constitution of the Republic of Ireland. Roman Catholic moral Britain is dead, but moral Ireland is, for the time being, alive, though not altogether well.

Since 1922, Ireland, first as the Irish Free State, and later the Irish Republic, has been an independent country, although it retains the English laws it inherited from the time when it was attached to Britain. The strange impending death of moral Ireland is both an adjunct to and an extension of the strange death of moral Britain and this is particularly true of the province of Northern Ireland or Ulster, which remains part of the United Kingdom. Yet it is also a contrasting story of a different country with a different religion, one closely tied to its separate national identity and with a different moral fate.

Behind the strange death of moral Britain lies the strange death of Christian Britain. Even in 1900 the leaders of Christian Britain feared that such a decline might take place. At that time, the churches had survived the secularization of many aspects of British society; in-

deed, they had flourished as agencies specializing in moral education and exhortation, and the energies of the religiously committed
had been enthusiastically employed in this work. Likewise they derived strength from their associations with national and indeed ethnic and political identities. Yet the leaders of Christian Britain were
already aware that their aspiration to evangelize the entire nation
was not going to be fulfilled, that they were no longer growing in
size and influence, and that decline was possible. Nonetheless, they
did not see and could not have foreseen how rapid the churches'
decline would be in the last half of the twentieth century, a decline
described in detail in chapter 1. Britain in the twenty-first century is
a thoroughly secular society in marked contrast to what it had been
a hundred years earlier.

The death of religion, the decay of commitment to a nation and its
traditions, and the breakdown of families mean the removal of the
most important foci of particular loyalties that in the past sustained
such moral traits as duty, service, sacrifice, loyalty, and fortitude.
What is left is not an amoral or an immoral society but one that can
make only limited moral demands on its members.

Notes

1.   "The Bill of Rights 1688, an act declaring the Rights and Liberties of the Subject and
      Settling the Succession of the Crowne." Also the Declaration of Rights 1689.
2.   It is perhaps at this point worth defining the many units that make up the United
      Kingdom that have been and will be discussed. The principality of Wales was
      incorporated into England by a series of Acts of Union, 1536-1543. After that time,
      Wales shared a common legal and political system with England and in the late
      nineteenth and twentieth centuries Welsh statistical data were collected on the same
      basis as in England, yet its culture, religion, and traditions differ. At this time, Wales
      was overwhelmingly Nonconformist in religion and predominantly Liberal and
      later Labour in its politics. For this reason Wales rather than some other less distinc-
      tive region has often been used to check whether generalizations about, say, trends
      in crime apply throughout Britain as well as in aggregate. For convenience, England
      and Wales taken together are often described as Britain and their people as British,
      there being no other convenient designation for the two occupants of the former
      Roman Britain. To use any other term would have been to call the Welsh "English,"
      which would not have pleased them. The Kingdom of Scotland has received here
      less attention than it deserves partly because both before and after the Act of Union
      between the two kingdoms of England and Scotland in 1707 it had and has a
      separate and distinctive legal system radically different from the English system that
      operates in England, Wales, and Ireland, and many commonwealth countries. In
      addition, the ways of gathering statistical data by the Scottish office have differed
      from those in England and Wales. Nonetheless, I must apologize to Scottish readers
      for not having a separate chapter dedicated to the strange death of moral Scotland,

particularly in light of that country's distinctively different Protestant history, the impact of which on everyday life and morality I have discussed elsewhere (Davies 2002: 17-49). Most of the legislative changes that will be discussed were debated in the British Parliament in Westminster by MPs elected by the English, Scots, and Welsh alike. There was at that time no political devolution, no Scottish Parliament, no Welsh Assembly. Nonetheless, it should be possible to tease out the differences resulting from Scotland's distinctive religious culture and legal system and to make comparisons with England and Wales, and I hope other scholars will be able to do so.

1

The Strange Death of Respectable Britain

During the last half of the twentieth century, the British people, who had long been remarkable for their honesty, peaceableness, propriety, and sobriety, ceased to be distinguished by these qualities. Britain at the beginning of the twenty-first century is characterized by levels of dishonesty, violence, illegitimacy, and drug and alcohol abuse that would truly shock an imaginary time-traveler projected forward from 1910 or 1925 or even 1955. The time-travelers would be shocked not only at the magnitude of the changes, changes that they would certainly deplore, but at finding such changes in a society that enjoyed a far higher standard of living and lower levels of deprivation than they had ever known.

The Collapse of Respectable Britain

At the end of the twentieth century, in 1999-2000, over 5 million crimes were recorded by police in England and Wales as compared with only 78,000 in 1900. The number of crimes recorded at the end of the century was more than sixty times greater than at its beginning. The century began with less than three recorded crimes for every 1,000 persons over the age of ten and ended with over eighty (Hood and Roddam 2000: 680; *Criminal Statistics* 2000). Most of the increase took place from about 1957 onwards. Between 1957 and 1967 recorded crime grew about 10 percent every year, more than doubled during that decade and doubled again over the next ten years. After that the rate of growth was slower, but during that twenty-year period (1957-77) Britain, Scotland, as well as England and Wales, moved decisively from being a society in which crime was rare to one in which both crimes of violence and crimes of dishonesty were serious social problems. In 1937, there were only about

1

10,500 persons in jail in England and Wales, of whom a mere 850 were serving sentences of over three years. However, the dramatic growth not only in crime but in the number of persons convicted of the more serious offenses meant that by 1997 there were 64,000 people in prison, with 24,000 of them serving sentences of three years or more (Hood and Roddam 2000: 676). Society had not become more punitive—if anything the opposite was true—merely more criminal, and the jails were increasingly reserved for the more serious offenders.

A similar transition occurred in relation to two other forms of deviant and anti-social behavior incompatible with respectability, namely illegitimacy and drug and alcohol abuse. Throughout the twentieth century, until the mid-1950s, the incidence of illegitimacy had been low in Britain except during the two world wars, and the proportion of births in England and Wales that were illegitimate remained steady at between 4 and 5 percent. However, from the mid-1950s the proportion rose to 5.4 percent in 1960 and 8.5 percent by 1968 (Hartley 1975: 39) and continued to rise steadily for the rest of the century to the point where over a third of live births were illegitimate.

For the first half of the twentieth century addiction to opiates was a rare and diminishing problem. In 1953, there were only 290 addicts known to the Home Office, the lowest number ever recorded, and no significant drug-related crime. In 1963, there were 635 registered addicts and by 1968 nearly 3,000 (Bean 1974: 103). At the beginning of the twenty-first century, there were 20,000 registered addicts and between 200,000 and 400,000 regular users of heroin (*Drugs Uncovered* 2002). There was a substantial black market in drugs in Britain; purchasers financed their habits with acquisitive crime and dealers regularly settled their disputes with violence and increasingly with firearms. Likewise, drunken and often violent hooliganism, which had been uncommon and sporadic in the early 1950s was regular and widespread in town centers on certain nights of the week.

The strange death of respectable Britain in the last half of the twentieth century brought to an end a moral order that had dominated the first half of the twentieth century but which itself had only been created in the last half of the preceding century. The full history of respectable Britain that will be described in this chapter consists of three linked stages: birth, maturity, and decline; Reforming Britain, Respectable Britain, and De-moralized Britain. The level of adherence to the respectable virtues by its very nature is more easily measured when respectability is departed from rather than when it is adhered to. The story of the rise and fall of respectable Britain is thus the story of a society in which crimes of dishonesty, crimes of violence, illegitimacy and drug and alcohol abuse first fell, then remained steady at a very low level, and then rose again, a striking pattern identified by the author (Davies 1983) in 1983 as the "U-curve of deviance": a U-curve of crimes of dishonesty and violence, including murder; a U-curve in the size of the prison population; a U-curve in the incidence of drug and alcohol abuse; and a U-curve in illegitimacy. The turning points differ slightly in each case but the common pattern is overwhelmingly clear. Respectable Britain was created in the last half of the nineteenth century, faltered at the time of the First World War, enjoyed an at times uneasy stability but with signs of decay until the late 1950s and then went into rapid decline. The last stage cannot be understood without an examination of its two predecessors, so we must begin at the beginning.

The Creation of Respectable Britain

The Decline of Crime

During the last half of the nineteenth century there was a remarkable fall in the incidence both of crimes of violence and of crimes of dishonesty in England and Wales. It was remarkable both in its scale and in its comprehensiveness, for many types of common crime declined in their incidence (Gatrell 1980: 257), and in its regularity and stability. The overall incidence of serious offenses recorded by the police in the 1890s was only about 60 percent of what it had been in the 1850s. Larcenies recorded by the police dropped from about 500 for every 100,000 of the population in 1857 and 1858 to fewer than 300 in the early 1890s (Gatrell and Hadden 1972: 373-77). Offenses against the person fell by 43 percent from their peak in the 1840s to their lowest point between 1906 and 1910. Trials for all indictable crime fell from an annual average of 288 trials per 100,000 of the population in the early 1860s to only 164 per 100,000 in the late 1890s (Gatrell 1980: 281-83). Gatrell and Hadden (1972: 374) noted that "the figures must reflect a real decline in criminal activity and a quite spectacular one." Given that the efficiency of reporting and recording crime was markedly improving during the entire period the actual fall in the crime rate would have been far greater than that indicated by the official statistics.

Indeed, C. E. Troup of the Home Office in his introduction to the Criminal Statistics for 1898 wrote:

> That the actual number of crimes brought into the courts has diminished appreciably during the last thirty years; that, if the increase of population is taken into account, the decrease in crime becomes very marked; that, if we also take into account the increase of the police forces and the greater efficiency in the means of investigating and punishing crime, we may conclude that the decrease in crime is even greater than the figures show; and finally, if we take into account the fact that habitual criminals are now for the most part imprisoned only for short periods and have much more frequent opportunities than formerly of committing offences, we must hold that the number of criminals has diminished in an even greater ratio than the number of crimes. (Troup 1900: 25. See also *Statistics Relating to Criminal Proceedings for 1894 Criminal Statistics* 1896: 19; *Statistics relating to Criminal Proceedings for 1895; Criminal Statistics* 1897: 21; Lee 1901: 405)

Britain then was not only a less violent and dishonest society in 1898 than it is today, but it also was less violent and dishonest than it had been half a century earlier, and the incidence of violent crime continued to fall until 1914. Even the incidence of murder, a rather rare and atypical crime in Britain, fell from 2.0 per 100,000 of the population in 1865 to 0.7 in 1914, and felonious and malicious wounding fell from 6.1 in 1875 to 2.8 in 1914 (Gatrell 1980: 343-47).

The findings of the research done by Gatrell and Hadden, which is the most thorough and sophisticated examination of the data relating to England and Wales that has been carried out, are strongly supported by local studies of Lancashire (Gatrell and Hadden 1972), Wales (Jones 1992), and London and Middlesex (Pierce, Grabosky, Gurr 1977). In rural, industrial, and urban Wales alike there was a dramatic drop to a much lower level in the number of serious crimes reported to the police from mid-century onwards (Jones 1992: 44). Jones (1992: 109) notes, "the overwhelming impression to be gleaned from the returns is that people's property at the end of the century had never been safer. Taffy was becoming less of a thief." Likewise, there was a striking fall in all forms of violence in Wales. Crimes against the person affected one person in 237 in 1871, but by 1899 it impinged on only one person in 375, and by 1931 it was lower still (Jones 1992: 67-68). In 1858, there was one violent crime for every sixty-three citizens of the largest port towns of Cardiff, Swansea, and Newport, but by 1931 the incidence of violence was negligible (Jones 1992: 71). Pierce, Grabosky, and Gurr (1977: 64-8) have demonstrated a similarly marked decline in theft and violence in London and Middlesex. The details of the decline in crime differ from one region to another but in each case there was far less crime at the end of the nineteenth century than there had been fifty years earlier and in each region the incidence of violent crime continued to decline until World War I.

Although the long-term trend in crime was clearly downwards there were marked fluctuations around this trend in line with, and due to, the trade cycle. During a boom when wages rose and unemployment fell there was a fall in property crimes, which rose again in the depression that followed when wages were squeezed and unemployment rose, particularly among the less skilled and less effective workers who were the first to be sacked when trade and output fell. Conversely, crimes of violence rose as output, wages, and employment rose and there was more money to spend on alcohol. In the downturn, when money was no longer so freely available, there was less drinking and less violence (Gatrell and Hadden 1972: 368-71). The direct link between being able to afford to drink more alcohol and violent behavior may be inferred both from the (not that easily measured) incidence of drunken behavior of all kinds and from the difficulty of finding any other explanation of why prosperity should make people more violent. These patterns of short-term fluctuations in violence, correlating directly with economic production, and of theft, correlating inversely with it, are also (with local variations) characteristic of particular areas that have been studied in detail, namely Lancashire (Gatrell and Hadden 1972: 376) and Wales (Jones 1992: 47, 68). What must be stressed, though, is that we have no reason to suppose that there is any connection, or even anything in common, between these short-term fluctuations with peaks and troughs perhaps ten years apart and the pronounced *long-term* fall in *both* violent and acquisitive crime. They are two separate phenomena. The only point at which the interaction of the two creates a degree of confusion is in the years before World War I, between 1900 and 1914. Crimes of violence continued to fall, but there was a rise in property crime (Gatrell 1980: 314, 323, 329, 343-60) during this time of economic difficulties when for many groups real wages fell. Given that woundings and assaults continued to decline until World War I, the continued rise in reporting and recording, and an increasingly lenient criminal justice system that gave shorter sentences to habitual criminals, it seems reasonable to regard World War I, rather than the end of the nineteenth century, as the turning point that brought Britain's era of falling crime to an end.

There is one further point to note about this era of falling crime—the criminals were getting older. The prison population in particular was on average older at the end of the nineteenth century than it had been earlier and contained more experienced criminals and fewer young delinquents. By implication, prisoners were drawn from a hardened criminal class that was less numerous and less representative of the population as a whole, than that from which most offenders had been drawn earlier in the century (Gatrell and Hadden 1972: 378). Likewise, the average age of offenders in Wales rose faster than might have been expected from the general ageing of the population (Jones 1992: 178). There were fewer juvenile recruits to crime at a time when crime was falling. The early social training of young people increasingly turned them away from crime, leaving a residue of older and often illiterate prisoners who had grown up earlier in the century in less moral times. Crime had fallen fastest among the young. It is a striking obverse to the rise of the youthful criminal in the latter part of the twentieth century.

None of these points would have surprised the Victorians. Despite the occasional outbursts of outrage in the press or the legislature about some particularly vile cluster of crimes, they saw themselves as living in an age of improvement when theft and violence were in decline. Even at the time of the so-called garrotting "panic" in the 1860s when there was a severe response to a sudden spate of street robberies with violence (Sindall 1990), many contemporaries saw it as a mere blip, an uncharacteristic interruption of a trend towards an ever-safer society (Pike 1876: 574-75; Street Terrors 1863: 535-37). Everyone knew that robberies in the open were less common than in the past and attended by less violence, just as in the twenty-first century we know that such robberies are far more common than they were in the 1950s and that a mugger may well gratuitously choose to injure his victim. There were only three robberies per 100,000 people recorded in 1862. There was more than fifteen times that number by the late 1980s (Sindall 1990: 162). It may well be that muggers were treated with severity in Victorian England precisely because the streets had become safe for inoffensive, respectable persons. Likewise those convicted of making use of firearms while breaking into a house were given savage exemplary sentences (Wiener 1990: 343) because gun crime was almost unknown despite widespread gun ownership and the lack of tight legal restrictions on such ownership in the nineteenth century. Carolyn Conley (1991: 67) comments in her study of criminal justice in Kent: "In Victorian Kent the judicial system was concerned with allowing respectable people to walk the streets safely. To a large extent they succeeded."

Their success was confidently announced at the time in 1876 by the barrister Luke Owen Pike (1876: 480-1);

> Meanwhile it may with little fear of contradiction be asserted that there never was in any nation of which we have a history, a time in which life and property were so secure as they are at present in England. The sense of security is almost everywhere diffused in town and country alike and it is in marked contrast to the sense of insecurity that prevailed even at the beginning of the present century...any man of average stature and strength may wander about on foot and alone at any hour of the day or the night, through the greatest of all cities and its suburbs, along the high roads and through unfrequented country lanes and never have so much as the thought of danger thrust upon him, unless he goes out of his way to court it.

Pike (1876: 472-80) was convinced of the decline of crimes of all kinds from murder to theft to the point where he feared that the lack of violent crime in England was a mark of feebleness and decadence and wrote:

> With the diminution of crime and especially of crimes of violence there has been a perceptible subsidence of the military spirit in England.... Hence arises the very grave question whether British civilisation is advancing towards its own destruction and incurs danger from a foreign military barbarism in proportion as it progresses towards its own perfection. (Pike 1876: 530-1)

Pike (424-25, 584) likewise was well aware of the differing ways in which theft and violence were related to the trade cycle, even though he used a different set of terms to describe the way in which theft rose in bad times and assaults in prosperity. Indeed, there seems to have been a widespread if more vague recognition of this dual relationship among contemporary judges and magistrates (Conley 1991: 144). Yet most people knew that in the longer term crimes of all kinds were falling and in particular that far fewer crimes were being committed by those under thirty (Escott 1885: 217, 239, 284).

Commentators who knew their own times well and had a sophisticated understanding of the problems involved in using official statistics were convinced that crime was withering away and were positively smug about this remarkable achievement of their society (Quinton, 1910: 6-13). They routinely spoke of the bad old times of the earlier part of their century in the way that their late twentieth-century successors were to speak of the good old times of their parents and grandparents. Just as it would be foolish to dismiss the latter as indulging in false nostalgia, so, too, we cannot dismiss the total optimism of the later nineteenth century.

Only one group of people consistently got it wrong both then and today, namely the sociologists and criminologists. In the nineteenth century at a time when the crime rate was clearly falling, "as diverse and eminent a lot of theorists as Durkheim, Ferri, Tarde, Engels, and Bonger were united in insisting that crime was rising" (McDonald 1982: 406). Marxists from Engels down to Bonger at the end of the century were convinced that crime must be rising because their theories predicted it would be, for as capitalist societies developed, the members of the working classes were bound to express their increasing rage and misery in an epidemic of theft and violence (McDonald 1982: 411, 415-16). Of course, this never happened, but why allow facts to spoil a much-loved theory? Likewise, Durkheim was permanently convinced that urbanization and modernization would lead to anomie and increased crime.[1] As we shall see later, he had a point and it may well be that Durkheim was a better prophet than an observer, but even in France crime rates were falling at the time he was writing (McDonald 1982: 413-14). Durkheim (1952 [1897]: 160, 165) had always found nineteenth-century England an anomaly in many other respects and perhaps for this reason he avoided confronting the evidence that crime had been falling in that most urban, most industrial, most commercial, and most global of all countries (Sindall 1990: 2; Pierce, Grabosky, and Gurr 1977: 37-9; McCabe 1925: 36; Jones 1992: 43-45.). In 1850, only half of the British population lived in towns and the biggest economic factor determining dearth or prosperity was still the size of the harvest. By 1900, nearly 80 percent of the population lived in towns yet crime had fallen. At the end of the nineteenth century, state intervention in Britain's thoroughly capitalist economy was minimal and a determined adherence to free trade exposed all sectors of agriculture and industry to a degree of global competition greater than in any other country and greater than in the late twentieth century (Gourevitch, 1977: 296, 299). Yet the incidence of crime was by the standards of the late twentieth and early twenty-first centuries very low.

During this time of falling crime the standard of living of the people rose considerably, if not always steadily or evenly. There were great inequalities between the different classes, between the rich who flaunted their wealth and the poor, many of whom were, or were on the brink of becoming, paupers. There was far more to steal in 1900 than there had been in the 1850s, as mass as well as luxury consumption rose. In the towns, things worth stealing became more accessible as traders took to displaying their goods outside their shops as well as within. A large proportion of the population worked as domestic servants in the homes of those wealthier than themselves and knew intimately the kinds of luxuries they enjoyed. By 1900, there was far more to steal—clothing, jewelry, watches, bicycles (Jones 1990: 112) yet there were fewer thieves. In large cities with greatly improved transportation it was far easier than in the past to travel to a district where one was not known and to use that anonymity to steal a purse or a wage packet, pilfer from a shop or a warehouse, abstract someone else's rent money from its receptacle in their home, or make off with a bicycle, and yet fewer people seized such opportunities. Envy, desire, access were all there in 1900 but fewer people became thieves than is the case today or had been in the more distant past. They were more honest, more respectable, more moral.

The Decline of the Prison

In the late nineteenth century, as the incidence of crime fell, the number of people imprisoned fell in relation to population, though with marked short-term fluctuations as the volume of crime varied with the trade cycle. Escott (1885: 254) and Du Cane (1893: 480) both noted at the time that the absolute number of prisoners was declining at a time when the population was increasing and ascribed this to the manifest decrease in crime (Du Cane 1893: 483-85). Towards the end of the century sentences became more lenient as crime was ceasing to be a serious problem. Increasingly, those convicted were released without sentence, fewer were sent to prison and prison sentences had become shorter (Wiener 1990: 371). The number and proportion of those convicted and sentenced to terms of imprisonment (including penal servitude) longer than one year fell to the point where in 1894 only 1,721 persons were given such sentences, about 4 percent of those convicted of indictable offenses. The vast majority of the 22,000 people sent to prison in a particular year received sentences of three months or less (*Statistics Relating to Criminal Proceedings for 1894, Criminal Statistics* 1896: 16-17; *Statistics Relating to Criminal Proceedings for 1895, Criminal Statistics* 1897: 12-13). One consequence of this greater leniency was that many recidivists were released back into the general population to commit more crimes earlier than they would have been, which tended to push up the crime rate (*Statistics Relating to Criminal Proceedings for 1895, Criminal Statistics* 1897: 21; Gatrell 1980: 284). However, the incidence of crime was falling and by now was so low and unthreatening that there was a willingness to pay this price for increased leniency. In Gatrell's (1980: 284) view it was the sense that the battle against crime had been won that made possible the marked shift towards more lenient sentences during the last half of the nineteenth century. Not only did the fall in the crime rate mean that fewer were convicted and thus liable to be sentenced to imprisonment, it also had the indirect consequence that those who were convicted received shorter sentences, if indeed they were imprisoned at all. Many contemporaries would have seen this trend as a natural outcome of a society in which the state and the law had become an agent for peaceably arbitrating the social and predominantly market-based economic relationships between its citizens and was less and less needed for the purposes of retributive punishment.[1]

Success and Doubts: An Early Turning Point

Those politicians and servants of the state who made penal policy were greatly pleased at the way in which crime had fallen as a result of and as an expression of the triumph of respectable Britain at their own part in this triumph and at the opportunity it gave them for relaxing the rigors of a moralizing and deterring sentencing and penal system. Yet their very deliberations in their moment of triumph at the end of the nineteenth century reveal their doubts not just about past policy but about the virtues and associated restrictions and constraints of respectability itself (Wiener 1990: 257-58). Not just they but other members of the educated and prosperous elite were ceasing to believe in the very idea and ideal of the autonomous, self-controlled, rationally choosing individual that had been and still was the very basis of respectable Britain. Among the majority of the people this ideal was reaching ever further in both extent and intensity in an ever more respectable population, but within that very section of the elite who had been its true believers, promoters, and exponents it was losing ground. For this particular influential elite the 1890s were a turning point, the point at which moralism began to lose ground in their thinking and their reflections about the moral nature of social relations began to go causalist (Wiener 1990: 338). They no longer held with their former confidence and certainty to the dividing of people into the deserving who were to be rewarded and the wicked who were to be punished, but rather saw below a mass of weak people divided into the virtuous and the offending only by chance opportunities and adversities that caused them to act as they did. They were not truly free agents and it was the duty of the high-minded to administer their welfare in such a way as to minimize harm regardless of merit or guilt of the individuals concerned. Such ideas were to become more influential and, as we shall see, to become dominant during and after the late 1950s, which was also the second and final turning point in the strange history of respectable Britain, the beginning of the final decline. The success of moral Britain by the 1890s contained within it the sources of its own ultimate collapse.

The Birth of Sober Britain

Unwise and excessive indulgence in alcohol, which it was generally agreed at the time was the source of most violence, was also declining in the later years of the nineteenth century and the early part of the twentieth. The match between the long-term decline in violence and in drunkenness over the entire period is not as good as when we consider only the brief span of the trade cycle, but a broad shift in a civilizing direction is clearly discernible. Men and indeed women became less violent when they were drunk and they were also less inclined to get drunk and in consequence to become violent. Everyone agreed in the late nineteenth century that drunkenness was declining both in its incidence and in its offensiveness and yet increasing numbers of people were arrested for and charged with being drunk. The society was becoming less tolerant of drunken behavior and as part of this change fewer departed from sobriety but the remnant who continued to get drunk were more likely to attract the attention of the police and more likely to be prosecuted. Whereas theft and violence have particular victims who tend to report and complain about their victimhood, public drunkenness unless it leads to violence is simply a general nuisance and it is at the discretion of the police, guided by public opinion, whether to do anything about it. It is this dual aspect of arrests for drunkenness that was remarked on by the Welsh historian David Jones (1992: 47) when he wrote of Wales that "Both the rise in the rate of these prosecutions (for drunk and disorderly conduct) in the second half of the nineteenth century and the decline early in the twentieth were regarded by experienced observers as a sign of progress. People were being and becoming civilized." Thus, there is no contradiction between the comments of Charles Booth (1903: 68-69) that public drunkenness had declined substantially in the last twenty years of the nineteenth century and with it drunken rowdiness and the fact that the numbers of both proceedings for drunkenness in England and Wales and convictions peaked in 1900-1904 (Wilson 1940: 286).

The same Luke Owen Pike who had praised the safety of Britain in the 1870s and yet worried about its martial spirit was likewise ambivalent about the increased assiduousness of the police in "apprehending persons guilty of very small offences, such as being drunk and disorderly" (Pike 1876: 479) and thus marring the purity of the statistics that he was using to demonstrate the fall in crime in general. He added that "the increased number of criminals can be made to appear formidable only by including in it persons guilty of offences which our hard-drinking great-grandfathers would have regarded as merits rather than as faults" (Pike 1876: 480).

In the eighteenth century, hard-drinking and even drunken brawls had been common in most classes, but customs had become more civilized among Pike's peers to the point where drunkenness "would be followed by expulsion from any respectable club" (Pike 1876: 587; see also 586, and Harrison 1994: 301). Among respectable people generally there was disapproval of drunkenness because it showed a loss of self-control both in that the drunk revealed that he or she could not control the degree to which he or she indulged and because drinking further undermined self-control and led the drinkers into forms of anti-social and self-destructive behavior that they would have shunned when sober. In the latter part of the nineteenth century, the respectable people were able both to persuade and to constrain the rest of the population to a greater degree of sobriety and moderation

After 1900 there was a steady decline in alcohol consumption in Britain that accelerated to such an extent during and after World War I that by the 1920s alcohol abuse no longer constituted a significant social problem, nor was it to do so for the next forty years. The bottom of the U-curve had been reached. In Arthur Marwick's (1965: 68) words "From being a melancholy but inescapable feature of the British scene, drunkenness became a limited and manageable problem." Britain had for the time being solved its most significant drug problem.

The Opium of the People

Meanwhile, another potential drug problem that might have come to challenge respectability was averted. For most of the nineteenth century opium was for many people almost a necessity. Its sale was not restricted to pharmacists and it could be bought across the counter in a variety of forms in ordinary shops (Berridge 1999: 27-31; Warburton 1990: 22), much as in the twenty-first century customers can buy aspirin or paracetamol, cough mixtures or cures for diarrhea. Opium was part of normal routine self-medication. It was the only effective pain-killer, the usual remedy for dysentery at a time when the quality of the water supply was dubious, and a standard remedy for a persistent cough. It might well be taken (in the absence of modern alternatives) to allay anxiety, depression, fatigue or sleeplessness, or to get through the ordinary tasks and troubles of the day. At different times in the nineteenth century such reputable figures as William Wilberforce, W. E. Gladstone, and Rudyard Kipling used it to enable them to complete a difficult or demanding task or one that required confidence, coolness, and a steady nerve. To take opium in this way was not an indication of a loss of self-control, nor did it lead to a further loss of self-control. At worst it produced a drowsy passive euphoria quite the opposite of the qualities expressed by fighting drunks who had abused alcohol. Opium did not in general lead to anti-social behavior nor threaten respectability.

Many of those who took opium became dependent on it. They took it regularly over many years and would have felt unwell if they had stopped, but it was a controlled addiction. They did not seek increasing sensation or increase their consumption. They did not drop out of or seriously neglect their work or family life. William Wilberforce, the great reformer and evangelical leader, took a four-grain pill of opium three times a day for at least thirty years of his life and Elizabeth Barrett Browning has been described as a well-balanced addict (Berridge 1999: 58-59; Lefebure 1977: 25).

Respectable opium taking and even respectable addiction was possible for many people because of the strong and successful pressures of respectability, of duty, responsibility, and moderation enforced through informal social controls. Those who took opium were not members of a deviant sub-culture of drug-takers encouraging one another's excesses but people for whom the self-control they exercised in other areas of life and which was demanded of them by their immediate associates was extended to their drug habit.

There were, however, problems. One was that some individuals did become seriously addicted to the point where their character was impaired and the drug enslaved them completely in a bondage of opium, as happened with Samuel Coleridge (Lefebure 1977). These individuals became uncontrolled addicts who required ever greater quantities of the drug, were unable to work, ran into debt, exploited their families and associates to pay for their habit, and became utterly untrustworthy in every way (Lefebure 1977: 65, 294, 383). They were seen by their respectable associates as weak-willed individuals whose vicious, character-destroying obsession set them apart from those in control of their intake. It was feared and it was perfectly reasonable to fear that the numbers of these hopeless cases would rise if the use of opium as a source of sensation and not merely sedation were to become common among the least respectable and least temperate sections of society. Accordingly in the latter half of the nineteenth century, there were moves to control and restrict the sale, availability, and supply of opium.

After the passing of the 1868 Pharmacy Act, only pharmacists were allowed to sell opium, though at first this had little effect on consumption. Contemporaries were well aware that a rapid and radical attempt to constrict supply would lead to a black market (Berridge 1999: 117). Control and constraint were established gradually through the pharmacists, who, in turn, were policed by their professional association and by government inspectors. Dispensing and dosage became more accurate and the use of opiates in patent medicines was reduced and often eliminated. By the early twentieth century, opium use was ceasing to be culturally acceptable (Berridge 1999: 236). The bounds of respectability had been extended.

It was a change encouraged and promoted by the medical profession that was coming to see addiction to opiates as a disease, yet a disease defined in such a way as to leave room for the condemnation of personal moral failure. Treatment involved self-control and self-help, the elimination of impulsivity, the inculcation of duty to family and society, and even an appeal to religion (Berridge 1999: 162-63). As less opium was prescribed by doctors and less purchased for self-medication by the early 1900s, deaths from the use of narcotics fell by two-thirds from what they had been in the nineteenth century (Berridge 1999: 236).

The Decline of Illegitimacy

Illegitimacy was also declining in the last half of the nineteenth century. The illegitimacy ratio (the ratio of illegitimate births to all births) fell from a peak of 7 percent in 1845 to less than 4 percent in 1900. During the latter half of the nineteenth century the illegitimacy ratio in the East End of London where the poorest people lived was consistently well below the national average: it was 4.5 percent in the middle of the nineteenth century and just below 3 percent by the beginning of the twentieth (Himmelfarb 1995: 223).[2]

Once again the statistics understate the magnitude of the Victorian achievement for as Lionel Rose (1986: 22) reminds us:

> Until 1874 registration of births in England was not even compulsory; in 1867 the proportion of non-registration in parts of London alone was estimated at anything between 15 and 33% and as the local registrars had to depend on their informants' word, many illegitimates were in fact being registered as legitimate.... The Registrar General believed that there was a 10% underestimate in the official returns of illegitimate births but the Infant Life Protection Society in 1870 put it as high as 30%.

That the illegitimacy ratio should have been falling at a time of improved reporting and recording of births indicates that the real fall in the incidence of illegitimacy was greater still. Also whereas in the first half of the nineteenth century there had been a marked concern about the level of infanticide and of concealment of births, by the beginning of the twentieth century it was "no longer regarded as a problem" (Keown 1988: 47). Many of the newly born that had been killed by their mothers shortly after birth or else abandoned in a public place, were the children of unmarried mothers, particularly domestic servants. The disappearance of infanticide is thus a good indication of the decline in illegitimacy and we may also infer a fall in the number of newborn illegitimates whose death and indeed birth had been successfully concealed by the mother and never come to the attention of the authorities.

The Triumph of Respectability

The decline in violence, dishonesty, drunkenness, and illegitimacy in the late nineteenth century and probably up to the First World War are all indices of the growth of the respectable virtues. At the core of the respectable Britain that its people had created were the moral qualities of self-control and self-restraint, of probity and prudence, of decency and sobriety. Far from existing in opposition to other moral qualities the virtues of respectability are the base on which the other virtues rest. Respectable Britain was not the whole of moral Britain but it was of necessity a major and essential part of it. These qualities were to endure during the years of crisis, hardship, and tragedy that followed, World War I and World War II, the slump and mass unemployment, and the postwar austerity that were the crucial experiences of respectable Britain between 1914 and 1955. They may not have been good times, but they were the times of a good people.

Respectable Britain: Triumph, Maturity, and Slow Decay

Neither Drunk nor Violent

During the 1920s, the incidence of violent crime fell and it remained steady at a low level in the early 1930s. This was probably connected with the marked decline in levels of alcohol abuse relative to the pre-war years. Britain between the wars was a society in which drunkenness was rare. It was a major social change. The consumption of spirits per head in England and Wales dropped by 80 percent and the consumption of beer halved (Wilson 1940: 11, 253) relative to the period before World War I. Changes in aggregate consumption alone are not a good guide to the incidence of alcohol abuse but in this particular case the two went together. In 1930-34, there was only a quarter as many convictions for drunkenness as there had been in 1900-04 (Wilson 1940: 286) and there is no reason to suppose that the police had become less vigilant or more tolerant of drunkenness.

In Scotland, the change was just as marked and proceedings for drunkenness fell to a quarter of their pre-war level. There was a corresponding reduction in proceedings for breaches of the peace and assaults of husbands on wives (Wilson 1940: 295). David Jones (1996: 128) notes that female habits changed in the interwar years and he cites a 68-year-old police matron as saying in 1948, "women don't get drunk like they used to. I remember the cells full with 26 in a night. They used to bring them in kicking on hand trucks." There seems to have been a general decrease in the rowdyism and hooliganism associated with drinking and, hence, a fall in violence as well as inebriety (Jones 1996: 127). The interwar period in Britain, a time of economic crises and prolonged strikes, of political tension and threats of war, was perhaps the safest time for the ordinary citizen in Britain's entire history; it was a time when the streets were relatively free of the aggressive drunks of the past and of the street robberies of today. As Norman Dennis (1997: 66) has vividly pointed out, in the best year, 1927, of the interwar period 1920-38 there were only 110 robberies and in the worst year, 1932, a mere 342. In 1970, there were 6,000 robberies and in 1990 about 36,000. Even those who were most critical of their own society boasted how peaceful it was as in George Orwell's famous comment:

[An] imaginary foreign observer would certainly be struck by our gentleness; by the orderly behaviour of English crowds, the lack of pushing and quarrelling, the willingness to form queues.... And except for certain well-defined areas in half a dozen big towns, there is very little crime or violence. The average of honesty is lower in the big towns than in the country but even in London, the news-vendor can safely leave his pile of pennies on the pavement while he goes for a drink. The prevailing gentleness of manners is new, however... (Orwell 1968 [1944] 2-3)

It is not much more than a hundred years since the distinguishing mark of English life was its brutality. The common people, to judge by the prints, spent their time in an almost unending round of fighting, whoring, drunkenness and bull-baiting.... What had these people in common with the gentle-mannered, undemonstrative, law-abiding English of today? (Orwell 1968 [1944]: 5-6)

Orwell's comment about crowds is particularly remarkable given the disorder that had marked sporting events both in the early nineteenth century and in the hooligan-ridden game of the late twentieth century when the supporters of the visiting team had to be escorted to the ground by the police and carefully segregated from their local rivals to prevent violence. The ex-Franciscan turned Rationalist, Joseph McCabe, used the example of England's football matches in 1925 to illustrate the civility and decency of a contemporary English crowd in contrast to the brutal coarseness of its ancestors. McCabe's juxtaposition of sporting contests reinforces his point:

> There was one fight in 1824 to which the London Press gave more space, on its front page, than to any other event of the year. Langan and Smith met on Worcester Race Course, and nearly all the gentry of the country—five thousand people—must have made the ten-hour coach ride to see it. No gloves were worn in 1824, and there were almost no rules. The men fought seventy-five rounds, in two and a half hours, with naked fists. The Irishman Langan, who lost—and was put to bed with fifty leeches on him!—was dissatisfied, and a few weeks later they fought for an hour and forty-eight minutes (seventy-six rounds). In April 1825, there was a seventy-round fight. Deaths were quite common. Naturally, working men and boys imitated the gentry all over Britain. It is not so well known that women engaged in prize fights. A Stockport paper of the year 1825 describes an appalling encounter between two women, and remarks that it is a "frequent spectacle" in that district. On February 28 (1825) the fourteen-year-old son of the Earl of Shaftesbury, the famous philanthropist and Churchman, fought *sixty* rounds with an older and heavier boy. The whole school were present, and every master in the school must have known of it. Young Ashley Cooper's friends plied him freely with brandy between the rounds. Witnesses said that he drank more than half a pint, and that it was customary at Eton to give the boys brandy when fighting. The boy was killed...(by contrast) a modern First League football match is a clean and stimulating spectacle to which any lady may be taken; and I have taken refined girls, who agreed. (McCabe 1925: 54-55, 57-58)

During World War II, there was a marked increase in violent crime despite a further decline in drunkenness due to the shortage and deliberate dilution of alcoholic drinks. The number of more serious violent offenses such as felonious wounding and malicious wounding nearly doubled and there was almost certainly a sharp rise in assaults, many of which were not recorded (Smithies 1982: 152-53). Whereas in World War I crime had fallen with a large part of the male population away fighting in France, in World War II much of the British army remained at home until 1944—millions of young men armed with guns living away from their families and local communities. Yet the guns were very rarely used for criminal purposes and the murder rate remained very low. Nearly all the crimes committed using guns during World War II in Britain were carried out by members of the American armed forces stationed in England prior to D-day in 1944 (Smithies, 1982: 153-54).

After the war the level of violent crime continued to rise until the late 1940s, but then fell back until the mid-1950s. In 1955, the anthropologist Geoffrey Gorer still felt able to say in his study, *Exploring English Character* (1955: 13) that:

> ...in public life today, the English are certainly among the most peaceful, gentle, courteous and orderly populations that the civilized world has ever seen...the control of aggression when it has gone to such remarkable lengths that you hardly ever see a fight in a bar (a not uncommon spectacle in most of the rest of Europe or the USA), when football crowds are as orderly as church meetings, when all the frustrations and annoyances symbolized by queueing are met with orderliness and good humor, modified, at most, by a few grumbles and high words, then this orderliness and gentleness, this absence of overt aggression calls for an explanation if the dynamics of English character are to be effectively described. This English gentleness would seem to be a comparatively new phenomenon.

From Honest to Delinquent Britain?

The incidences of crimes of dishonesty followed a similar pattern but with some important differences. The incidence of recorded thefts (the largest category) and other crimes of dishonesty rose in the 1920s and early 1930s, but the absolute incidence was very low by the standards of the late twentieth and early twenty-first centuries and it is very difficult to say how much of the modest rise in the statistics was part of a long-term upward trend, how much due to improved reporting and changing patterns of recording, and how much a short-term cyclical rise due to the severe depression and high unemployment experienced in Britain in the interwar period. The size and nature of the impact of extremely high levels of unemployment on the crime rate, particularly in the North of England and South Wales, is a particularly difficult question (Mannheim 1940; *Criminal Statistics England and Wales 1929,* 1931: xv-xxii). What *was* regularly commented on at the time (in contrast to the Victorian period when in an era of falling crime the criminals were getting older) is that the criminals were getting younger. For the *older* age groups the incidence of crime as measured by convictions *fell* but there was a noticeable increase in juvenile delinquency in England and Wales (*Criminal Statistics England and Wales 1929,* 1931: vi-xiv).

There was little growth of crime in England and Wales until the late 1930s, but in the 1920s and early 1930s it is possible to discern a curious precursor of what was later to become the strange death of moral Britain. Between 1921 and 1934 there was a decline in the numbers of adult offenders per 100,000 of the population but a rise in the number of juvenile offenders as shown in Table 1.1.

Table 1.1
Proportion of Offenders per 100,000 of Population of England and Wales

Year	Adults (16 and over)	Juveniles
1911	232	288
1921	197	267
1925	169	297
1929	173	307
1932	201	354
1933	189	370
1934	189	439

(Based on *Criminal Statistics England and Wales 1934*, 1936: xiii.)

The steady decline in adult crime shown in Table 1.1 remains even when allowance is made for the changing age and sex structure of the British population caused by World War I and by the fall in the birth rate. Likewise the number of juveniles aged 10-16 was about the same in 1934 as it had been in 1911, but the number of juveniles charged with indictable offenses had risen from 12,000 in 1911 to 18,000 in 1934. It is as if the older generation was still part of the earlier tendency for crime to fall but was beginning to be overshadowed by a new breed of juvenile criminals.

There does though appear to be a turning point in the mid-1930s after which the annual increase in crimes of dishonesty and particularly the more serious ones become significantly greater (Pierce, Grabosky, and Gurr 1977: 159). It can be argued that this is merely because a steady proportionate increase in the incidence of crime year on year produces ever greater increments. Such is the nature of compound interest, but what on earth is the point of using a model based on compound interest in discussing crime? From the point of view of society it is the absolute increase that matters and so far as that is concerned it is reasonable to regard the mid-1930s as a turning point.

The Withering Away of Imprisonment

The number of people going to jail and the total prison population remained very low indeed throughout the interwar period when the average number of people in custody was only about 10,000 at any one time (Hood and Roddam 2000: 695-96). This was a matter of pride to the politicians and indeed in the 1920s to those who believed they were living in a time of progress (McCabe 1925: 77). Even though crimes of dishonesty were by now rising again, albeit slowly, the increased use of non-custodial sentences such as probation led to entire prisons being closed down (Morris 1989: 17). The number of people sent to prison continued to decline during the interwar period and the average number of people in custody in England and Wales was only about 10,000, drawn from a population of over forty million. In Scotland in 1932 only 5,000 people were sentenced to imprisonment, less than 7 percent of those convicted (*Criminal Statistics Scotland 1932*, 1933: 9). These very low figures at a time of very high unemployment, significant strikes (notably the General Strike of 1926), and political tension make a mockery of the argument that prison in Britain is used as an instrument for political coercion and intimidation or as a way of mopping up unemployment. In the 1920s and 1930s, this phenomenon was an obvious feature of the socialist sixth of the world, the U.S.S.R., where labor camps were consciously used for both these purposes, but was absent in Britain.

Alcohol, Drugs and the State in Respectable Britain

One striking aspect of the creation of respectable Britain is the relatively unimportant role played by the state. Respectable Britain was a form of spontaneous order (Barry 1982) that emerged from the efforts and aspirations of ordinary people; it was not designed or enforced by the country's rulers. There is one notable exception: the slow shift towards sobriety, towards temperance and moderation in the use of alcohol in the late nineteenth century and the years before World War I was greatly accelerated by the decisive measures taken during that war to curb and control the supply and sale of alcohol in order to prevent drunkenness and inefficiency (Wilson 1940: 289). Britain was a far less drunken and a less violent society in the 1920s than it had been before the war because of coercive measures taken during a military emergency that were not seriously relaxed when peace returned. There was no attempt during or after the war to enforce prohibition and the efforts of the lone member of the left-wing Prohibition Party in the British Parliament, Edwin Scrymgeour, to introduce prohibition in the 1920s had little support and were greeted with derision by the Conservatives. In Britain, there were few extremists for respectability seeking to use the power of the state as part of their war against alcohol or against sin in general. In any case, they would have been defeated by an alliance of libertarian Conservatives and their supporters in the drink trade. Britain in the 1920s remained free and became sober. Because there was no Prohibition there were no speakeasies, no bootleggers, no multiplying of illicit stills, no gangsters, no upsurge of violence or corruption of public officials. Britain in the 1920s was less violent than it had ever been before and far less violent than it was to become in the latter part of the twentieth century, and the policy of restrictions on but no prohibition of the sale of alcohol was one of the bases of its peaceableness.

The key change introduced during World War I was the severe restriction of licensing hours, the hours during which a public house was allowed to sell alcohol. It involved earlier closing in the evening, later opening in the morning, and for the first time a compulsory break of at least two hours in the afternoon (Wilson, 1940: 134-38). These changes were broadly retained in the Licensing Act of 1921, and a widely accepted (Wilson 1940: 159) enduring and distinctively British pattern of restricted public drinking was established. It was a particular legal embodiment of respectable Britain. For those who found the regulations too onerous, there were numerous licensed clubs for all classes in society serving members only (i.e., known individuals) to which the more stringent rules did not apply but which were models of self-enforced propriety.

The war-time changes had an immediate impact on public behavior. In the early days of the World War I, the London County Licensing Authority at the urgent request of the military officer commanding the London District changed closing time from 12:30 a.m. to 11:00 p.m. (and subsequently to 10:00 p.m.). The *Brewers Gazette* (24 September 1914, quoted in Wilson 1940: 128) reported:

A transformation of the night scenes of London has followed from the closing of the public-houses at 11. Great traffic centres, like the Elephant and Castle, at which immense crowds usually lounge about until one o'clock in the morning, have suddenly become peaceable and respectable. The police instead of having to "move on" numbers of people who have been dislodged from bars at 12.30 at night found very little intoxication to deal with, the last hour and a half being responsible for the much of the excess of which complaint is made. Journalists, who are necessarily out late, have quickly noticed the effects of the change upon public conduct.

What the authorities had realized was that extended drinking hours at this time of night, far from encouraging the consumers to drink more slowly and calmly, merely gave them more drinking time and produced a greater likelihood of their getting drunk and quarrelsome. No doubt nightlife and streetlife became less "colorful," but then "colorful" is merely a euphemism for ribald disorder. It is interesting to note that the particular change in 1914 described above, exemplifying a general shift in the direction of state-guided temperance, was initiated by Britain's military commanders, a group notably tolerant of drinking but terrified of any possible breakdown of order and control, particularly in wartime. It is ironic that the change was a reflection of the priorities of military and Conservative Britain who before the war had been more tolerant of alcoholic excess than the left-leaning temperance movement with its links to the pacific Nonconformist churches, Labour and Liberal Parties and Co-operative movement (Wilson 1940: 180, 243-44, 258-93). It would have taken the latter decades to bring about such changes in peacetime against Conservative opposition.

There were, though, other important, if slower and measured, changes that do reflect the influence of the temperance advocates on the actions of the state. Between 1870 and 1930 there was a steady fall in the number of licenses to run a public house granted or renewed, and those granting the licenses took advice from the police both about the conduct of a particular licensee and about the possible impact of the distribution and density of public houses on disorder in the streets (Wilson 1940: 236-38). Also taxes on alcohol, which had been substantially raised during the first world war (Wilson 1940: 128-29, 195), were kept high, high enough to deter heavy drinking but not so high as to encourage large-scale smuggling or illicit distilling. It was an altogether different world from the heedless sale of cheap alcohol of the early nineteenth or late twentieth centuries.

As was the case with alcohol, the government extended its powers to control opiates during World War I and these powers were confirmed by the Dangerous Drugs Act of 1920 (in part because of international pressure and agreements) (Bean 1974: 23). In particular, there were tighter controls over the use of the more powerful and injectable opiates, morphine and heroin. However, the size of the problem was minimal. In 1921, there were only 251 prosecutions for offenses against the Dangerous Drugs Act of which 190 involved opium or manufactured opiates such as heroin or pethidine. In 1925, the number of prosecutions involving opiates had fallen to thirty-five and in 1938 there were only six (Bean 1974: 98; Spear 1969: 246). The Rolleston Committee stated in its 1926 report that "addiction to morphine or heroin is rare in this country and has diminished in recent years" (cited in Schur 1963: 118). Respectable Britain had triumphed over the abuse of opiates.

In 1926, the Rolleston Committee report was approved by Parliament which placed the management of addicts in the hands of individual doctors who were free to prescribe to their individual patients such quantities of opiate drugs as they thought appropriate. Doctors and pharmacists were monitored by the Home Office, but there was little need for strict regulation. In 1935, there were only 700 addicts known to the Home Office and the number steadily declined to 519 in 1938, 367 in 1945, and 290 in 1953, the lowest number ever recorded (Bean 1974: 97, 103). No doubt there were some addicts not known to the Home Office either because their doctors had not reported them or for some other reason (Schur 1963: 121), but there is no doubt that overall the number of addicts was very small and declining and the black market in drugs miniscule (Bean 1974: 41).

Most of those who were addicted came from respectable backgrounds. Many had become addicted as a result of medical treatment or belonged to professions (nurses, doctors, dentists, pharmacists) with easy access to those drugs. Most of them were over thirty years of age and at least half of them were female (Bean 1974: 97-103; Schur 1963: 119-22; Spear 1969:247-48). It is likely that given the decline in the number of addicts that their average age was increasing, much as had happened with criminals and prisoners as crime rates fell in the late nineteenth century.

It was the low number of addicts, their social origins and demographic characteristics that made it possible to operate the so-called "British system," leaving addicts largely in the hands of the doctors with the police and the criminal justice system rarely being involved (Schur 1963: 80, 119). It was a non-system confronting a non-problem. Many of the addicts had, as a direct result of their addiction, problems in their work and in their family relationships and they may well have been difficult and mendacious patients to deal with. However, it was rare for them to be involved in illegal drug dealing or criminal activities, partly because their drugs were provided for them (from 1948 they were provided free under the National Health Service) but also because women, people over thirty, and professionals would be disinclined to become criminals anyway. Even when their character was in some degree undermined by their addiction they retained a higher degree of self-control than they would have if recruited from less respectable backgrounds. Also most addicts were isolated individuals who did not know or mix with other addicts with whom they could have created a deviant and destructive subculture. They were surrounded in their everyday life by respectable non-addicts who pressed them into conforming to normal standards of self-control. It was respectability that kept the "British system" in equilibrium and gave it an appearance of stability. Schur's (1963: 140) contention that "by refusing to treat the addict as a criminal, Britain may have kept him from becoming one" is only one side of the picture. It may be said equally that because Britain's addicts had never been involved in any kind of crime it made sense not to treat them as criminals. The British system was also kept in equilibrium by the overall respectability of British life in the first half of the twentieth century. In a society where there was very little crime and established patterns of moderate alcohol consumption were hedged in by generally accepted laws concerning sale and supply there were not enough deviant individuals to be potential customers for drugs unloaded by rogue registered addicts or recklessly prescribing doctors. Most addicts were not minded to be pushers; those who were had nowhere to push it to. There was as yet no mass of demoralized and delinquent male youths in search of novel forms of sensation to provide a market either for an addict trying to proselytize or merely hawk part of his or her prescription or for local or foreign criminal entrepreneurs seeking a new source of illicit profits. Respectability still ruled.

Those in charge of the British system did not understand how precarious it was and how dependent on the taken-for-granted respectability of British social life. They radiated smugness. Smugness on moral issues on the part of the powerful or of those able to get their views recorded is an extremely significant social phenomenon. It is often missed by those who seek to understand a period by dredging the popular press and recording the outbursts of the indignant in a search for moral panics. It is always possible to find moral panics because a scandal is what sells copy and the indignant know that if they show any sign of going moderate they won't get quoted any more. Most moral panics are not panics, they are mere excitements. Only a few result in significant change, the rest are epiphenomenal. The lurid horror stories in the press of drug taking in high society in the 1920s and 1930s were a tiny wave on a flat sea of smugness. The most important story about drugs from the 1930s is a comment in the *British Medical Journal* in 1936 that "Britain might serve as a model for other countries" (cited by Bean 1974: 70). The comment is reasonable given that it accurately reflects the almost complete absence of a drug problem in Britain at this time, but it also shows that the medical establishment had no understanding of the social forces of respectability that made this possible, no appreciation that this very respectability was already slowly beginning to ebb away.

The Disturbance of War and Back to Stability

Crimes of dishonesty rose markedly during World War II and remained high in the immediate postwar years, which is not surprising given the degree of internal social disruption caused by the war and the growth of a massive black market due to rationing and price controls, controls that were retained into the late 1940s, well after the war had ended. The black market resulted in very large numbers of ordinary respectable citizens routinely breaking the law as had happened in America during Prohibition and also gave an incentive to the large-scale thieving of everyday consumer goods. Pent-up demand created dishonest supply. The high black market prices also enabled anyone who stole or who dealt in stolen goods to make a much higher profit than pre-war and the existence of the black market made it easier to dispose of them safely. Crime paid better. Recorded levels of crime peaked in 1948 and then fell again until the mid-1950s. The real fall in crime at this point may well have been far greater than that implied by the statistics. Many now thought that the postwar crime wave in juvenile delinquency had merely been the result of the disruption to the childhood and adolescence of those who had grown up during the war, caused by bombing, evacuation, and fathers absent in the armed forces. Now everything seemed to be going back to normal in the calm years of the early 1950s and it was possible to be optimistic about the prospects of conquering crime. Likewise after a predictable rise in the incidence of illegitimacy during World War II, the incidence of illegitimacy had now fallen back to its low, long-term, steady level of between 4 percent and 5 percent of all live births. The early 1950s were, however, to prove to be the last days of Respectable Britain.

The Transition to De-moralized Britain

The Rise in Crime

From the mid-1950s there was a marked and sustained rise in both crimes of violence and dishonesty, which lasted for forty years. Britain moved during this period from being a society in which theft and violence were minor social nuisances to one in which they were a major social problem. An honest and peaceable society became a dishonest and violent one. It was a massive and rapid qualitative change as significant as the disappearance of public drunkenness described earlier. An equally striking collapse in family life and a marked rise in illegitimacy also took place. After 1960, public drunkenness was to return in force and other forms of drug abuse became a serious problem for the first time in the twentieth century. There is a clear and definite turning point in the social and moral history of British society, which is located in the late 1950s and early 1960s. Britain was now firmly embarked on the final leg of a U-curve of deviance. From this point onward there was for the next forty years a more or less continuous growth in all forms of deviant behavior regardless of the state of the economy. Respectable Britain decayed steadily.

The years 1955-57 mark a turning point after which there was a sustained and rapid rise in the recorded rate of crimes of *both* violence and dishonesty in England and Wales (Hood and Roddam 2000: 681; McClintock and Avison 1968: 3-27; Morris 1989: 90-91; Radzinowicz and King 1979: 15-16) that was to last until the mid-1990s. The twenty-first century will decide whether crime then stabilized at a very high level or merely paused and dipped before rising to a yet higher pinnacle. In the early 1950s, crime was not a serious social problem. By the 1990s crime was regarded by ordinary British citizens, particularly those who lived in the most crime-ridden areas, as one of the most serious problems they faced in their everyday lives. In 1957, just over half a million notifiable offenses were recorded by the police and in 1997 just under four and a half million. In 1957, just under 11,000 crimes of violence against the person were recorded and in 1997 a quarter of a million. Recorded crime in general in 1997 was seven times as high as it had been in 1957 and violent crime was twenty times as high. Even the more serious crimes of violence had grown nine-fold. In 1957, there had been fewer than 1,200 robberies reported and in 1997 over 63,000, which is fifty-one times as many. The end of the twentieth century was a totally different world from that least violent of all decades the 1920s. In 1927, fewer than 2,000 offenses of violence against the person were recorded, of which just over 500 were classed as serious. In 1927, at the very lowest point of the U-curve in robbery, there were only 110 robberies. Even if we allow for the rise in population there were nearly thirty times as many crimes recorded in 1997 as in 1900 and most of the increase occurred after 1955 (Hood and Roddam 2000: 676, 680-83). The last leg of the U-curve of violence and dishonesty had been completed, and after forty years of decline respectable Britain was dead.

The Rise in Violence

It is worth noting, too, that the rate of increase in violent crime greatly exceeded that of crimes of dishonesty. It is sometimes suggested that as a society gets wealthier theft increases because there is more to steal. The marked fall in theft at a time of rising incomes and wealth in the last half of the nineteenth century and the rise during the time of austerity during and after World War II clearly disproves this. However, the most striking refutation of this thesis lies in the very sharp rise in the ratio of violent crimes to crimes of dishonesty in England and Wales since 1955. Indeed, there has even been a U-curve in the ratio of violent crime to crime in general (most of which is theft) in Britain that matches the general U-curve in violence. In 1900, violence against the person was 2.4 percent of all reported crime. It fell to 1.0 percent by 1937 and 0.9 percent in 1967, but rose to 5.6 percent in 1997 (Hood and Roddam 2000: 682-83). By the end of the twentieth century once peaceful Britain had become one of the most violent societies in Western Europe (Kesteven et al. 2000).

Although murder remains a rare and atypical crime, there has also been a U-curve of homicide in Britain following roughly the same pattern as other violent crime, though as might be expected it was a flatter, saucer-shaped U-curve with marked fluctuations year on year. The incidence of recorded homicide, both murder and manslaughter, fell (Pike 1876: 468-472; Pierce, Grabosky, and Gurr 1977: 116-17; Gatrell 1980: 287-343; Gurr 1989: 31) in the nineteenth century and indeed the actual fall may well have been greater than that recorded in the statistics. By the end of the nineteenth century an experienced coroner or indeed police officer would have been able to identify and record murders that might have been considered accidents or death by unknown causes fifty years earlier (Gatrell 1980: 247). There was likewise a slow but steady rise in homicides in the latter part of the twentieth century (Rock 1998: 10-13) as respectable Britain was dying. The number of offenses initially recorded (and indeed eventually recorded) as homicide by the police rose consistently if irregularly between the mid-1950s and the end of the century. There were 279 offenses initially recorded as homicide in 1955 and 761 in 1999-2000. The number of offenses eventually (after elimination of those initially but no longer recorded as homicide) recorded as homicide in England and Wales rose from 7.3 per million of the population in 1967 to 13.2 in 1999/2000.[3] (*Criminal Statistics England and Wales 1999*, 2000: 71-6, *Crime in England and Wales 2001/2002 Supplementary* 2003: 7). The real rise in the incidence of homicide was probably even greater as the medical profession's skill in resuscitating the severely injured had improved. Many a victim of an attack who might have died in the 1920s from a blow or a wound would have been saved in the 1990s. Gurr (1989: 31) likewise notes that "the criminal conviction rate for murder and manslaughter gradually declined from about 0.5 per 100,000 in the 1870s to half that in 1930" but "increased from about 0.7 per 100,000 in the 1950s to more than 2.00 in the 1970s." These are still very low figures by comparison with other countries and by the 1970s remarkably low for such a violent country as Britain.

The Rise in Crime Was Real

The significance of the recent rise in homicides lies not in the absolute incidence but in the fact that it is not possible even to begin to try to explain it away in terms of increased reporting and com-

plaining by the victims and increased concern on the part of the
police. There is a corpse and the vast majority of British murders get
reported to the police and are thoroughly investigated. The doubling of the incidence of murder is undeniably real, real beyond
quibble.

It is important to note that the fastest rise in the incidence of crime
overall in England and Wales occurred in the late 1950s and in
the 1960s, a time of rapidly rising incomes, negligible unemployment, and a narrowing of the gap between rich and poor
(Dennis 1997:31-58), with a slowing down of the rate of increase
during the more difficult economic times of the late 1970s and
1980s (Hood and Roddam 2000: 680). It would be nonsense to
argue that this massive rise in crime has been caused by poverty
or increasing relative deprivation. In the short run it may well
still have been the case in the last decades of the twentieth century, as it was in the nineteenth century, that property crime rose
faster when there was a check to the growth of consumption and
that crimes against the person increased most when levels of consumption were rising faster (Hood and Roddam 2000: 704), but
this has no relevance whatsoever to the explanation of the massive
upward climb of both forms of crime in the last half of the twentieth
century.

A significant part of this huge rise may well be due to the greater
reporting and more efficient recording of crime, but that is beside
the point. All that is being argued here is that behind the figures
cited there took place so large a rise in the actual incidence of crime
in Britain as to constitute a *qualitative shift* from a low crime to a
high crime society. All the evidence that we have from the official
crime statistics, victimization studies, local area studies, insurance
companies' perceptions of rising claims made by the victims of crime,
the memories of those who lived in the period, or the increase in
facial injuries points in the same direction.

What was true of England and Wales as a whole was equally true
of areas as diverse as the British capital, London, and South Wales,
a declining industrial area. In London, there was a marked decline
in the total number of indictable offenses known to the police and in
convictions by the higher courts in relation to population after World
War II to a low point in 1955 and then a very rapid increase. Indictable assaults grew slowly before 1955 and much faster afterwards.

Murder and manslaughter fell in the late 1940s to a low point in 1950 before rising markedly, if erratically (the absolute number was, of course, small), after that time. Rates of acquisitive crime, larceny, burglary and robbery, which were not much higher in London in 1955 than they had been in 1935, rose rapidly after 1955 (Pierce, Grabosky and Gurr 1977: 158-66). Pierce, Grabosky, and Gurr were particularly scornful of the idea that this rise could be explained away as reporting and recording and noted that "it is unlikely that in London in the early 1950s there 'really' were 80,000 to 90,000 burglaries (the 1974 level) but people chose to report only 12,000 or 14,000. Phones by which to report offenses have been within walking distance of most Londoners throughout this period." Indeed, they concluded that due to the enormous increase in theft people were less likely to report petty thievery and that theft had probably increased more than the official figures indicated (Pierce, Grabosky, and Gurr 1977: 167).

Likewise, writing about the U-curve in robbery in London 1877-1977 with particular attention to the marked rise after 1955 (Pratt 1980: 72), Michael Pratt (1980: 73) noted dryly:

> But none of this, it is suggested, can begin to explain why the apparent pattern of robbery has changed so dramatically, particularly in more recent years. The "dark figure" and similar considerations may offer some explanation but they cannot account totally for an apparent increase of something like 25,000 per cent in less than fifty years. Moreover, although it is difficult not to be attracted by the argument of Daniel Bell (1961) (ably supported by Bernard Crick [1974]) that it is "obvious' that there *must* have been more crime 150 years or so ago than there is now, it is, at least in the case of robbery, simply not supported by the only facts that are available.

Similar patterns emerge from Norman Dennis' (1997) accounts of the North East of England and David Jones' (1996) study of South Wales. In each case what comes across is that nearly all the crime is committed by young males and yet that crime has risen steadily *even* when this group has been a constant or declining proportion of the population. This is particularly clear from the figures for Wales from Jones' (1996: 61) research shown in Table 1.2, which demonstrates clearly that crime has not been driven by demographic factors. In Wales, young males became an increasing problem to the community in the course of the twentieth century because they were *more criminal*, *not* because they were more numerous.

Table 1.2
Crime and Demography in Twentieth-Century Wales

Year	1901	1911	1921	1931	1951	1961	1971	1981	1989
Males as % of Welsh population	50	51	50	50	49	49	49	48	49
% of population aged									
0-14	34	33	31	27	23	24	24	21	19
0-19	44	42	40	35	29	30	31	29	26
15-24	19	18	18	17	13	13	14	15	15
Indictable offenses recorded per 100,000 of total population in Wales	222	279	385	392	979	1720	3395	5057	6818

Just as it was only the sociologists and criminologists who insisted that crime was rising in the nineteenth century when in fact it was falling substantially, so, too, it has been only sociologists and criminologists who have doubted the existence of the explosion of crime of the last half of the twentieth century (see account in Dennis 1993: 37-48). Just as many thought that crime "must" be rising in the "anomic," capitalist, inegalitarian nineteenth century (McDonald 1982), so, too, there have been those in the latter part of the twentieth century who found it difficult to believe that an enormous expenditure of public money on welfare, education, slum clearance and new council houses, community and leisure centers, and general social uplift not only had failed to bring about the fall in crime that they had hoped for and expected but was followed by an unprecedented rise not just in crime but in all manner of deviant behavior. Worse still was the suspicion that these very reforms may well have caused this crumbling of the social order. It is better to deny that any such rise in crime has occurred and put it all down to reporting and recording. Their instinct to do this is reinforced by a fear that politicians, press, and public alike will respond to this fearful increase in crime with a demand for punitive vengeance; they see this as having happened in the United States and are anxious lest it spread to Britain. Even the civil servants of the British Home Office have tended to talk down the increases in crime and to speak rather of the, by implication, irrational fears of those who know about crime merely through experiencing it directly or through their close associates. The spin put on the data in their reports does make the reading of official publications a richly humorous experience. The impact of crime on victims is always minimized unless the victim comes in a category where it is departmental policy to amplify the intensity as well as the frequency of victimhood, as with, say, domestic violence, sexual assaults, or racial attacks. The standard Home Office gloss on the crime figures is to stress that the vast majority of offenses do not involve violence and that most violence does not result in serious injury. In the early 1980s, responses to the British Crime Survey suggested that there were about 1,800,000 crimes of violence against persons over the age of sixteen in any one year (many of them not reported to the police) but readers of the report were reassured that in only 12 percent of these did the victim need any sort of medical attention and in less than 1 percent of cases was the victim admitted to the hospital (Hough and Mayhew 1983: 9-14). Yet, presumably, this means that 216,000 individuals who had been attacked did need medical attention and that many thousands were admitted to the hospital. It is a totally different style of presentation from, say, government health statistics which tend to overemphasize the dire effects of any departure from officially approved diets or sexual practices. Why should the British people have been encouraged to fear their own behavior but not that of other people?

On the whole, far from becoming more punitive, the British criminal justice system has become more lenient. When the prison population rose in Britain in the final stage of the U-curve such that by 1997 there were 64,000 prisoners, it was entirely a consequence of the marked rise in crime and particularly serious crime. The numbers serving sentences of less than twelve months had decreased and that of those serving more than three years had increased sharply. In 1937, there were only 800 male prisoners serving sentences of over three years, a mere 9 percent of the total. By 1997, there were 23,000 men serving over three years, who made up more than half the prison population. In relation to the number of crimes committed, the size of the British prison population *diminished* over these sixty years. The ratio of prisoners to those found guilty or cautioned was lower in 1997 than it had been in 1937 (Hood and Roddam 2000: 695-99). What emerges is a picture of a society trying to make less use of imprisonment, notably with the Criminal Justice Act of 1991 that became known as the Criminals'Charter (Davies 1993), but overwhelmed by the sheer rise in the volume of crime and particularly serious crime. The number of prisoners has risen because and only because there is far more crime and not because Britain has become more punitive or particularly given to sending people to prison. On a list of twenty-seven democratic societies England and Wales came in eighth in 1997 in relation to prison population per 100,000 population but only sixteenth in relation to prison population per 100,000 crimes, well below Spain, Portugal, Japan, Ireland, Italy, Switzerland, France, and Greece, who seemed superficially to make less use of imprisonment. The situation in Scotland was similar to that in England and Wales and both countries were roughly comparable with Australia and Canada (Hood and Roddam 2000: 701). British prisons were full mainly because far more people in Britain had been victims of crime and especially serious crime than had been true in the past or than was the case in other European countries. The U-curve in Britain's prison population in the late nineteenth and twentieth centuries was a reflection of the U-curve in crime on which had been superimposed a steadily increasing reluctance to send people to prison. As is now clear, respectable Britain began to crumble in the late 1950s and the incidence of crimes of violence and dishonesty rose rapidly. The rise in crime was not at first related to addiction; it was driven neither by the effects of drugs on individuals nor by the need to get money to pay for drugs. It was part of a general collapse of moral order which, in turn, was about to include an escalating orgy of drug taking, producing yet another massive crime wave. Another corner was being turned in degenerating Britain.

The Rise of Drug Abuse

In 1955, there were only 335 known addicts, with women outnumbering men. By 1963, there were 635 known addicts, of whom more than half were male, and by 1968 there were nearly 3,000 of whom nearly three-quarters were male. The new addicts had not become addicted as a result of medical treatment nor were they in medical or allied occupations. Indeed the total numbers of addicts in these categories were actually declining, as was the number of older addicts. By 1968, there were 764 addicts under twenty years of age and 1,530 between twenty and thirty-four; nearly three-quarters of the total number of addicts were now under thirty-five (Bean 1973: 104-7). There was very little illegal importation of heroin and other opiates into Britain prior to 1968, so far as we can tell from the levels of seizures by customs and excise, so that the drugs used by the new addicts were derived from those legally prescribed by the doctors. The system collapsed because it was not designed to deal with addicts who lacked respectability in a society that was also losing that quality. There had probably always been a few addicts willing to sell part of the drugs prescribed to them and a few doctors willing to over-prescribe but now there also existed a generation of young male delinquents willing to buy their drugs in order to seek new forms of excitement. Indeed, Schur's (1963: 235-51) survey in Willesden in the late 1950s had revealed the existence of just such a constituency, who did not at that time abuse opiates but only because they lacked knowledge of and access to them. What was now happening was that a new, young male experimenter would buy heroin for injecting from a registered addict, become addicted, register with a doctor and get a supply of his own and then sell part of it to other new experimenters thus creating an escalating number of new addicts. There were no safeguards in place to prevent this because in the previous respectable era they had not been needed and by the time they were put in place in 1967 it was too late, since a black market and an addict sub-culture based on legally prescribed drugs was well established. There has been much futile argument as to exactly why and when the system began to spiral out of control; the burglary of a pharmacy, over-prescribing by one or two uncontrollable doctors and the arrival of experienced Canadian addicts have each been fingered as the trigger. It is an irrelevant question since the general demoralization of society meant that the system of prescribing was in a position of unstable equilibrium and any minor perturbation could have dislodged it. In the late 1950s, there already existed a substantial black market in amphetamines and barbiturates, which were very widely prescribed (Griffith-Edwards 1978: 4, 12) by doctors for a variety of disorders. Heroin was simply added to the menu of illicit drugs being bought and sold.

The mortality of the new young users of heroin and morphine by injection was far greater than that of their predecessors (Bewley et al. 1968: 726). Although they were given clean needles, strict instructions about hygiene and dosage, and accurately measured quantities of the pure drug, they had a high death rate from overdoses, hepatitis, tetanus, and septicaemia. They shared needles and neglected the most elementary hygienic precautions (Stimson and Osborne 1970) because the very lack of the respectable virtues that had led them to becoming addicted rendered them incapable of dealing with their addiction. The drugs they took further undermined what little self-control they had. They associated mainly with other addicts who shared what were not merely a lack of prudence and foresight but a rejection of these very virtues. Injecting drugs is by its very nature a more hazardous procedure than the alternative ways of taking them and whereas the addicts of the 1930s were sufficiently in control of their own behavior to survive the risky routines of injecting drugs, the new addicts were not.

The addicts' hedonistic search for dangerous new forms of pleasure linked them to those responsible for the huge increase in theft and violence from the mid-1950s onward who were also young and male. Indeed, many of the new addicts had criminal convictions before they ever turned to drugs (Mott 1978: 81-85). Criminals were also in search of quick excitement. Their thefts were not planned enrichment nor was their violence purposeful. Rather theft, violence, and drug taking were all different ways of pursuing risk and sensation in a society that had ceased to value and enforce respectability. Indeed, such forms of deviant behavior are both an index and a consequence of the death of respectable Britain. The self-destructive behavior of the addicts in the 1960s links them also to the strange rise in the suicide rate of males under twenty-five between 1960 and 1970. It was strange because it happened at a time when the suicide rate of women and older men was falling (Robertson and Cochrane 1976: 79, 84). There were to be further falls in the suicide rates both of women of all ages and of men in the older age groups and the overall suicide rate in England and Wales was lower at the end of the twentieth century than it had been in 1970. By contrast, the suicide rate among males aged 15-34 continued to rise as did deaths from drug and alcohol abuse (Charlton et al. 1994: 6-7, 21; see also Fitzpatrick and Chandola 2000: 109). There is no reason to suppose that these movements in opposite directions are a reflection of changes in patterns of reporting and recording.

Rather, the collapse of respectable Britain in the prosperous years of the 1960s created an anomic situation for those under twenty-five who had been constrained previously by the forces of respectability. When the constraints collapsed, young males not only turned to criminality, alcohol, and drugs but also increasingly succumbed to the self-destruction that Durkheim (1951[1897]: 246-47) had long before associated with a lack of constraints on human desire. Durkheim was wrong to think of late nineteenth-century societies as increasingly anomic and increasingly given to crime and suicide. As we have seen, crime rates were actually falling. However, Durkheim's insights have proved to be prophetic and his theory of anomie explains precisely why the suicide rate of young males rose even at a time of falling suicide rates generally; it was the young males who were most in need of protection from self-destruction by a framework of moral constraints (Durkheim 1952 [1897]: 275).

Neither suicide nor the high mortality of addicts were ends originally sought by those seeking the higher levels of excitement that the death of respectability seems to make possible. In that respect, they are as phenomena quite different from crimes of violence and dishonesty, which are in themselves a means of finding, gaining, and experiencing excitement. However, all four phenomena were products of a society in which, for young males at least, wants had become infinite once the restraints of respectability had been repudiated.

From 1968 onward, the main source of illicit drugs in Britain became illegal imports. There was a market for these drugs, which from 1967 were no longer being provided as freely by the National Health Service. The gap between the high price addicts and even would-be addicts were willing to pay not just for heroin but for a wide variety of drugs and the trivial cost of growing and manufacturing them meant that very large profits could be made in the new black market. Those who were addicted often financed their habit by pyramid selling whereby an addict would finance his or her own consumption by selling at a profit part of the drugs that he or she had bought, which, of course, expanded the size of the market very rapidly. Dr. John Marks has suggested to the author that it might well have expanded faster in those areas where the new clinics that had a monopoly of prescribing heroin tried to cure addicts by severely restricting the amount of drugs given to them than in the areas where the clinics took a more lax approach; this was quite contrary to what the tough-minded doctors now running the clinics assumed (see Griffith-Edwards 1978: 14). The doctors grossly overestimated their ability to cajole and coerce the addicts into abstinence and the politicians overestimated their ability to suppress the black market in drugs. The only result of their efforts was a further increase in crime since restricting the supply pushed the price higher and addicts turned to crime to pay for their habit. The crime rate was already rising rapidly in Britain in the 1960s *before* the illegal trade in drugs took hold and at a time when the number of addicts was negligible but a substantial part of the rise in theft, burglary, and robbery from the 1970s onward was due to addicts seeking money to pay for drugs (Clutterbuck 1995: 3, 180; Merry 1994: 78-79; Stevenson 1994: 30-31). Likewise a degenerate culture of drug takers developed in which the thrill of drug taking was supplemented by the excitement of illegal dealing.

Survey data at the beginning of the twenty-first century suggests that there could be anywhere between 200,000 and 400,000 regular users of heroin in Britain (*Drugs Uncovered* 2002) as against 25,000 Home Office registered addicts. A fair proportion of them do not inject, pay for their habit out of their earnings, and have sustained periods of abstention. They do not turn to acquisitive crime to pay for their drugs and they do not have a markedly high death rate (Benson and Rasmussen 1996: 7-13; Stevenson 1994: 21; Yates 1990: 9-14; see also Cohen 1990: 212-22). Nonetheless, the large rise in the number of consumers will have brought with it a rise in the absolute number of addicts out of all control.

In post-respectable Britain discussion of the drug taker's moral character and the impact of the drugs on that moral character is minimal. A causalist ethic of harm minimization is central to the way policy is discussed (see Clutterbuck 1995: 192-213; Stevenson 1994: 45-46). It may well be that in many cases the assessments of the relative levels of harm entailed by adopting one particular policy rather than another merely reflect the moral values and biases of particular assessors, but the dominant form of argument that they are forced to use has come to be what I have termed causalism (Davies 1980: 13-14).

A further indication of the move away from a concern with self-control towards an emphasis on minimizing harm may be seen in the normalization of recreational drug use (Parker et al. 1998) and the decline in the use of and campaigns against tobacco in the last half of the twentieth century. At the beginning of the twenty-first century, a national survey revealed that 13 million people in Britain, including over half of those in Britain aged 16-24 and a large proportion of those aged 25-44, said that they had taken an illegal drug, the most frequent choices being cannabis and ecstasy. By contrast very few people over 55 had ever taken such drugs (*Drugs Uncovered* 2002: 12). Clearly, there had been a marked increase in the use of those drugs and local surveys indicate that it was particularly rapid in the 1990s when a substantial proportion of young people of both sexes from respectable backgrounds and with no history of delinquency came to take illegal recreational drugs paid for from their own legitimately acquired money on a fairly routine basis. (Parker et al. 1998: 153-54; Stevenson 1994: 20-21). They had decided that any health risk involved was worth it for the sake of the sensation. In post-respectable Britain, they were not concerned by the fact that the drugs were illegal (Parker et al. 1998: 155, 159), nor, as the previous generation might have done, did they perceive the activity as a questionable form of self-indulgence involving a loss of self-control.

By contrast, the number of tobacco smokers fell remarkably, during the very time when respectable Britain was crumbling. At the smoking peak in 1948, in the last years of respectable Britain, 82 percent of all men over sixteen smoked tobacco, the highest ever. Smoking rose and fell *with* *r*espectable Britain. The consumption of tobacco by men rose in the last half of the nineteenth century, and the first half of the twentieth century was the era of high, mass consumption of cigarettes. In 1948, the average male smoker got through nearly fifteen cigarettes a day (Hilton 2000: 83-115, 148; Fitzpatrick and Chandola, 2000: 118-20; Wilson 1940: 253-54). For men at least[4] it was the drug of respectability, the drug of the steady worker and the steadfast warrior. It could be used according to choice and circumstance as a drug that improved concentration and performance in the face of fatigue and distraction or as a drug that provided calm and relaxation under conditions tending to induce stress and fear. Above all, tobacco does not intoxicate and as such it did not threaten the central concerns of a respectable society. It does not interfere with the smoker's control over his or her own actions nor, in general, lead the smoker into anti-social behavior.[5] Indeed, it can be shown experimentally that nicotine enhances cognition and improves performance on a variety of tasks in marked contrast to alcohol, which has a debilitating and impairing effect, "a behaviour toxicity" even in small doses (Hindmarch et al. 1994: 52-57). Smokers consciously use tobacco to assist them to complete tasks that are difficult or tedious or both (Lowe 1994: 100-101; Mackenzie 1957: 335, 343). Tobacco as a drug was thus entirely compatible with the values and institutions of respectable Britain. It is almost certainly coincidence that the discovery of its long-term and fatal consequences occurred just at the point where respectable Britain was about to go into steep decline. If medical research had shown tobacco to be harmless it would still be flourishing alongside alcohol and other drugs of enjoyment. The vast majority of women as well as men would have become smokers, as its association with women's enhanced importance in the labor force and greater sexual freedom would have been ever more skilfully exploited by the advertisers. The critical minority who had long condemned tobacco as a dirty form of self-indulgence and as a vicious addiction revealing a lack of character and self-control would have dwindled away.

The Rise in Illegitimacy

The final index of the collapse of respectable Britain was the upward explosion of the incidence of illegitimacy after the mid-1950s, although it was not quite as dramatic as a simple examination of Britain's fast-rising illegitimacy ratio suggests. There was certainly a substantial rise in that ratio for England and Wales, from 4.7 percent in 1955 to 8.5 percent in 1968 (Hartley 1975: 39), which was as good an indication of the onset of demoralization and collapse of respectable Britain as the rise in the crime rate during the same period. Subsequently, it rose to the point where 35.8 percent of children were born outside marriage in 1996 (Coleman, 2000: 51), but many of these children were being acknowledged and brought up by both parents. As Coleman (2000: 52) notes:

The greater part of the post-1960's increase in these births was to couples living together in some form of informal union. This can be inferred from the joint registration on birth certificates of illegitimate births.... This increased from 38.3% (of a much smaller number) in 1966 to 58% in 1981 and to 78% in 1996. Just over half the registrations of illegitimate births are not only jointly registered but give the same address for both parents (58.1% in 1996). Correspondingly, the more "traditional" type of unmarried motherhood where the mother registers the child only in her own name has fallen from 61.7% of the total (41,400 births) to 21.9% in 1996. Nonetheless given that overall fertility markedly declined between 1966 and 1996, the growth in the number of such children born every year from 41,400 to 51,000 indicates a very large increase in illegitimacy indeed. A high and increasing proportion of the truly illegitimate children were born to mothers under the age of 20. (Coleman 2000: 53)

A large proportion of the latter category of illegitimate children will have no contact with their father and will only ever know a frequently changing succession of boyfriends temporarily associating with their mother. Some of these children will not even know who their father is (and indeed possibly their mother doesn't know either; it is ironic that at a time when it was proposed to reveal the identity of sperm donors to their offspring, no such right was available to those conceived as a result of natural insemination by donor). It is here that the moral significance of illegitimacy lies and not in sexual conduct. Throughout the entire history of respectable Britain a very substantial proportion of brides were pregnant at the time of marriage but children who were pre-maritally conceived were not discriminated against or stigmatized or seen as a particularly deviant phenomenon. Those who (in desperate search for proof that little has really changed) use the figures on premarital conception of the past as an index of hypocrisy or immorality have misunderstood the motives and relationships of the couples concerned and failed to see that legitimacy is a form of contract between parents and children. Those who married "because they had to" fulfilled this contract. From an anthropological point of view the function of marriage is to legitimate children and thus to provide them with a secure social location and also with a complete set of relatives, both father's and mother's, on whose assistance they can call (Murray 1994: 10). There is, likewise, an implicit contract in the case of cohabitees who jointly register their children; the problem does not lie in the informal nature of these relationships but in their greater instability (Coleman 2000: 60-61), that is, in their tendency to break up and produce fatherless children by another route. Only 36 percent of these children will spend their entire childhood with their biological parents, compared with 70 percent of those born legitimate. What is needed is a new and more sophisticated index of fatherlessness or, to be more precise, of the deliberate or reckless bringing about of a situation of which fatherlessness is the likely consequence.[6] Such an index would be a good measure in a family context of the absence of those qualities of prudence, foresight, and restraint that are the essence of respectability.

The rises in crime, illegitimacy, and drug and alcohol abuse that characterized the period 1955-1995 began as independent expressions of the collapse of respectability but soon became intertwined. Crime was already rising rapidly before drug abuse became widespread in the 1970s, but the growth of a population of addicts using theft, burglary, and robbery to pay for their drug habits provided an additional reason for a further rise in acquisitive crime and in the long run also of violence stemming from disputes between gangs. Likewise, the return of public drunkenness fuelled by the erosion of the legal controls and restrictions on the sale of alcohol was a stimulus to a further increase in violent crime. The rising proportion of illegitimate births after 1955 will have led to increased crime as a higher proportion of children grew up without fathers. Fathers are an indispensable source of personal, social, and economic stability, of moral influence and constraint, and of protection (Dennis 1993: 2-5; Dennis and Erdos 1993: 66-71, 120; Halsey 1993: xii; Murray 1994). Their increasing absence was both an indication of and a cause of the strange death of moral Britain.

The Measure of Respectable Britain

Thus far we have spoken mainly of the fall and subsequent rise of forms of deviant behavior indicating an absence of respectability. It is after all easier to demonstrate the existence or absence of dishonesty, violence, illegitimacy, fatherlessness, drunkenness, and addiction than to show directly the extent to which people display the virtues of honesty, concern, self-control, uprightness, prudence, sobriety, fortitude, and sense of duty, the elements that go to make up what was once called "character." Virtue is silent; indeed, when it is not we suspect it. An attempt to measure the strength or prevalence of the respectable virtues (rather than their absence) would soon become a mere catalogue of inspiring stories of ordinary people struggling to maintain standards in difficult circumstances. Such stories are a good way of inculcating the virtues of respectability and were often used as such in the hagiographies of the humble given out as Sunday School prizes, but we can not easily gain access to the real world respectability of the past. Anthropologists cannot travel back in time and the memories of the very old are uncertain and selective. Besides, acts of honesty, decency, and prudence are all too easily forgotten in a society where they are the normal mode of behavior. The white sheep of the family are invisible. Respectability is not exciting or amusing and its virtues are those of moderation, and attention to the regular duties of everyday life, not sudden and heroic responses to extremity. Respectability leaves few tales. There were no glittering prizes associated with respectability, no acclaim, no awards and titles, no gongs, no ribbons. It could be attained by anyone and was within the reach of those of modest earnings and talents, and in the past to have a good name and a good character were both necessary and sufficient for self-esteem and for gaining the respect of others. However, that respect depended on remaining respectable; if you lost your respectability others ceased to respect you. This kind of respect was available to everyone, but it had to be earned. Respect was not the cheap and impudent demand of today for automatic acceptance regardless of qualities of character or patterns of behavior.

It is necessary rather to look at the rise and fall of the institutions that promoted respectability, institutions that were both exercisers of respectability in themselves and the training ground for respectability elsewhere. Their success is both an index and a cause of respectability. The most notable and influential of these institutions was the Sunday School, a great engine of respectability rooted in religion. During the time of its rise, deviant behavior fell, and as religion decayed the Sunday Schools declined; both religion and Sunday Schools collapsed together from the late 1950s, and, as we have seen, a tide of deviance swept over the land. The trajectory of the Sunday Schools is that of respectable Britain.

The Rise and Fall of the Institutions That Created and Promoted Respectable Britain

The Rise and Fall of the Sunday Schools

The Sunday Schools run by the churches provided children with a moral training whose effects may well have endured for the rest of their lives. The pattern of their rise and fall can be seen in Table 1.3 (based on data from Gill 1992: 96-97), which charts the proportion of population under fifteen enrolled in Sunday School in England and Wales.

A very similar picture emerges if we look at the absolute numbers of children in the Sunday Schools at its rise and fall over time (based on Laqueur 1976: 246).

Table 1.3
Percentage of Population under Age 15 Enrolled in Sunday School in England and Wales

Year	Percentage
1818	12%
1851	38%
1891	52%
1901	53%
1911	51%
1931	46%
1961	20%
1989	14%

Table 1.4
Numbers Enrolled in Sunday Schools in Britain

Year	Numbers
1851	2,614,274
1881	5,762,638
1901	5,952,431
1906	6,178,827
1911	6,129,496
1916	5,572,194
1921	5,256,052
1931	4,823,666
1941	3,565,786
1951	3,047,794
1961	2,547,026

At the peak of their influence in the late nineteenth and early twentieth centuries the Sunday Schools reached a large number of young people and a high proportion of their age group. Not only was there high enrollment but it has been estimated that "between two-thirds and three-quarters" of enrolled pupils generally attended on a particular Sunday (Gill 1992: 96). By 1888, about three out of four children attended Sunday School, "a remarkable proportion when it is remembered that parents of the higher social groups did not particularly favor attendance" (Wilkinson 1978: 7). In 1910, at their peak, the president of the Sunday School Union claimed that more than 700,000 teachers taught more than 7 million pupils Sunday by Sunday. On an average Sunday more than a fifth of the entire population was at Sunday School (Horton 1910: 57; see also Munson 1991: 12). In 1957, of those over thirty years of age 76 percent had attended Sunday School at some time in their lives. However, the age of decline had already begun and the corresponding figure for those under thirty was only 61 percent (Martin 1967: 42). By the year 2000, fewer than a tenth of children attended a Sunday School (Brown 2001: 3). An entire culture had been lost.

The pattern is the inverse of the U-curve of deviance with the Sunday Schools growing in strength in the late nineteenth century as the incidence of deviant behavior fell, reaching their peak at the end of that century, and then a long, slow decline that accelerated in the late 1950s, the time when crime, illegitimacy, and drug and alcohol abuse began to become serious problems in British society. It is difficult to resist the inference that there is a connection between the two phenomena.

The Sunday Schools at their peak were a great force for inculcating the virtues of respectability in the young. Their leaders knew that they had not created a devout church-attending population, but the president of the Sunday School Union in 1910 was convinced that the "comparative cleaness, truthfulness, kindness, and beneficence of our people in Great Britain" was due to their efforts. He believed that the Sunday Schools had transformed the "tone and temper, the habits and possibilities of our country" (Horton 1910: 58). Indeed, this was one of the main reasons why such a very high proportion of working-class parents insisted that their children attend them. In the latter part of the nineteenth century, the basic literacy and numeracy increasingly needed for survival in the labor market were freely available in ordinary week-day schools (Springhall et al. 1983: 223); if the acquisition of these secular skills had been the reason for sending children to Sunday School, the Sunday Schools would not have flourished as they did in the decades before World War I. Even in London at the turn of the century where levels of adult church attendance among the working classes were low (Mudie-Smith 1904) perhaps three-quarters of a million young people would receive moral and religious instruction each Sunday (Mann 1904: 274) because their parents wanted this. In the Midlands and the North of England the Sunday Schools had an even stronger hold over their scholars (Green 1996: 212-3). Many middle-class children attended church with their parents or received instruction at home instead of going to Sunday School (Green 1996: 217; Laqueur 1976: 248; Wilkinson 1978: 7), but attendance at Sunday School was "a norm of working-class juvenile life in the late Victorian manufacturing town" (Green 1996: 214; see also Laqueur 1976: xi; McLeod 2000: 273; Springhall et al. 1983: 22). This was no doubt the source of the, by present day standards remarkable, absence of serious juvenile delinquency in these towns at the end of the nineteenth century. In many parts of Wales, attendance at Nonconformist Sunday Schools was also usual for adults; men, women, and children felt equally at home in an institution that provided the country with the main basis of its popular culture (Davies 1981: 37-39, 64). It was in consequence a moralized culture, a source of the respectable virtues and of resistance to the temptations of urban and industrial as well as rural life.

The strength of the Sunday Schools lay in their popular character. They were to a substantial extent created by ordinary people, their teachers were drawn from the respectable working and lower middle classes, and they catered to the aspirations of parents from these classes for the proper moral upbringing of their children. It was part of a widely held culture of self-restraint, self-help, self-improvement, orderliness, and respectability (Green 1996: 214-15; Laqueur 1976: 231). The Sunday Schools were not in any sense an imposition of social control on an otherwise rumbustious and rebellious working-class by a distant and powerful elite. They were a form of social control but it was one based on age not class.

Parents and Sunday Schools were in agreement that children should be faced with a single, uniform, consistent set of moral precepts.

Anti-social behavior was condemned and self-respect, respectability, and a reputation for decency and probity were taught as fit and proper aspirations in life for all. However much the members of the various social classes might differ on other directly political questions, they could and did agree on these basic and straightforward moral points. It was very much in the parents' interests that their children turn out sober, diligent, and provident rather than dishonest, defiant, feckless, and wanton. No doubt the acquisition of these virtues also benefited the political and economic elite, but the wiser and more cynical members of these elites would have noticed that the leaders of the radical organizations that were to challenge their authority with far more determination, stamina, and methodical effectiveness than any mob of drunken rioters could have done were the products of the Sunday Schools (Laqueur 1976: xii, 171, 228). Nonconformist Protestantism was a source of political radicalism (McLeod 2000: 194-95; Munson, 1991: 301) as well as of the stability of every day life.

The Importance of Religion

It is important to stress the religious inspiration for and underpinning of the Sunday Schools and to link the rise and fall of their influence to the parallel rise and fall of religion in British society. Britain has become a strongly secular society with relatively low levels of Christian belief, church attendance, participation and membership, and even *rites de passage* such as baptism, but this is a surprisingly recent phenomenon. As late as the 1950s, religion still mattered in Britain and secularization only set in at the end of that decade when a previously religious people abandoned organized Christianity (Brown 2001: 1-6). Their abandonment of religion coincided with the rise of a society plagued by high levels of deviant behavior.

In some ways the process of the secularization of British society is a very old one, one going back to the Enlightenment and also proceeding hand in hand with modernization and the differentiation of society into separate specialized areas each with its own pattern of knowledge and belief. Individual merchants, scientists, manufacturers, lawyers, bureaucrats, artisans, factory workers, soldiers or scholars might well be devout Christians, but the ordinary activities that occupied most of their lives were not informed by, nor much influenced by, sacred or supernatural considerations; they had become secular, purely mundane, matter-of-fact objective activities from which religion was excluded. In the late eighteenth and nineteenth centuries when Britain became the world's first urban and industrial society, this aspect of secularization undoubtedly became stronger, but it does not follow that Britain became irreligious. Rather, religious institutions came to specialize in providing moral and spiritual socialization (Green 1996: 385), and in providing consolation, often in the form of a belief in an afterlife, for the sufferings and bereavements that the secular world, then as now, could only alleviate and postpone. Within this sphere it is arguable that the church institutions that continued to be based on a belief in the supernatural and in a morality revealed by God, became more influential over time in an increasingly urban and industrial Britain. In Britain at least secular competitors with the Sunday Schools were singularly unsuccessful and the market in providing an education in respectability was dominated by competing Christian denominations whose ultimate justification lay outside this world. It was religion and religion alone that gave the stamp of authenticity to the moral training of children on Sundays, a training infused with and informed by distinctively Christian beliefs. This is hardly surprising given that the majority of the population, even though they rarely went to church and did not see church-going as a duty or obligation (much to the despair of the clergy), possessed a taken for granted and largely unquestioned popular religion that included an attachment to church-based rituals, a fondness of hymns, a rather vague acceptance of central Christian beliefs, a profound respect for sacred things, and a conviction that it was a religious duty to help others (Green 1996: 17; McLeod 2000: 272).

Nowhere in Victorian and Edwardian Britain was there any marked antipathy towards or rejection of the Christian religion (Green 1996: 199), nor, except among a few intellectuals, a sense of alienation from it or attempts to seek a substitute for it in exotic forms of spirituality or rationalist secular ideologies. Even those who sought direct contact with the dead through spiritualism did so alongside rather than in competition with conventional religion (Davies 1999: 350-51). The growth of urban life and industrial employment had not in general undermined religion and given that the nature of its impact was so very varied it is not surprising that in some areas it led to an intensification of religious life (Green 1996: 18-19). The period from the 1850s to the 1880s, the time when Britain finally and decisively became a predominantly urban and industrial society, was a time of remarkable success for the churches and one that touched the entire population (Brown 2001: 162-66; Davies 1981: 16; McLeod 2000: 48).

Even in the more uncertain period between the 1880s and the outbreak of World War I there are other indices of continued success besides the thriving of the Sunday Schools. There were increasing levels of church adherence and membership in relation to population rising to a peak in England and Wales in 1904 and in Scotland in 1905. Religion marked all the key-turning points in people's lives. In England, the proportion of infants baptized in the Church of England rose steadily to a peak of 700 per thousand live births in 1913, and confirmations were at their highest ever in 1914. In 1900, 85 percent of marriages in England and Wales and 94 percent in Scotland were religious. Likewise the highest levels of Easter Day communicants in relation to population in the Church of England were in 1903 and 1913 (Brown 1992: 42-45; Brown 2001:7, 163; McLeod 2000: 264-65; Marrin 1974: 211). Yet the leaders of the churches were uneasy about their failure to evangelize the entire country and create an inclusive Christian society. The last great religious revival took place in Wales in 1904 (Evans 1969) and it sputtered out in 1905 in the midst of criticism from doctors and from the drier ministers of religion for its emotionalism and indeed hysteria. No single clear turning point can be identified, but somewhere in the early years of the twentieth century a corner was turned.

In the 1920s, after the devastating losses and social upheaval of World War I it was clear that Britain was ceasing to be a Christian society, such that Simon Green could speak of the strange death of religious Britain (Green 1996: 380). A corner had indeed been turned. Yet the rate of decline was relatively slow. Attendances fell but there was only a small decline in membership until the mid-1950s and levels of baptism and marriage remained high. Indeed, there was a brief recovery in Sunday School enrollment between 1945 and 1955 (Brown 2001: 5-6,162-69). It is only from the mid-1950s onwards that religion ceased to matter in Britain. During the last forty years of the twentieth century every single index of Christian activity, adherence, and religiosity demonstrates collapse. Seventy-two percent of marriages in England and Wales in 1957, and 83 percent in Scotland, were religious; by 1997, it was 39 percent in England and Wales and 55 percent in Scotland. The proportion of infants in England baptized in the Church of England fell from 602 per 1,000 live births in 1956 to 228 in 1997. Levels of church adherence at the end of the twentieth century were less than half of what they had been at the beginning and most of the fall occurred in the last half of the century. The state of religion in Britain in 1955 was far closer to 1900 than it was to the millennium (Brown 2001: 6-7,163; see also Brierly 2000: 665). In 1955, Britain was what it had been in 1880, a fundamentally Christian country, most of whose adult population rarely attended church but who accepted the legitimacy of the Christian religion even though they were not strongly committed to things otherworldly. "Yet," as Callum G. Brown (2001: 142) put it, "what made Britain a Christian nation before 1950 was not the minority with a strong faith but the majority with some faith." The minority is still there though diminished in size and influence, but there has been a marked rise in disbelief. In the 1950s in Britain, two-thirds of those questioned said that they believed that Jesus was the Son of God and less than a fifth expressed disbelief. By the 1980s, less than half of those asked said they believed Jesus was the Son of God and nearly 40 percent said that they did not believe this (Brierly 2000: 663). In the 1950s, believers in the *central tenet* of the Christian religion were in a majority in Britain or at the very least it was conventionally accepted in the society that this was what ought to be believed and few people chose to dissent. When people say they disbelieve we can take it they mean it, and it is the doubling of expressed disbelief in thirty years that is the real index of change. In the United Kingdom in the twenty-first century, disbelief predominates except in Northern Ireland. The majority neither believe nor retain any kind of institutional link with religion even by passive association or *rites de passage*. The second corner has been turned, and Simon Green's (1996: 380) "strange death of religious Britain," which marked the end of confidence and fervor by the 1920s, has been succeeded by Callum G. Brown's (2001) *The Death of Christian Britain*, in which the entire Christian identity of the society has been effaced. Thus, behind the rise and fall of those great factories of respectability, the Sunday Schools, lay a more fundamental change, the rise and fall of the churches in Britain.

Religion, Respectability, and Deviance

It seems fairly clear that the rise and fall of the fortunes of the churches in British society produced the rise and fall of respectable Britain, which, in turn, lies behind the otherwise inexplicable U-curve of deviance in crime, illegitimacy, and drug and alcohol abuse. It is difficult to specify precise turning points, given the many different aspects of human behavior that have been discussed and the problems of measurement involved. Somewhat arbitrarily, I shall take World War I as one turning point and the late 1950s as the other and divide the era of the rise and reign, and fall and death of respectable Britain into three reasonably consistent stages.

Table 1.5
The Rise and Fall of Respectable Britian

	The Rise of Respectable Britain 1850-1914	Respectable Britain 1919-1955	The Strange Death of Respectable Britain 1955-1995
Acquisitive Crime	Falls to a very low level	Rising slowly. Stabilizes in early 1950s	Rising Rapidly
Violent Crime	Falling	Falls then rises slowly	Rising Rapidly
Illegitimacy	Falling	Steady at a low level except in wartime	Rising Rapidly
Drug and Alcohol Abuse	Falling	Falling then steady at a low level	Rising Rapidly
Sunday School Enrollment	Rising Rapidly	Falling slowly. Recovery in early 1950s	Falling Fast
Church Adherence	Rising unevenly	Falling slowly. Recovery in early 1950s	Falling Fast

Given that it is unlikely that a falling incidence of crime, illegitimacy, and drunkenness drove parents to enroll their children in Sunday Schools and given that those who organized and taught in the Sunday Schools were motivated by religion, it seems reasonable to describe the period from the mid-nineteenth century down to World War I as "religion and the rise of respectability." The fortunes of respectability rose and fell with those of religion. The difficult question to answer is whether or not there is some common factor in the background promoting and then undermining both respectability and religiosity. Why, in a world where religion was no longer important in the central, secular, and clearly expanding sectors of society, namely science, commerce, and manufacturing, did differentiation and a specialization in personal morality initially lead to a strengthening of religious institutions and later to their abandonment? There are no easy answers to such a question; for the time being it is perhaps better to accept that religion is an autonomous force in society, shaping as well as being shaped by other institutions. If this assumption is made then respectability did grow out of religion.

Towards the end of the nineteenth century doubts appeared both about religion and about respectability not among the mass of the population but among those most influential in shaping society. Those who had the power to influence the policy of the state on moral questions were beginning to shift from a mode of thinking based on moralism, the allocation of rewards or penalties on the basis of dessert to individuals seen as autonomous decision-makers, to causalism, a form of harm minimization, which that will be the subject of chapter 2. This did not in itself set off the decline and collapse of respectable Britain but it was an indication that above the apparent stability lay considerable doubt. The moral forces that drove the system were losing their dynamism by the end of the nineteenth century; indeed they had been stronger earlier in that century. Moral Britain was close to the top of its trajectory. As Martin Wiener (1990: 337) stated with great insight:

> In the late nineteenth century a gradual but ultimately profound reshaping of the human image took place—normal as well as deviant. Even as the image of autonomous and effective but self-restraining, Protestant man established in the first half of the century was strengthening its hold on social classes *beneath* them, members of the official classes were finding that image increasingly unconvincing intellectually and unsatisfactory emotionally. (Emphasis in original.)

Immediately below the official class, those who remained earnest were becoming uneasy by the end of the nineteenth century, both at the shift to causalism of those who exercised power and at the realization that yet further efforts on their part were not going to give them any further increments of influence over the mass of the people in their society. They had peaked. They went on winning, probably until World War I, but they were faltering; they knew they were reaching the limits of what they could achieve. Those who graduated from their Sunday Schools remained respectable, but most showed little interest in joining or taking part in the churches whose Sunday Schools they had attended (Horton 1910: 58). As adolescents they were not violent or dishonest by the standards of the late twentieth century, they did not produce illegitimate children, and they were increasingly disinclined to get drunk in public, but the males in particular did not take seriously admonitions as to the virtues of teetotalism or the sins of gambling and impurity. The organizers of the Sunday School movement were proud of the social transformation of Britain "in the direction not only of civilisation but of Christianity," which they saw as the result of their own "voluntary and devoted labours" (Horton 1910: 58), but they realized that the limits of respectability had been reached and that the achievement of this level of respectability had not produced a corresponding growth in piety. They had reached an impasse.

Voluntary Institutions and the Material World

With the exception of the drastic reform of the laws relating to the sale of alcohol during World War I, respectable Britain was not planned or designed by the state, which played a very limited role in its creation. Indeed, if the state had played a more substantial and coercive role, as some of its more fierce promoters wanted, this would have led to social conflicts that might have thwarted respectability. Rather it is an example of a spontaneous order emerging out of the independent actions of many individuals and voluntary organizations (Barry 1982).

Voluntary institutions rooted in religion were perhaps the most important and persuasive because they came to control the moral socialization of children, both directly and through their influence on the state educational system. However, voluntary institutions concerned with the economic welfare of their members were also important. Indeed, the author's earliest (Davies 1983) explanation of the U-curve of deviance was based on an economic analysis of social change. In the nineteenth century, welfare institutions tended to moralize the population, whereas in the last half of the twentieth century they have had a demoralizing effect. In the late nineteenth century, when the incidence of deviance was falling, welfare was provided either by families or by voluntary institutions. Families did not want either the economic burden or the loss of respectability associated with one of their members being a criminal, or a drunkard, or producing an illegitimate child. Individuals knew that they were dependent on their families for economic support if they ran into difficulties and that it was necessary to conform to respectable standards of behavior if this was to be forthcoming.

The dominant trend in welfare in the last half of the nineteenth century when crime and other forms of deviance were declining was the development of mutual aid. It was the time of rapid growth for the friendly societies and social and benevolent clubs whose subscribers were entitled to sickness benefits, medical care for themselves and their families, support for widows and orphans, and funding to assist members to travel in search of work (Green 1993: 40). They might also provide unemployment benefit and old age pensions for their members, most of whom had very modest earnings and very little in the way of personal assets. The numbers enrolled in registered societies rose dramatically in the late nineteenth century from 2.75 million in 1877 to 3.6 million in 1897, to 6.6 million in 1910 (Green 1993: 31-32; Gosden 1960: 212-13; Gosden 1973: 91, 103-4). The friendly societies were initially based on direct relationships between individuals who felt able to trust one another and to work together in running a local society or branch of a society on a democratic basis. Their sense of fraternity and solidarity was reinforced by shared rituals and celebrations (Gosden 1960: 115-57). The societies were based on personal contact, trust, and mutuality and there was an absence of the kind of individual dependence upon and exploitation of state welfare that has characterized the last half of the twentieth century. The members could and did watch over their fellow members' actions, not just in relation to claims for benefit or to restrain imprudent or wicked behavior that might damage the society financially or damage its good name, but as part of what they saw as a necessary aspect of a character-building association

(Green 1993: 46-53, 56-57). Some were temperance organizations that added sobriety to the other prudent and respectable virtues (Wilson 1940) and in others fraternal ties were cemented by regular convivial meetings and celebrations.

The friendly societies were a means of combining autonomy and self-help with collective action. Lecture 5 of the Ancient Order of Foresters (1879 cited in Green 1993: 51) demonstrates this synthesis well:

> Forestry recognises and practically enforces the great truth, that man is not formed for himself alone; that he has been designed for far nobler purposes than the practice of selfishness, or for the satisfaction of his own single pleasure —that for so mean and narrow a purpose his endowments are too excellent, his capacities too large. Forestry, therefore, acting on the reality that man is a social being, dependent on his brethren for comfort, enjoyment, aid and succour, endeavours so to develop and direct the best sympathies of our nature that human distress may be alleviated, anguish abated, suffering relieved and affliction blunted.

The lecture emphasizes the essentially moralizing character of these associations in contrast to the bureaucratic and often adversarial and demoralizing character of modern welfare.

The first turning point in the history of the friendly societies came in 1911 with David Lloyd George's Insurance Act. The societies gradually began to decline in importance and were replaced by bureaucratic state welfare. The second turning point came in the late 1940s when the modern welfare state was put in place. Despite numerous periodic political controversies about its funding the welfare state's extent, functions, and cost are far greater today than they were in 1950. David Green (1993: 98-120) has aptly labelled these two turning points "the crowding out of Mutual Aid" (after 1911) and "the Eradication of Mutual Aid" (in 1948). Thus, there is another *inverted* U-curve, the curve of mutual aid that coincides with but moves in the opposite direction from the U-curve of deviance.

Work and Character

There is a further economic factor linked to the moralization and subsequent demoralization of British society, which has been identified by Bryan R. Wilson. Wilson argues that with the growth of an urban industrial economy in Britain in the nineteenth century there was a need for a new kind and degree of morality in which the routine social controls of the rural village order were replaced or, at least, supplemented by a more intense socialization of the individual:

> Work was being moralized. It had become a separated and well defined sphere of activity, no longer embedded for the mass of men in home, kinship and local community...There grew up an increased awareness that good work depended on willingness, sobriety, trust and commitment and the moral undertaking to give of one's best. (Wilson 1985: 320)

In this new moral order the idea of personal responsibility, though already important in the old face-to-face world, came to be stressed ever more strongly because of the 'need for self-regulation and self-control on the part of individual workers. It was necessary for them to be diligent, honest, and reliable even when they were not under the surveillance of others. As Wilson (1985: 319) noted:

> ...the best guarantee of a man being a good worker is the assurance that he is also a "good man".... It became quite common in nineteenth century Britain, for any worker of the humbler sort, to rely not merely, and perhaps not mainly, on any certification of his technical skills (that day was still to come)...but on evidence of his moral worth. He often had, sometimes literally in an envelope in his breast pocket, what he called "my character"—a testimonial from some employer which affirmed that he was the possessor of those prized moral virtues: honesty, willingness, industry, conscientiousness, a sense of responsibility, punctuality, and sobriety.

Finally, speaking of the last half of the twentieth century, Bryan Wilson (1985: 320-21) commented:

> ...The third phase of my model is that of the de-moralization both of work and of the wider reaches of the social order.... The new work order gradually ceased to be dependent on the general morality inculcated in earlier industrialization.... Once conveyor belts, electronic controls, automation and computers came into wider use, it became less necessary to depend for performance on the moral commitment of the worker.... The good worker need not now be the "good man"; indeed his moral quality as a man could now be regarded, industrially and commercially, as a matter of indifference. It follows that the modern worker does not need to have been socialized for a predominantly moral role.

Wilson's model is an excellent comment on and provides a possible explanation for both the moralization and the demoralization phase of the U-curve rooted in changing patterns of work within British society. Yet it is difficult to see why it would ever have been profitable for employers to abandon their search for workers imbued with the old morality merely because new technologies became available that were an improvement on the older impersonal incentives and forms of coercion provided by clocking on and off, payment for piece-work rather than by the hour, incentives and bonuses, fines and deductions. Machine minding then was much like machine minding now and much of modern industry continues to depend heavily on the dependability and trustworthiness of its more skilled and reliable workers. The alternative is the kind of economic collapse that occurred in the Soviet Union where intensive surveillance failed to produce high levels of productivity from an alienated workforce that was addicted to vodka and whose main efforts were devoted to their alternative and illegal sidelines in the black economy.

It is more likely that employers have come to neglect moral worth as a criterion for recruiting an employee or retaining one because the culture of which they are a part does not emphasize moral qualities and because they cannot easily be quantified—their assessment depends on personal judgment. Such judgments are transmitted through networks of trust and a heavy reliance on such networks leads to accusations of discrimination. In Northern Ireland, a more traditional society than Britain and (politics aside) one with a much lower crime rate, it was until recently customary for employers to ask a valued employee when they left their employment to recruit their own replacement. They would naturally as an extension of their own reputation seek out someone who was known as sharing their own good moral qualities. However, they also tended to recommend someone from within their own religious community, whether Protestant or Catholic, which reinforced the segregation between the two communities. Even in contemporary societies it makes sense for any organizations to choose between individuals with sufficient technical aptitude to do the job effectively on the basis of moral criteria determined by reputation. Reliability, diligence, sobriety, honesty, and sense of duty in an employee are as much economic assets today as they were in the nineteenth century, perhaps more so in an economy where the service sector is larger than that devoted to manufacturing and the biggest provider of employment. However, such qualities are intangible and cannot be fitted into a managerial culture of measurement and a political culture of equality. To prefer one individual over another because of intangible moral qualities can be perceived as infringing the latter's rights and it is seen as impermissible to make broad judgments about another's worth rather than specific assessments of their performance at a limited range of tasks. It is the growth of this kind of ideology that has undermined morality rather than economic change as such. It is not that moral qualities no longer have a value in the market place but rather that it is unfashionable to take note of them and decision-makers who did so openly and explicitly would meet resistance. The truth is that no one knows what, even from a narrowly economic point of view, is the optimal balance between a reliance on the general moral sensibility of a person performing a role and on attempts to monitor and control that person's performance according to narrow and often arbitrary criteria. Wilson's insights make more sense if his functionalist model is recast in terms of the anxieties of those who exercise managerial power. Those in power now prefer to have more detailed information and a delusion of control rather than to have to rely on a morally directed but autonomous individual, even when the latter course of action would be more profitable or effective. They are choosing not rationality but the appearance of rationality. It is in *this* way that moral worth was initially devalued, thus setting off a self-reinforcing movement towards demoralized work and a demoralized society.

Inflation and Crime

In the context of a discussion of economic issues it is also worth asking the question whether there is any relationship between the incidence of deviant behavior and indices of the performance of the economy as a whole. The growth of crime since the mid-1950s has sometimes been linked to the growth in levels of income and wealth since that time, supposedly because most crime is property crime and there is now more to steal. Yet there was far more to steal in the far wealthier society of 1900 than there had been in 1850 when most people owned very little; the increased temptation was there, but fewer people took it. Likewise, it is only in the short run that unemployment and hard times have had a significant impact on the incidence of property crime. Neither unemployment nor poverty nor deprivation nor inequality have any explanatory power whatsoever when it comes to assessing long-term trends in crime and may be safely discarded. There is, however, one neglected economic variable that does seem to correlate with the long-term trends in property crime and that is inflation. Skeptical as I am of attempts to discern meaningful links between aggregate economic variables and long term changes in social behavior, let me put forward for eager econometricians the hypothesis that it is inflation that is the key to an understanding of the rise in property crime in Britain and that in both cases there is a significant turning point in the mid-1930s. Before the mid-1930s, there was relatively little property crime and prices had been reasonably stable since the 1850s (with the exception of the blip in prices during and immediately after World War I). Indeed prices, like crime, had been falling in the latter part of the nineteenth century. Then from the late 1930s there was sustained inflation (Smith 1983: 219) and a sustained exponential increase in the incidence of property crime. Since that time there have been short-term fluctuations in the level of inflation and in the rate of growth of property crime; indeed, there have been brief periods when it has looked as if they may have halted, as in the last years of the twentieth century. However, if the price level and the crime level for 1936 were taken as the base of an index then the long run trend in both has been one of exponential growth and this is quite unprecedented. Peter Smith has calculated that if the year 1281 is taken as the base then prices had risen by 29,309 percent by 1981, but that nearly 96 percent of that rise took place from 1936 onward, the year in which John Maynard Keynes (1936) published *The General Theory of Employment, Interest and Money* [7] (Smith 1983: 219). Yet nearly all the rise in property crime since 1900 has also occurred since 1936. To say that this is merely the working out of compound interest is to beg the question of why such growth persisted over such a long period of time.

The *long-term* relationship that I have suggested between inflation and crime in Britain does not mean that I subscribe to a model in which the independent variable inflation is responsible for changes in the incidence of property crime or indeed of illegitimacy. Thieves are just as happy to steal money as goods except during hyper-inflation, which, not surprisingly, puts forgers out of business (Mannheim 1940). Rather the link between the two is a cultural one. Inflation is a form of theft that steals from savers and particularly the poorer ones, whose meager savings are held as money in a savings bank or in mattresses or as bonds rather than as real assets, in order to pay for excessive government expenditures that the state dare not finance by taxation. After a time, business gets used to inflation and it is built into everyone's calculations such that it is difficult to halt inflation without causing a slump; if there is a slump there is then a clamor for more inflation to get the economy out of it. In a slump, thrift now comes to be seen as a vice, as a selfish refraining from buying and consuming that has led to the collapse in trade, production, and earnings: the destructive paradox of thrift.

Inflation is corrosive of some of the virtues that in the late nineteenth century acted as a preventative of crime and the support of a system of welfare based on mutual aid, namely, prudence and foresight. Inflation arbitrarily transfers money from the prudent to those who live by deliberate indebtedness and is thus similar in its operation to a modern bureaucratic welfare system. Ironically, it is the increasing demands of the latter that in turn drove governments to finance them stealthily through inflation. Property crime and inflation alike are all the result of people taking things for which they are not willing to pay, usually at the expense of the respectable poor.

It is perhaps too much to ask whether there is a common element to the decline of religion, the replacement of voluntary welfare systems by bureaucratic systems, the adoption of employment criteria that exclude qualities of character, and the promotion of inflation, which, in turn, led to the death of respectable Britain. Yet one aspect of the late twentieth century does seem to underpin all of them, the change in the scale of society, a change that has been partly a consequence of technical and economic development and partly a result of political choice. It is not inevitable as we can see from the counter-examples of Switzerland or Japan where sophisticated production and involvements in global markets has coexisted with the preservation of local ties and communities (Clinard 1978; Segalman 1986; Segalman and Marsland 1989).

Britain in 1900 was a predominantly industrial and urban society; few people worked in agriculture or lived in villages. However, the size of their local communities and even places of employment remained small by the standards of the latter half of the twentieth century. People solved the problems caused by urbanization or movement from town to town by creating essentially personal institutions that were adapted to such movements and indeed facilitated them, such as the nonconformist chapels not tied to a parish system or the friendly societies. These institutions did not survive the subsequent replacement of communities by bureaucracy, a bureaucracy whose existence might have been necessary to perform particularly large-scale tasks but which then became an end in itself because so many people had an interest in its efflorescence.

Notes

1. It is strange that Durkheim (1933 [1893]: 68-69), who emphasized the shift from criminal to civil law and from retribution to restitution, was unwilling to accept that crime was falling in accordance with the growth in the division of labor, but he seems to have been too obsessed with notions of the abnormality of his own times. The trend towards both a diminution in crime and greater leniency also fitted Herbert Spencer's thesis of the withering away of the state in a capitalist society extremely well, but from a Spencerian point of view this was offset by the proliferation of the quasi-criminal law, of mere "police-offenses" that no one thought of as crimes, administrative regulations to do with vaccination or truancy or terms of sale whose breach could nonetheless lead to a conviction. The late-Victorian state was increasingly running people's lives in the furtherance of their own welfare, not something of which Spencer (1884) would have approved.

2. At the time this was often ascribed to the high proportion of Jewish immigrants settled there who had a particularly strong ethic of self-control. Most of them were destitute on arrival but demonstrated from the start that poverty need not be associated with crime, drunkenness, and illegitimacy.

3. The figure for 2001-2002 was 16.0, but it will fall slightly as a few suspected murders get retrospectively reclassified. This is why I have taken the lower 2003 figure for 1999-2000 rather than the previous 2001 estimate. The number of male homicide victims rose by 73 percent in the decade after 1991, whereas the number of female victims was constant, that is, murders in public places and in pursuit of crime or drug disputes rose far faster than family murders. In an increasing number of cases guns were employed, showing up the ineffectiveness of Britain's ultra-strict gun controls (*Criminal Statistics England and Wales. Crime in England and Wales 2001/2002 Supplementary* 2003). It would be interesting to hear the comments on this of any surviving upholders of the 1957 Homicide Act.

4. Female smoking and its link to respectability needs a different interpretation. In the nineteenth century, it was not considered respectable for women to smoke and in the earlier years of the twentieth century they did not smoke in the street. In the twentieth century, the incidence of smoking among women rose until 1948. It was not considered respectable in the nineteenth century because most smokers smoked pipes and cigars, which were and are considered distinctively masculine. Even in 1948 when female smoking was well established few women smoked pipes whereas many men used them as a form of male display. It was not considered respectable for women to smoke because it was cross-gender behavior, almost a form of cross-dressing. For women to smoke was also seen as a form of sexual wantonness, a presumption that they had the kind of sexual freedom conventionally enjoyed only by men. The situation changed partly due to the decline of these concepts of female respectability in the twentieth century and partly due to the development of a mass market in machine-produced cigarettes, which were much more neutral in their image. The manufacturers and their advertisers promoted both masculine and feminine images of the cigarette smoker. Cigarettes were seen as milder and cleaner. Today all smoking is seen as dirty and polluting, a sooter up of the lungs, an irritant to the eyes and throats of others, a source of an unwanted and persisting stink in an otherwise odorless house or office, and men as well as women seek to appear deodorized. In the nineteenth century, dirt, smells, and sweat were more acceptable among men than women and indeed often an inevitable aspect of certain occupations. Male pipe smokers would have exuded a perpetual reek of tobacco, their teeth, beards, and moustaches as well as their fingers would have been stained brown, and they would

have rasped and spat on the ground or in a cuspidor. It would have been considered unseemly for women to do this, and, indeed, even for men pipes and cigars were often restricted to all-male occasions, occasions when they could revel in distinctively masculine behaviors that did not undermine their respectability but would have done that of women. At a time when the health hazards of smoking were not securely known nor extensively publicized the "new" cigarette seemed far more compatible with female refinement.

5.   "Addicted" smokers may, however, cause serious problems if they continue smoking illicitly when there is a danger of fire or explosion. They are apt to go to lengths that would do credit to a terrorist to smuggle tobacco into hazardous places and smoke despite very strict prohibitions and the danger to others. The company or its insurers then has to pay damages to the victims, which is fair enough, but the blame lies with those whose vicious indulgence leads them into such evil paths.

6.   The decline in mortality in the late nineteenth century will have reduced another form of fatherlessness and thus assisted in the creation of respectable Britain, but the children of young widows were not particularly noted for their delinquency. They still had their father's kin and his memory and reputation; in many ways they were less fatherless than many fatherless children of today whose fathers are alive but absent.

7.   Keynes was well aware of the dangers of inflation, but those operating Keynsian policies recklessly used low interest rates and deficit financing to try to preserve full employment and induce growth, resulting in inflation and, in Britain's case, the severe economic crisis of the 1970s.

2

The Strange Death of Moralist Britain

The strange death of respectable Britain was an account of the marked changes in the moral behavior of the British people. The strange death of British moralism is a related story, but it concerns changes in the thinking of a policymaking elite, again with two marked turning points, one before or around the time of World War I and another in the late 1950s and 1960s. There is a rough coincidence here with the turning points in the rise and subsequent decline of respectable Britain and the two phenomena are clearly related though it is not a relationship that can be easily elucidated; the two changes did, after all, occur at quite different levels in the society. One is about everyday behavior and the other about the framing of legislation. Also whereas the legacy of the collapse of respectable and religious Britain was mere anomie and fragmentation, the policymakers who abandoned moralism did adopt a new moral framework of a consequentialist kind, causalism.

The shift from the world of moralism, one based on the principle that the main purpose of policy is to reward the virtuous, protect the innocent, and penalize the wicked, to the world of causalism in which the purpose of policy is to minimize harm in aggregate regardless of dessert was a process that can be said to have begun towards the end of the nineteenth century (Wiener 1990: 338). The ideas on which causalism is based were far from new even then, but it is at this time that we can see them start significantly to replace moralism. Moralism assumed the existence of the autonomous and responsible individual freely choosing between modes of conduct. Causalism, by contrast, assumed that the actions of individuals were to a large extent caused by their circumstances. It was a change that coincided with and probably influenced the first turning point in the U-curve of deviance, when the zeal of reforming Britain ran out, leaving an apparently stable and at first complacent and confident but later uneasy and crumbling respectable Britain. However, the main or at least most spectacular shift towards causalism occurred in the late 1950s and in the 1960s. In this chapter, this later shift will be examined in detail and particularly in relation to four major legal changes that took place at that time, none of which have ever been reversed or even seriously challenged, namely (1) the abolition of capital punishment in stages in 1957 and 1965; (2) the liberalization of the law on abortion in 1967; (3) the reform of the divorce laws in 1969; and (4) the decriminalization of male homosexual behavior in 1967. There are many other legal changes to which the same analysis can be applied, such as the relaxation of several kinds of censorship in Britain (Davies 1978: 9-36) or the extension in 1959 of the possibility of legitimation by subsequent marriage to the case where the partner had not been free to marry at the time of the birth of a child because he or she was married to someone else (Davies 1980: 9-36), but these four examples best illustrate the decisive move to causalism that took place.

In the case of capital punishment, it was not abolition as such that marked the transition to causalism but the change in the way in which the punishment for murder was debated within the British Parliament and, in particular, the way in which capital murders came to be distinguished from non-capital. When this division was first proposed in the late nineteenth century the suggested distinction between them was based on culpability; when it was enacted in 1957 the difference between the categories was based on the effectiveness of deterrence. Likewise it was not only the fact of the liberalization of abortion that indicated a shift in the direction of causalism but the central and repeated use made by the reformers in Parliament (almost to the exclusion of other reasons) of the argument that women were having abortions anyway, and it was better that these be carried out safely by qualified medical practitioners rather than by unskilled and dangerous "back-street abortionists." A second measure of the dominance of causalist thinking in Parliament is that the particular circumstances under which abortion was permitted under the 1967 Abortion Act were all justified in causalist terms; others that did not fit this pattern were rejected. The criteria that were accepted were all based on the minimizing of harm, those that were proposed but rejected related to the moral status of the woman concerned. There was no significant discussion of rights. No one argued that a woman should have a right to choose abortion, a right to privacy or rights over her own body; none of these arguments had any practical import in Britain when the vital question of the state's power to permit or forbid abortions was being discussed. Likewise, those opposed to liberalization found it difficult to argue convincingly that the fetus should have a right to life, since no such right had ever been recognized in Britain; such a right was not to be found in a moral Britain in which a mother and child were viewed almost as a single unit. To kill a young child was primarily a crime against its mother and when a mother killed her own child it created moral dilemmas that society found very difficult to resolve. In moral Britain in the first half of the twentieth century, murder was a very rare crime and regarded with singular horror because it involved the deliberate extinction of a particular person with hopes, expectations, memories, and relationships; abortion did not arouse that kind of horror, and in the 1930s as many as 60,000 respectable and otherwise law-abiding women obtained illegal abortions every year. When from time to time a woman seeking an abortion was injured or even killed due to the operation being botched, she was an object of popular sympathy not condemnation, much as happened in the case of those who committed suicide. Only among the leaders and the more fervent members of the more hierarchical churches and particularly among Roman Catholics was there much concern with what has been termed the "sanctity of life" and this concern, one not shared by others, will be analyzed in detail elsewhere in chapters 3 and 5. For most people, the fetus was not regarded as a person but as a mere potential person, and its demise did not arouse the moral outrage caused by the wanton killing of a full particular person, an outrage that was the basis of the substantial and consistent popular support for capital punishment on the part of the British masses.

Likewise, male homosexuality was decriminalized in Britain on the causalist grounds that it would reduce harm, not just the suffering of those convicted and punished but of those who lived in fear of arrest, exposure, or blackmail. No one in the British Parliament defended homosexuality or even the rights of homosexuals to liberty or privacy.[1] The reasons for the harsh treatment of homosexuals in Britain are complicated and difficult to unravel and will be given suitable detailed consideration elsewhere in chapter 4. All that concerns us here is that in moralist Britain the fact that male homosexual activities were widely perceived as being morally wrong was enough to justify their being penalized; in causalist Britain, it was concluded that the harm caused by keeping the existing law greatly exceeded any harm it might have prevented and that regardless of whether or not male homosexual behavior was immoral the law would have to be abolished. In 1967, the view that homosexuality was morally wrong was waning and this no doubt made it easier to pass the legislation, but condemnation of homosexuals and their behavior was still strong at the time. Decriminalization was a necessary precursor of the eventual toleration and acceptance of homosexuality, but these future developments were neither foreseen nor intended by the leading reformers (Davenport-Hines 1990: 326). Many of the reformers agreed to the legalization of behavior that they themselves thought was wrong and disgraceful (or at the very least something disgusting and distasteful) because they considered that on balance decriminalization would reduce harm and suffering, albeit among guilty men.

Divorce became steadily easier to obtain throughout the entire history of moral Britain, despite opposition on religious grounds by the leaders of the powerful hierarchical and in many respects catholic Anglican Church and the even stronger opposition of Britain's Roman Catholic minority. The members of the strongly Protestant Nonconformist churches of England and Wales certainly disapproved of divorce as being contrary to accepted standards of respectable behavior but they were not inclined to support strong action by the state to prevent the remarriage of those whose first marriage had ended; for them the state's powers should rather be directed towards the suppression of drunkenness, gambling, and prostitution. Divorce was undesirable, an indication of the breakdown of the family, an institution to which they were strongly committed, but not in and of itself an affront to their central beliefs; they did not perceive marriage as indissoluble and viewed with equanimity the laxer rules on divorce of Protestant Scotland or Protestant Prussia. Much of the moralist opposition to divorce took the form not of resisting divorce altogether but of insisting that the processes and consequences of divorce should pillory and penalize the guilty party and protect and favor the innocent one. It was only in 1969 that no fault divorce was (to a substantial extent) instituted on the grounds that the aim of divorce should be to dissolve a marriage that had irretrievably broken down in such a way as to minimize the aggregate harm done to the parties concerned regardless of past conduct. However, only in 1996 did causalism finally triumph in the field of divorce and the reforms of 1996 have never been implemented.

Let us now look in detail at the way in which the shift from moralist to causalist Britain took place, examining in turn capital punishment, abortion, homosexuality, and divorce.

The Death of Capital Punishment

No one has been executed since 1837 in England for any crime committed in peacetime other than murder. After 1861, murder was, in effect, the only crime for which British subjects were even liable to be executed in peacetime.[2] After 1868, there were no public executions and murderers were hanged behind prison walls out of sight. So far as capital punishment was concerned, the 1860s were the time when moral Britain began. During the time of moral Britain's triumph, the late nineteenth and early twentieth centuries, a high proportion of British murderers were caught, a high proportion were convicted, the death penalty was mandatory, and there were few reprieves, so that nearly 60 percent of those convicted of murder were executed. Moral Britain was a world apart from the eighteenth and early nineteenth centuries when thieves and sodomites, forgers and rapists, robbers and arsonists were liable to be hanged in public. The chances of this happening were small for they were rarely caught and convicted and the vast majority of those convicted were reprieved. It was a case of a severe penalty being rarely and erratically carried out. People were not hanged as an act of just retribution, for few contemporaries thought that the majority of those hanged for minor offenses got their just desserts; the justification was deterrence alone. In consequence, juries increasingly refused to convict, particularly for minor crimes of dishonesty. Their refusals were a sign of the approach of moral Britain.

In the moral Britain that emerged in the later nineteenth century, by contrast, capital punishment for murder was not perceived in this expedient way. It was reserved for the punishment of one crime alone, because it was seen as a fitting retribution for that crime. The ultimate crime deserved the ultimate penalty. The justice of this view seemed to be reinforced by the certainty with which execution followed conviction. Where there were doubts about the justice of capital punishment they concerned the differing degrees of culpability involved as between one murder and another. The 1866 Capital Punishment Commission sought to draw a distinction between unpremeditated and premeditated homicide (with express malice aforethought), with only the latter attracting the death penalty (*Report of the Capital Punishment Commission* 1866: xlix-l). The purpose of making such a distinction was not that murders on impulse were less likely to be deterred but rather that the wickedness of the premeditated murderer was seen as greater than that of someone acting under sudden provocation. Eight attempts were made in Parliament to introduce Bills defining degrees of murder on the basis of culpability between 1866 and 1894 (*Report of the Select Committee* 1931: xl-xli; Wiener 1990: 277). No agreement was ever reached. It is not that considerations of deterrence were unimportant but that notions of guilt and retribution took first place, both in the formal debates of those with the power to change the law and in the imagination of the people as a whole. The decision in any individual case was indeed made by the latter for all murder trials were decided by the verdict of a jury and the death sentence was mandatory. It was the apogee of moralist as well as moral Britain.

As we shall see in chapter 3, there was a turning point in attitudes to capital punishment after World War I because of its use as a military punishment for desertion as an act of pure deterrence; this was truly shocking to opinion in moralist moral Britain. It also led to divisions among the political and religious elite, such that support for capital punishment became a specifically conservative cause, the cause of those who upheld the principle of hierarchy in church, state, and the armed forces. The opposition to capital punishment was to be found in the Labour and Liberal parties and in the Free Churches as opposed to the Conservatives, the Anglicans, and Roman Catholics. As a result of these political and religious divisions there was, after World War II, a major clash in Parliament over the question of capital punishment between those adhering to two opposed moral frameworks. The abolitionist MPs saw hanging as wrong in and of itself; they, too, were moralists. In keeping with their principles they forced Parliament to vote on the issue in 1948. Both those in favor of abolition and those wishing to retain capital punishment were unwilling to see it as a merely pragmatic and utilitarian question, and the debates had a strongly "moralist" tone on both sides (*Hansard*, House of Commons 1948, vol. 449, col. 1014-1070).

For many abolitionists, capital punishment was absolutely wrong; they could not perceive any circumstance in which it might be justified even if its exercise saved the lives of others. For the retentionists, murderers received their just desserts; it was an appropriate punishment for a horrible crime and properly a part of moral Britain, a social order whose duty it was to protect the innocent, reward the virtuous, and punish the guilty. There was a clash of irreconcilable moralities, each intensified by the memory of the events of World War II. For the abolitionists, capital punishment was associated with the evil regimes that had been defeated, notably National Socialist Germany which had wantonly taken so many human lives (*Hansard*, House of Commons 1948, vol. 449, col 1014). However, as Quintin Hogg, who wished to retain capital punishment, pointed out there had been no protest from the abolitionists at the time of the trial and execution of the German war criminals at Nuremburg (*Hansard*, House of Commons 1948, vol. 449, col. 1016). Likewise, the abolitionists had not protested when three men had been executed in England *after* the war had ended for forms of treason committed during the war, two condemned by civilian courts after trial by jury, one by court-martial. Such executions were retribution in its purist form since they were neither carried out to deter others from committing such crimes in the future, nor to incapacitate the accused from carrying out further atrocities. The point was presumably not lost on Sir David Maxwell Fyfe M.P. (later the Lord Chancellor, Viscount Kilmuir), the Deputy Chief Prosecutor at Nuremburg, who as Home Secretary in 1951-54 proved to be a notable upholder of capital punishment. War criminals were guilty. Traitors were guilty. Murderers were guilty. They all deserved to be executed. The judges who sat in the House of Lords were particularly insistent on this point. The Lord Chief Justice, Lord Goddard, spoke at length of the wickedness of particular murderers over whose trials he had presided and upon whom he had passed the sentence of death. Lord Goddard in his speech in favor of retaining capital punishment did not emphasize questions of deterrence or expediency or policy but spoke in moralist and retributive terms. "Murder is a crime *sui generis*—it stands by itself; the man who commits the supreme crime should pay the supreme penalty," he said (*Hansard*, House of Lords 1948, vol. 156, col. 116; see also Gowers 1956: 52-55; Smith 1959: 143). It was not surprising that he should take this line, for as a judge he was concerned with assessing the guilt and innocence of particular individuals. It is interesting to note that when after 1957 capital punishment ceased to be clearly linked to the culpability of individual murderers, the hanging judges lost their former enthusiasm for it.

The House of Commons voted by a large majority for an amendment to the Criminal Justice Bill abolishing capital punishment in 1948, but the House of Lords, knowing they enjoyed the support of more than two-thirds of the electors (Cameron, 2002: 139), refused its consent. The Archbishop of Canterbury, Geoffrey Fisher, sought a compromise; he raised the old possibility that it might be possible to make a distinction between more heinous and less heinous murders, with only the former being subject to capital punishment. He said: "I think it might be as well to amend the clause so as to distinguish between foul murder—for murder is always foul—and what I would call 'murder most foul'.... I believe Judge and jury would have no difficulty in deciding which murders were in the category of murder most foul" (*Hansard,* House of Lords 1948, vol. 156, col. 47). The Archbishop was speaking in moralist terms, in terms of a murderer's degree of guilt, with only those guilty of murder most foul rather than mere foul murder being sentenced to death and executed. The House of Lords rejected his idea. However, a Royal Commission on Capital Punishment was set up to look into the question of whether or not it was possible to find a compromise between the existing situation where there was a mandatory death sentence for anyone convicted of murder and total abolition. The Royal Commission was unable to find or devise any satisfactory half-way measure (*Report of the Royal Commission on Capital Punishment* 1953). The Report is a sober, pragmatic, empirical document, much concerned with considering the strengths and weaknesses of the contention that capital punishment is a unique deterrent to the committing of murder by sifting through data from European and Commonwealth countries and each of the states of the United States. It is an assessment of cause and of consequences, a thoroughly "causalist" document. Relatively little attention in the Report is paid to the moralist issues of retribution, reprobation, atonement and expiation, and indeed there are explicit comments about the decline in their importance in contemporary thinking about crime and punishment (*Report of the Royal Commission on Capital Punishment* 1953: 17-18; see also Davies and Trivizas 1994).

In 1956, the members of the House of Commons again voted on a free vote on a Private Member's Bill in favor of the abolition of capital punishment and once more the matter came before the House of Lords. As we have seen, the Archbishop of Canterbury, in 1948, had suggested the division of murder into capital and non-capital murders according to degrees of heinousness (*Hansard*, House of Lords 1948, vol. 146, col. 47) and he had made the same point in his evidence to the Royal Commission on Capital Punishment (Potter 1993: 151, 158). However, in 1956, the Archbishop shifted his ground and argued that the categories of capital and non-capital murder should be defined entirely by reference to the relative strength of capital punishment as a deterrent for each particular type of murder; he had abandoned the retributive "moralism" of moral Britain and was arguing a "causalist" case. He now urged that only those committing "deterrable" murders should be subject to the death penalty even though this would mean that those responsible for the most vile of murders would escape execution. The Archbishop argued that

> Within these given categories the deterrent power of the death sentence obviously would have its maximum possible effect, for a murderer would have to put himself into the reach of the death penalty by deliberate act.... It is true that some murders, some of the most abominable murders would fall outside the categories and would escape the death penalty. They would be murders of a specially beastly and passionate kind (*Hansard*, House of Lords 1956, vol. 198, col. 751).

It was a significant shift in the Archbishop's thinking and it may have made him the original begetter of the 1957 Homicide Act. It was certainly the case that when the Lord Chancellor, Viscount Kilmuir (formerly Sir David Maxwell-Fyfe) introduced the Homicide Bill in the House of Lords on behalf of the then Conservative government in 1957 (*Hansard*, House of Lords 1957, vol. 201, col. 1168-9), he went out of his way to acknowledge the importance and significance of Archbishop Fisher's speech the previous year. Fisher had set off a moral revolution, though probably without any understanding of what he was doing.

However, the immediate cause of the government's sponsorship of the Homicide Act of 1957 was the agitation among the influential that had followed yet another defeat in the House of Lords in 1956 of a Private Member's Bill suspending (and in effect abolishing) capital punishment. The Bill had been carried by the House of Commons on a free vote but had once again been thrown out by the House of Lords.

The Conservative government was now trapped since there was a considerable majority in the more democratic of the two Houses of Parliament in favor of capital punishment and also a considerable minority of Conservative MPs had become abolitionists. Opinion among MPs and among the influential was against capital punishment, but public opinion was strongly in favor. The Conservative government now took the unusual step of bringing in its own legislation on capital punishment and obliging its MPs to vote for it (by tradition legislation on this kind of moral issue had been decided on a free vote of the members of the two houses, with the leaders of the political parties refraining from instructing their members how to vote).[3] That the government should seek a compromise by dividing murder into categories of capital and non-capital murder was not surprising, but the nature of the compromise was radically different from previous attempts to enact such a division into types of murder.

The distinction between the categories of capital and non-capital murder was entirely causalist and justified in terms of minimizing harm. The capital murders were: killing in the course of theft; killing of policemen and prison officers; killing by shooting (by 1957 few people in Britain owned guns and even fewer kept guns at home), or an explosion and the committing of murders on separate occasions (Tuttle 1961: 128). These were chosen *not* because they were especially vile, atrocious, or brutal murders, manifesting exceptional depravity but because those committing murders belonging to these categories were seen as being more likely to be deterred from killing by the threat of execution. Some of the categories also referred to murders seen as not merely causing harm to a particular victim but as putting the safety of the public at risk. The murders that would continue to be punished by execution were instrumental murders, murders undertaken as a means to an end by criminals who were seen as calculating and weighing up in advance both the possible gains from crime and the penalties for crime involved in a criminal enterprise that might end in murder. The justification was *not* the moralist one that premeditation is more wicked than a sudden emotional outburst, but rather that by executing in these cases, murders by other persons in the future would be prevented. Harm would be minimized. Other kinds of murder widely held to be especially abhorrent and culpable such as murder following rape, the wanton killing of children by strangers, poisoning, or the cold-blooded killing of an innocent passer-by for the sheer pleasure of doing so were not subject to the death penalty because the execution of murderers of these types was seen as not having any deterrent effect. An attempt to amend the Act to retain capital punishment for rapists who killed was withdrawn and another amendment concerning poisoners was defeated. There was nothing new about the argument from deterrence; it had always been strong. What was unusual was that it now stood alone, a marked departure from the dominant ethos of the late nineteenth century and the first half of the twentieth. There had been earlier, unsuccessful, proposals in Britain for dividing murder into capital and non-capital categories (Bedau 1983: 4-6; *Report of the Royal Commission on Capital Punishment* 1953: 158-162, 206-7) but none was as emphatically and exclusively causalist as that of 1957. Retribution, repudiation, denunciation, dessert and degree of moral culpability had all been abandoned. In the future, instrumental murderers were to be executed for instrumental reasons; the murderers had become a means to an end and were to be executed, not for the moral qualities of their own crime but in order to prevent someone else's crime, an unknown and unknowable crime that by definition could not be specified in moral terms. It was an important stage in the death of moralism and in the strange death of moral Britain.

The Archbishop of Canterbury, Geoffrey Fisher, an enthusiastic supporter (Potter 1993: 178-79) of the Homicide Act, said:

> I sought for myself something which would limit the field in which the death penalty operated but would make it in that limited field almost certain to be imposed, thus creating, if there is such a thing as a deterrent in this world, a real deterrent (House of Lords 1957: vol. 211, col. 1190)...the Bill does not proceed on that line; it does not attempt to distinguish degrees of murder nor to measure (and this I do not criticise) their moral evil. The Bill does create certain clearly defined categories of killing which shall carry the death penalty There has already been discussion on those categories. In the main they seem to me roughly speaking, right. They are clearly defined and easily understood. Anyone can know that a killing in one of these categories will carry the death penalty and their deterrent effect is, therefore, at the maximum. The law is not trying to legislate by degrees of horror.... The whole matter I suggest, is not one of deep

principle but one of expediency...The State has in this matter a power and a duty. How is it to exercise this penalty? (*Hansard,* House of Lords: 1957, vol. 211, cols. 1192-3)

Fisher's views in one sense stretched back to the very beginning of the nineteenth century, to the time before the creation of moral Britain when capital punishment, even for relatively minor offenses was acceptable to his predecessors as Archbishop of Canterbury, not as the satisfaction of justice but for the prevention of crime. Yet Fisher had also become in a rather muddled way a representative of post-moralist Britain, a world in which the designation of a particular type of murder as capital rather than non-capital was rooted in speculative calculations of future harm and not considerations of past dessert. He had stepped right outside moral Britain; that an Archbishop of Canterbury should do so was an indication of its weakened state. The causalist argument was that if we agree to take these lives today, it will save other lives in the future and the overall level of harm done will be less than if we had done away with capital punishment altogether. However, once the link backwards between the execution of a murderer and a particular act with a particular victim having particular moral qualities has been attenuated in this way it becomes far more difficult to describe capital punishment as the special denunciation of the uniquely horrible crime of murder. It was a point that led Britain's senior judges, formerly the strongest of the upholders of capital punishment, to come to prefer total abolition to selective execution by category on the basis of presumed deterrence.

Between 1957 and 1964, the judges had to carry out Parliament's will and administer the 1957 Homicide Act and they found the experience contrary to their own perceptions of justice as the making of distinctions based on degrees of guilt. When capital punishment was again debated in Parliament in 1964-65, the Lord Chief Justice, Lord Parker of Waddington, speaking on two separate occasions on behalf of most of the senior judges sitting in the House of Lords, said:

I suppose it is probably true that no one, perforce and not by choice, has seen more of the many types of murder and of the circumstances in which they are committed than the holder of my office. I am sure that my noble and learned friend Lord Goddard would agree. For this simple reason, that nearly every murderer, certainly every capital murderer, appeals to the Court of Criminal Appeal over which the Lord Chief Justice is the almost constant presider. Therefore, I hope you will bear with me if I express my views—and I am afraid rather strong views—on this proposal for the further abolition of the death penalty.... I confess looking back eleven years, that if anybody had then said that I should come out as a full-blooded abolitionist, I should have been surprised. But during that time, and particularly during the last seven years...I have seen the complete absurdities that are produced and have been completely disgusted at the result.... They (the judges) sit in court, they see where the shoe pinches, they see where justice does not appear to be done and when it is not done. I think I can say that the judges are quite disgusted at the results produced by the Homicide Act...(*Hansard*, House of Lords 1965, vol. 268, col. 480-13).

For seven years I have presided in the Court of Criminal Appeal to whom almost every capital murderer appeals and for the last four of those seven years I have been so disgusted (if I may put it that way) with the anomalies that arise, with the injustices that are done as between man and man—one man is hanged and another equally blameworthy, imprisoned for life—that I determined four years ago that something ought to be done and I was in favour of abolition. (*Hansard*, House of Lords 1965, vol. 269, col. 541)[4]

Despite Archbishop Fisher's view that the legislation on capital punishment of 1957 would endure because it was so soundly based, it lasted a mere eight years and capital punishment was suspended for five years in 1965, and abolished altogether in 1969. It has never been reinstated, nor has there ever been any chance that it might be. Capital punishment in Britain is long dead and buried. Once it became a purely causalist matter it was just a question of time before a new recalculation of the net value of the suffering resulting from its exercise (the suffering caused by its exercise less the suffering prevented by its exercise) led to its abolition. There is certain arbitrariness about these estimates and there was and there is no really decisive proof that capital punishment was or is a greater deterrent to murder than all the possible alternative punishments.[5]

There were several reasons why the abolitionists were bound to win in 1965 and there will be a further discussion of capital punishment in chapter 4. However, for our present purposes, the key point to be stressed is the way in which the question of deterrence dominated parliamentary debates in 1964 much as it had done in 1957. The retentionists could no longer employ the argument that capital punishment was a unique penalty for a unique crime and a maximum penalty reserved for the worst of crimes, for in the years between 1957 and 1964 many of the most evil murderers had received life imprisonment while less heinous crimes had led to their perpetrators being hanged. The retentionists were forced to argue in terms of deterrence yet for many of them the ghost of retribution lurked behind their espousal of deterrence and the abolitionists in Parliament taunted them with the arguments they had abandoned and put beyond use by pressing hard the anomaly that the most wicked often went to prison and men less guilty than them had been hanged. The abolitionists were willing to give a hostage to fortune that they knew fortune would not take and claim, in fairness often sincerely, that they would be willing to support capital punishment if proof of its deterrent effect could be provided and its ability to save lives demonstrated. Even the ones who did not hold this view argued their case not in terms of sentiment but in terms of the reasoned and pragmatic argument that capital punishment did not work in order to gain maximum support in a causalist climate (Davies and Trivizas 1986). Henry Brooke, who had been Home Secretary in the previous Conservative government and at that time an upholder of capital punishment now became a conditional abolitionist, having changed his mind on the facts of the matter, and now said:

> I do not share the view that the taking of life by the state is contrary to moral principle. I think that, if it can be shown that by retaining the death penalty for some or all types of murder one is lessening the likelihood of innocent people suffering death by murder, then there is no ground of moral principle on which one should dismiss the death penalty.... But I believe that retention of the death penalty can be justified only on the grounds that it is a unique deterrent. If it is a unique deterrent there is justification. If it is not, I do not think that the case for it can be upheld. (*Hansard,* House of Commons: 1964, vol. 704, cols. 908-9)

This was the causalist argument that captured the middle ground in 1964 (Davies and Trivizas 1986). Much of the argument was about who should get the benefit of the doubt in the face of the highly uncertain evidence about the power of deterrence, those facing execution or those unknown persons saved by the deterrence effect. For the moralists, saving the life of an innocent victim in the future presumably carries more weight than sacrificing the life of a guilty murderer. For a causalist, the harm done is the same in each case and to justify execution it would be necessary to show that each execution saved more than one life in the future; so far as Britain was concerned there was no convincing evidence that this was the case. However, those who argued in favor of retaining capital punishment on causalist grounds faced a further objection, namely that the person being executed is a full particular person with a known identity, whereas the persons whose lives are potentially saved in the future by the deterrent effect of today's execution are mere statistical persons. When other more mundane calculations about risk are made in a causalist society, this is a crucial distinction and in post-moral Britain, deterrence had become a matter of risk management like any other.

The way in which statistical persons rank lower in our scale of concern than full particular persons is demonstrated in the British Medical Association's study, *Living with Risk* (1987: 163):

> Everyday experience shows us that as a community we are willing to spend far more on some lives than on others and this has very little to do with how economists might value those lives…cost-benefit analysis is always liable to moderation on a case by case approach with the importance of the individual generally being believed to be paramount. Unlimited resources might be released to save the life of a miner trapped underground with his plight clearly visible to the nation through the news-hungry media. Yet nearly a miner a week dies in Britain from routine accidents. Take another rather more complicated example of individual exposure to risk. Imagine that a huge food store required fumigation to prevent the growth of a mould which could result in the death over the next 20 years of (say) a dozen people. However, the necessary fumigant chemical (for which there was no alternative) was hazardous to the workers to the extent that one or two would be likely to die within this period. It is unlikely that this fumigant would be permitted for use although there would be a net community gain, because the near certain death of one or two people is regarded generally as a matter of much greater concern than the possible death of more people but among a very large number.

Such a conclusion is far from being universally true; indeed, in a socialist society it would be regarded as mere bourgeois sentimentality. Nonetheless, the British Medical Association's authors' point was true for Britain. In a society where it is considered wrong to impose an enhanced involuntary risk on a few known people in order to diminish the risk faced by the majority, it is difficult to justify a death penalty based only on deterrence. Once the central importance of retribution and denunciation were undermined by the 1957 Homicide Act, the death penalty was doomed. There were thirteen attempts to restore capital punishment for murder by means of a Private Member's Bill in Parliament after its final abolition in 1969. All thirteen attempts failed and the abolitionist majority grew over time. The decision taken in 1965 had proved to be irreversible.

Public opinion remained strongly in favor of capital punishment because ordinary people did not see the issue in the same terms as members of the ruling political elite. The public probably did not make fine distinctions between retribution and deterrence, but felt that capital punishment for murder was both fitting and a contribution to their safety. At the 1966 general election, an independent candidate, Patrick Downey, stood against Sidney Silverman (the leader of the successful campaign to abolish capital punishment) on the sole issue of restoring capital punishment and obtained more than 5,000 votes, 13 percent of those who voted (Richards 1970: 56). Such a high vote for an independent, vastly higher than any anti-abortion candidate has ever obtained at a general election, showed that people felt strongly on the issue. Since then social attitude surveys have consistently shown that two-thirds of the British people support capital punishment and some polls give a figure of over 80 percent (Cameron 2002: 139). The political parties have agreed not to make it an electoral issue and voting in general elections is almost entirely on the basis of party. Those individuals elected under this system were then allowed by their parties to vote as they wished on this "moral" issue. The shift from moralism to causalism was a shift in the thinking and rhetoric of this group, not of the British people as a whole. It was partly a real shift in the way the members of this group thought and partly because those whose sentiments on an issue are clear but whose thoughts are multifaceted and could give rise to many kinds of arguments tend to select that argument which they think will carry most weight and enable their faction to win. So long as Britain had a political system based on parliamentary sovereignty where the judges were kept in their place, causalist arguments ruled because they were the winning arguments in Parliament. Arguments "adapt themselves" according to where power lies. With the waning of parliamentary sovereignty and, indeed, the undermining of Britain's national independence in the twenty-first century, the nature of the dominant arguments will no doubt change yet again.

Abortion

The law on abortion in England and Wales was substantially liberalized in 1967 for reasons that had nothing to do with rights. No right to choose abortion was established nor did the reformers appeal to any right to privacy. Reform took place on the grounds that women in Britain were having abortions anyway, often under harmful and even dangerous circumstances, and that if abortion were clearly made legal these terminations would be carried out safely, hygienically, and competently by qualified doctors, and there would be a reduction in harm and suffering. The causalist argument is that the state's duty is to reduce the level of suffering among the individuals who make up society regardless of their moral status or past behavior. Likewise, no right to life was being denied, for none had ever existed. As we shall see in chapter 5, many of those who opposed the liberalization of the abortion law, notably the Roman Catholics, did so in defense of a supposed fetal right to life, but they were defending something that had no secure existence or significance either in the laws of England or in the minds of the British people.

In principle, the sections of the Offences Against the Person Act of 1861 dealing with abortion, which were swept away in 1967, constituted a remarkably severe, stringent, and inflexible prohibition of abortion. Section 58 of the Act (after the wording was simplified in 1892 and 1893 [see Keown 1988: 167]) reads:

> Every woman being with child, who, with intent to procure her own miscarriage shall unlawfully administer to herself any poison or other noxious thing, or shall unlawfully use any instrument or other means whatsoever with the like intent, and whosoever, with intent to procure the miscarriage of any woman, whether she be or be not with child, shall unlawfully administer to her or cause to be taken by her any poison or other noxious thing, or shall unlawfully use any instrument or other means whatsoever with the like intent, shall be guilty of felony and being convicted thereof shall be liable (at the discretion of the court) to be kept in penal servitude for life. (Keown 1988: 167; see also Smith and Hogan 1978: 342)

In theory, the woman seeking an abortion was herself liable to prosecution and severe punishment and no external "exploiter" need be involved in any way. What happened in reality, though, was quite different, for "it was not the practice to prosecute the mother" in cases of illegal abortion (Smith and Hogan 1978: 342; Williams 1958: 195-96). The British authorities and even more strongly the British public had too keen a sense of humanity to take action against someone perceived as having already suffered a great deal from the circumstances that led them desperately to seek an abortion and from the risk and damage involved in such an undertaking. The use of the word "unlawfully" in the statute relating to abortion necessarily implied that there were circumstances in which abortions could be lawfully carried out (Williams 1958: 151-52), and in practice this meant that qualified medical practitioners acting in good faith did perform abortions for therapeutic reasons. Doctors, lawyers, and judges were all agreed on this point and prosecutors were reluctant to challenge medical discretion (Keown 1988: 52-57). Therapeutic abortion was not contrary to the conscience of Protestant moral Britain and the more stringent views of Britain's Roman Catholic minority were seen as aberrant (Williams 1958: 177). Indeed, in this context the moral outlook of Roman Catholic Britain and even more so of Britain's close neighbor, Ireland, were sufficiently different from that of mainstream moral Britain that the fate of their morality deserves a separate chapter of their own (chapter 5). There were disagreements about when therapeutic abortion was permissible, although no one doubted that it was allowable to save the life of the mother. The problem lay rather in the uncertainty of the law, in locating the boundary between lawfully and unlawfully, in deciding which of those cases where there were medical reasons for an abortion that fell short of an immediate threat to life were lawful and which were not. Much of the early pressure to reform the laws on abortion in the 1930s and again in the 1950s stemmed from a wish to clarify where this boundary lay.

Both these points have relevance for an understanding of the nature of moral Britain and confirm that the wish to arrange matters so as to minimize the level of harm and suffering by full and particular persons regardless of their moral standing was already present and growing stronger. In the 1950s and 1960s, the causalist ethic was to become dominant, but it had long been present in British thinking and had gained in power from the 1890s onward among policymakers (Wiener 1990: 338). In the later twentieth century, causalism was to prove stronger than any concern for rights. Both causalism and assertions of rights are based on a concern for individual persons, but in very different ways. Here we shall try to show, in turn, how a special concern for the difficulties and suffering of mothers and the lack of any general moral outrage about the wickedness of abortion as such were part of an established and distinctively British outlook that made inevitable the eventual reform of the law on abortion in 1967; it also indicates why that reform did not convulse and divide British society in the way it did the United States.

Such was the reluctance to punish the mother in cases of abortion in Britain that a social fiction was created to the effect that the mother was not an active agent in the procurement of her own abortion. Abortion was, in effect, defined as a crime against the woman seeking one, particularly if it went wrong and she died or was seriously harmed; the villain in the case was the so-called "back-street" abortionist who had brought this tragedy about. It is, of course, a common, convenient and not unreasonable assumption (as in the case of drugs or prostitution) that it is the seller not the purchaser who brings a market into existence and is the one who sets up a particular transaction. However, it seems a particularly inappropriate assumption in the case of abortion where the purchaser may be desperate and the provider is unwilling to comply but is persuaded into it by the other's desperation. Sometimes the person bringing the abortion about was a reluctant accomplice, often another woman trying to help out a desperate friend, relative, or neighbor (Brookes 1988: 34-36), yet if it went wrong and the mother died the "abortionist" was liable to be prosecuted for manslaughter.

Abortion was widespread in England and Wales long before the law was liberalized there in 1967 (and even more so in Scotland where it was only a common law offense). There was a reluctance to prosecute doctors acting within their own generally accepted professional ethics and these ethics had expanded from a concern to save the life of the pregnant woman to the prevention of her suffering permanent physical ill-health. In 1938, Aleck Bourne deliberately invited prosecution after he had performed an abortion on a fourteen-year-old girl who had been raped by a group of soldiers. He was seeking to secure an explicit declaration from the courts that abortion was permitted in circumstances where there was no real danger to life but a strong possibility of damage to the woman's health. Bourne's defense was *not* that his patient had been raped but that the operation was necessary to the preservation of her mental health (Keown 1988: 75). The judge summed up in Bourne's favor and he was acquitted (*R v Bourne* 1938). The judge in the case, Mr. Justice McNaughton, drew upon the wording of the Infant Life Preservation Act of 1929, which prohibited the destruction around the time of birth of a child capable of being born alive, but which also specified that no one was to be found guilty if the act was done in good faith for the purpose of preserving the life of the mother. McNaughton J. ruled that the mother was entitled to be preserved, not just from instant death but from a serious impairment to her health, which by implication might in some measure shorten her longevity. Mr. Justice McNaughton stressed *both* that the law of England did not permit women freedom of choice in abortion *and* that it did not uphold the absolute objection to abortion under all circumstances on religious grounds held by some. On the contrary, the judge held in regard to the latter that it was a doctor's duty to perform an abortion if it were necessary to save the life of a patient and that if on religious grounds the doctor refused to perform the operation and the patient died, he or she could be prosecuted for manslaughter by negligence. He added that a doctor holding such a view should not be practicing in this branch of medicine at all and, in the event of the mother's death, such a doctor would be in no different a position from a parent who for religious reasons allowed a child to die rather than seek proper medical treatment. It was a strongly causalist statement that clearly denied the right to choice, the right to life, and the right to conscientious objection (*R v Bourne* [1938]; Smith and Hogan 1986: 224-26),

The Bourne case confirmed what most doctors already thought the law meant but it was only one judgment, albeit one that was widely admired and unlikely to be reversed. Most doctors were reluctant to carry out abortions regularly for fear of being prosecuted as not acting in good faith or even making a business out of it. Indeed, a few doctors did end up in prison as well as being struck off the register (Brookes 1988: 35-75, 65). For most doctors the risks were too great. It was not moral obloquy that they feared but conviction. If any other medical operation or procedure went wrong and a patient died, a doctor who had taken all the relevant precautions had nothing to fear from the criminal law, but if a woman died as result of a termination he or she was likely to end up in jail and unlikely to practice medicine ever again. It is no wonder that most doctors, even those who had no moral reservations about abortion, resisted the pleas of their patients to provide abortions. Those who were known to carry out abortions often enjoyed popular esteem. In 1921, a Dr. Starkie was acquitted by a jury on the criminal charge of performing illegal operations despite very strong prosecution evidence, but received nine months imprisonment for administering drugs to procure an abortion. When he was released from Wormwood Scrubs prison after serving his sentence, 600 of his patients gave a banquet for him (Browne and Tullett 1952: 135-36). Starkie, a former police surgeon, would probably not have been investigated and prosecuted at all but for a suspicion that earlier in his career one of his patients had died as a result of his activities (Brown and Tullett 1952: 104).

In some cases, highly regarded doctors were acquitted by juries to an outburst of cheering. In the case of Dr. Daniel Powell of Tooting his patients subscribed £1,700 for his defense when he was prosecuted and when he died in 1938 women came from all over England to be at his funeral (Brookes 1988: 35-36). In other cases, thousands of people signed petitions asking for leniency whether from the court or from the General Medical Council for a convicted doctor (Williams 1958: 196). Women actively sought abortions from their doctors and those who obtained them would speak about their decision afterwards without any sense of guilt.

The problem rather was that most abortions were performed under unhygienic conditions by unskilled back-street abortionists. In the 1930s, there were probably as many as 60,000 abortions a year and possibly 8 percent of all pregnancies were terminated, nearly all of them illegally. Only about 200 of the 60,000 mainly illegal abortions were known to the police and there were only sixty convictions a year. Between 0.3 and 0.4 percent of abortions ended in death, about the same mortality rate as for childbirth but far higher than the estimated 0.01 percent for abortions in jurisdictions where abortion was legal (*Report of the Inter-Departmental Committee* 1939: 21, 39, 44-45, 117, 139; Williams 1958: 192). Most of the women who had abortions were married women with children who did not want another child. They were ordinary, respectable, and in other respects, law-abiding women, but they did not hesitate to break a law that prevented them from doing something that they did not perceive as wrong. The law was unenforceable (Brookes 1988: 117; *Report of the Inter-Departmental Committee* 1939: 15, 143; Williams 1958: 189-192).

It was this situation that the reformers sought to remedy in 1966-67 by making it legal for doctors to carry out abortions under a wide range of circumstances. They were emphatic that their aim was to eliminate the dangerous activities of the back-street abortionists and they specifically repudiated the idea that abortion should be available on request as a right (Simms and Hindell 1971: 161; David Steel, *Hansard*, House of Commons 1966, vol. 732, col. 1075). The reformers' entire argument was based on the moral imperative of reducing harm. If the law was left in its existing state, many women would go on suffering from the negative consequences of bearing unwanted children in difficult circumstances or from the dire effects of a desperate resort to an unskilled and unqualified abortionist. If the law was reformed and safe legal abortions were more widely available, the amount of suffering from these two causes would be reduced. That was the whole of their case.

The Roman Catholic opponents of the Bill, as we shall see in chapter 5, phrased their objections to abortion law reform in terms of the right to life. They represented the proposals for reform as a "barbarous" undermining of the "principle on which the whole security of society rests, namely, the principle of the sanctity of life" (Norman St. John Stevas, *Hansard,* House of Commons 1966, vol.732, col. 1157). However, no such strict principle existed in relation to abortion in British law and medical practice, nor in the minds of the women of Britain. The reformers were thus in a position to say that they were merely widening the *existing* grounds on which an abortion could be granted by defining health more broadly while leaving the crucial decisions in the hands of the doctors, the official guardians of health and monitors of harm. No change in principle was involved. The Roman Catholic opponents of liberalization were trapped for they knew that they would be easily repulsed if they attacked the status quo (Richards 1970: 97). The citadel was already, and long had been, in the hands of those whom Dr. St. John Stevas had deemed 'barbarians'; the security of society does not seem to have been undermined by this. The Roman Catholics were thus to a substantial extent forced to argue, at times not very convincingly, about the new risks and the danger of increased suffering for particular women that would arise under the more liberal regime that was being proposed. The medical practitioners' main concern was to be confirmed in their position as guardians and gatekeepers and to be free from hassle. They were after all the profession that in many areas of life had a monopoly over the most important means for the reduction of suffering. They had in the early nineteenth century supported tough laws against abortion as a way of eliminating competition by quacks and now they were prepared to support liberalization for the same reason.

The final wording of Section 1 of the 1967 Abortion Act regarding the grounds on which an abortion could be obtained reads as follows:

(1) Subject to the provisions of this section a person shall not be guilty of an offence under the law relating to abortion when a pregnancy is terminated by a registered medical practitioner if two registered medical practitioners are of the opinion, formed in good faith—

(a) that the continuance of the pregnancy would involve risk to the life of the pregnant woman or of injury to the physical or mental health of the pregnant woman or any existing children of her family greater than if the pregnancy were terminated; or

(b) that there is a substantial risk that if the child were born it would suffer from such physical or mental abnormalities as to be seriously handicapped.

(2) In determining whether the continuance of a pregnancy would involve such a risk of injury to health as is mentioned in paragraph (a) of subsection 1 of this section, account may be taken of the pregnant woman's actual or reasonably foreseeable environment. (Simms and Hindell 1971: 249-50)

Given the long process of argument and controversy in both Houses of Parliament that led to this wording, it is a remarkably succinct and coherent expression of the causalist ethic. It is about minimizing harm. It is not an elective law granting a free choice. The woman seeking an abortion has no rights and the fetus is not mentioned at all. There is a further respect in which a study of what has been *left out* of the law enhances our understanding of how causalist Britain worked. There is no mention in the Act of abortions being performed on the grounds of an absence of a proper consent to the intercourse that caused the pregnancy; there is no mention of abortion on the grounds of rape or of the mental incapacity or very young age of the pregnant woman or girl concerned. Each of these cases was discussed in detail and in all these cases it was decided not to make them part of the new legislation. There were those MPs who did want rape to be spelled out as grounds for abortion and they were often drawn from the ranks of those who in general were opposed to abortion. They believed in the special status of those who were innocent, which included both fetus and rape victim. Causalists are not concerned with rights or with questions of guilt or innocence. All suffering on the part of the particular person counts equally, regardless of the moral status of the sufferer.

The causalists were quite clear that they did not wish to see abortions withheld from the victims of rape, but on the basis that such a woman was liable to suffer great harm if her request were refused and not specifically because she was free of all blame for the sexual act that had led to conception, an act which had been unwilled on her part. Alice Bacon, a minister of state at the Home Office, in rejecting an amendment to the Bill to include a rape clause, was explicit on this point:

> The Clause [i.e., 1a] as amended, provides that it [performing an abortion] shall not be an offence if the doctor is of the opinion that the continuance of the pregnancy would involve risk to the life or injury to the physical or mental health of the pregnant woman or any existing children of her family and in determining whether or not there is such a risk of injury to life, account may be taken of the patient's total environment, actual or reasonably foreseeable. I cannot think of anything that would affect the mental health of a woman or a girl more than having to bear a child as a result of rape or sexual assault. I hope that the mover of the Amendment will ask leave to withdraw it because it would put us in a difficult position if we were driven to vote on this issue when practically everybody in the House would not want a woman to bear a child as a result of rape. It is not so much a question of what we want in the end, it is a question of the way to go about providing it. (*Hansard,* House of Commons 1967, vol. 750, cols. 1176 and 1177)

The decision that rape should *not* be specifically included as grounds for making abortion permissible does fit in with the causalist approach that asks, "What do we do now to minimize harm?" rather than "How should we be assessing the moral standing of someone's past behavior?" It was consistent with the previous legal position. When, in 1938, Aleck Bourne was prosecuted for terminating the pregnancy of a fourteen-year-old who had been gang-raped he did at first consider using the fact of the rape as his defense (he was himself of a moralist turn of mind), but before the trial took place he decided to go with the more acceptable and winnable defense that he was averting a danger to the mental health of his patient (Keown 1988: 79; Simms and Hindell 1970: 71).

There are hints in the parliamentary debates that some of those who were opposed to abortion law reform but had conceded its inevitability and were fighting over the details would have preferred that abortion be awarded to those women who were seen as victims and denied to the women whose conduct could be designated as sinful. It was not an acceptable view to put forward in a strongly causalist legislature, but it was one emphatically and explicitly made outside Parliament in the campaigns associated with The Society for the Protection of the Unborn Child (SPUC), which seems to have been more concerned with protecting the lives of the unborn children of sinners than those in the wombs of the virtuous. Simms and Hindell commented:

The Rev. K. Ward, Rector of Daventry...told (his congregation) that as Christians they must be certain that abortion was not "made available for all and sundry who behave promiscuously and irresponsibly." This notion that abortion if it was to be tolerated at all should be a reward for virtue, whereas the wicked and irresponsible should be punished with unwanted babies was a recurrent theme throughout the SPUC (Society for the Protection of the Unborn Child) campaign and was probably the attitude most often voiced in the campaign against reform. (Simms and Hindell 1970: 99)

The law on abortion in the long run proved stable and by the beginning of the twenty-first century abortion was no longer a matter for controversy in Britain. There was little support for the marginal "voice for choice" faction, there were no significant attacks on clinics or abortionists, and there was a widespread availability of pharmaceutically tested drugs that induce very early abortion. The legal provision and even state financing of abortion was not the divisive issue it was, and still is, in the United States. The rights and wrongs of abortion do not occupy political or legal thinking. No one has bothered to invest their time in devising new and far-fetched reasons to justify a right to abortion or to deny its availability with an eye to winning a political or legal conflict. The law on abortion did not become part of a culture war about rival rights (Davies 1983b). In Britain, the members of the medical profession had long been assigned the role of gatekeepers in the case of abortion and as they came to be familiar with and used to working within the 1967 Act, they came to interpret its provisions more and more liberally. Abortion, when carried out by those with appropriate medical qualifications and skill under appropriate conditions, is statistically far less of a threat to the pregnant woman's life or health than the continuation of her pregnancy. The phrase "injury to the physical or mental health of the mother or any existing children of her family" used in the Abortion Act is so vague and broad as to give ample scope to sympathetic doctors to agree to almost any request made. The improvements in screening for genetic disorders and the free and encouraged provision for screening in the National Health Service have made the early abortion of an abnormal fetus ever more feasible. The easier, earlier, more certain diagnosis of genetic risk provides another opportunity for minimizing harm. It is worth noting here the close connection between causalism and "risk," a word used three times in the first four paragraphs of the 1967 Act. The importance of avoiding risk, even when others had moral objections, was central to the political arguments about abortion in Britain. In the last three decades of the twentieth century, British society became more risk conscious and the protection of full particular persons from all manner of danger became of central importance and at times an obsession in all walks of life. This inevitably had an effect on the attitudes of doctors faced with a patient seeking an abortion. At the beginning of the twenty-first century, it was far easier to obtain an abortion in Britain where it is not a right than in the United States where it is.

The moralist opponents of abortion in Britain were not able to mount as massive a counter-offensive against the provision of abortions as had been done in the United States after *Roe v Wade* in 1973, but for many years they regularly tried in Parliament to recover some of the ground they had lost. Between 1967 and 1992, they introduced sixteen Private Member's Bills (Lee 2001: 44) into Parliament (the main ones were in 1974, 1977, 1978, 1979, 1985, 1986, and four in 1987), seeking to restrict the terms on which abortion would be allowed, but none of them aimed to outlaw abortion altogether or to introduce a right to life for the fetus. Those who had moralist objections to abortion were forced to restrict themselves to making limited proposals such as lowering the time limit for abortion, tightening up the definition of risk so that there had to be a "serious" risk of "grave" injury before abortion was permitted and regulating the provision of abortions by the private sector (abortions provided outside the National Health Service for those who paid). No doubt these were seen as stepping-stones towards the re-prohibition of abortion, but to a very considerable extent they had to be argued within the new causalist moral framework of harm and risk. None of the bills ever succeeded despite there being a majority of Conservative MPs in Parliament between 1979 and 1997 and increased numbers of Roman Catholic MPs in all three parties. The bills were, as is customary, put forward by individual members of the legislature, as was the case with the moral legislation of the 1960s, but, whereas the Labour governments of the 1960s had provided sufficient time in Parliament for these to be debated and passed, the Conservative governments of the 1980s declined to help in this way those who wanted new restrictions on the provision of abortion. Abortion had become a taken-for-granted fact of life in Britain and the free-market, post-1979 Conservative governments had no real wish to disturb this situation. There was no possibility of the Conservatives making abortion an electoral or party issue or mounting a moral crusade against it in the way that had happened in the United States.

On the contrary, the anti-abortion organizations such as Life and SPUC gradually found themselves pushed to the margins. There was no support for their attempt to create a secular ideology of fetal rights and they were forced to seek new issues on which to fight, such as the use of embryos in research in order to remain in being. There was also an absence of any widespread agitation for a right to choose or a right to privacy on the part of those content with a status quo that came very close to offering abortion on demand. In this way the language of rights was removed from the debate altogether (Davies 1983b).

The anti-abortionists were forced to move into causalist territory and to fight on issues very distant from their main concerns in order to get a hearing at all. In 1987, David Alton, a Roman Catholic MP, speaking in favor of a bill to restrict the legal time limit of abortion to 18 weeks, was the first politician in Britain to speak of "post abortion syndrome," a psychiatric condition allegedly experienced by women after abortion (Lee 2001: 41). Although the not very convincing or innovative research on which "PAS" was based was entirely American, the idea that abortion damages women's health was exactly what was needed by anti-abortion campaigners in Britain who were by now forced to argue within a causalist framework of harm minimization. Together with scares about abortion leading to an increased risk of breast cancer or of infertility, it enabled them to gain attention in a Britain where the mass media increasingly stressed the need to protect individuals from all manner of risks associated with artificial procedures (as distinct from letting nature take its course) even if this meant restricting their liberty. The risk of post-abortion syndrome was, in fact, very small and far less than the risks to mental health associated with pregnancy, but in many other contexts bad research statistics, the arousal of public anxiety by the media and its subsequent exploitation by politicians often did lead to restrictive legislation as, say, with the panic over genetically modified food or the banning of "beef on the bone." That such a campaign did not succeed in this particular case is a sign of the extent to which abortion had become normal and ordinary in Britain. PAS was not taken seriously in Britain and likewise there was no strong residue of basic anti-abortion sentiment available from which to derive a political demand for a requirement of "informed consent" or of compulsory counseling designed to impede women from seeking and obtaining abortions.

At the beginning of the twenty-first century, the British were in practice willing to allow women to choose abortion if their personal circumstances led them to seek it. However, most of those who publicly and politically defend the British status quo, in which abortion is freely available, do not do so in terms of rights, nor do they seek to establish a formal and explicit right to abortion, for to do so would be to go against British conventions governing public arguments about moral issues. Why should those in favor of abortion, whose success has been gained through a strict adherence to the rules of causalist argument, place that success at risk merely to win a rhetorical victory about rights? Meanwhile, the British anti-abortionists have lost out at all levels. Not only has abortion become almost universally available in Britain, but there is an even greater general indifference to anti-abortionist central values and concerns than there was in the past, in marked contrast, as we shall see in chapter 5, to neighboring Ireland. In Ireland, the anti-abortionists could argue about principle, about religion, about national identity and about natural and constitutional rights, but in Britain they were forced to argue in bad faith on other people's terms and failed to convince anyone (Davies 1988a).

Causalism Not Rights: Homosexuals and Law Reform

During the entire period between 1954 and 1967 discussions in the British Parliament about the decriminalization of male homosexual acts rarely made reference to questions of rights. This is both curious and significant since a lead had been given in the *Report of the Committee on Homosexual Offences and Prostitution* (1957: 9-10) which, in effect, argued that there were matters of private, sexual morality that were none of the law's business. Supporters of decriminalization in Parliament would refer to the principles of the 1957 Report with great respect, but they would then return to their main theme, the need to reduce the harm, suffering, and enhanced unhappiness caused by the law. We can see a good example of this causalist emphasis in the contribution of Dr. David Owen, a medical practitioner. Dr. Owen first asserted the importance of freedom of choice and action (David Owen, *Hansard,* House of Commons, vol. 738, col. 1110), but then slid quickly to an acceptance of society's moral condemnation of homosexuality, sandwiched between two strong declarations that the homosexual's lot is not a happy one, justified by a scatter of speculative references to homosexuality being a kind of disease. The purpose of the latter was not to demonstrate diminished responsibility on the part of the homosexuals but to emphasize that people who have symptoms and ailments suffer in consequence and that it is our duty to reduce this suffering. It was not so much the medicalization of homosexuality but the "awfulization" of homosexuality, a phenomenon also to be found in the debates about abortion. Dr. Owen argued that we must sympathize with the fate of the homosexual not because it is unchosen but because it is so very awful. It was a very characteristic speech indeed and its conclusion was well tailored to convince the members of a causalist institution. Dr. Owen stated:

These people, suffering from what I would prefer to call a symptom of homosexuality, already suffer very deeply from social ostracism. They are to a great extent alone in the world. But, because of the present law, a law which the Hon. Member for Ilford North (T. R. Iremonger) himself dislikes, they live in perpetual fear. Much has been made of the possibility of blackmail, and this is very important, but it is not the only fear. The real fear these people have is fear of prosecution. They know that they can be prosecuted. These are people who often, for other reasons, are mentally unstable in that they are anxious and nervous, and the threat of prosecution is very real. Those of us who have seen these people know how tortured they are. They come from all walks of life. We are not talking of the stage picture of the "queer," the "nancy boy." Often, these people go through life with those in closest contact with them not having the slightest knowledge that they live this tortured existence. My Hon. Friend the Member for Rochester and Chatham (Mrs. Anne Kerr) told us of the difficulties for them when they are forced by society's pressures to marry. These can be very severe, too. But so often they live in loneliness and fear. We cannot stop their loneliness. Society, I submit, will always condemn homosexual practice, and it would not be my wish that the House should be seen to condone it. But I ask the House to vote to remove the fear from those men who so order their lives that they do not inflict themselves and their ailment on society, and to allow them in the privacy of their own homes to pursue their lives as they are driven to do. (David Owen, *Hansard*, House of Commons 1966, vol. 738, cols. 1110-1111)

At the end of the many and lengthy debates on male homosexual activities and the law, when the vote was about to be taken to give the Sexual Offences Bill its Third Reading, one that made decriminalization certain, exactly the same line was taken by Roy Jenkins, who, as Home Secretary and a man with considerable influence over the allocation of parliamentary time, had indirectly but deliberately made sure that the legislation would pass.

It would be a mistake to think—my Hon. Friend the Member for Preston South (Mr. Peter Mahon) has some curious views on this—that by what we are doing tonight we are giving a vote of confidence or congratulation to homosexuality. Those who suffer from this disability carry a great weight of loneliness, guilt and shame. The crucial question, which we are nearly at the end of answering decisively, is, should we add to those disadvantages the full rigour of the criminal law? By its overwhelming decisions, the House has given a fairly clear answer, and I hope that the Bill will now make rapid progress towards the Statute Book. It will be an important and civilising Measure. (Roy Jenkins, *Hansard*, House of Commons, 1967, vol. 749, col. 1511)

The word *civilizing* is characteristic of self-consciously progressive causalist discourse. It refers to the ending of the infliction of, and particularly the aggressive infliction of, harm or even the threat or appearance of the infliction of harm not just by the state but by private individuals. The abolition of capital punishment and of corporal punishment in schools was civilizing—so was the decriminalization of homosexuality.

As far as the British legislature was concerned almost the entire case for setting the old laws aside was that it would lessen harm and suffering. Even though the laws against homosexual acts in private were only rarely enforced, with perhaps a hundred convictions a year, the consequences, which could include prison and inevitably meant exposure and public obloquy, were disastrous for those individuals unlucky enough to be caught. Those who escaped detection, nonetheless, lived in fear, not only that they might be caught next time but that some chance admission by a former sexual partner might lead to their being prosecuted for an old and stale offense. As one retired RAF Wing-Commander said in an interview many years later after the law had been repealed:

You may find it difficult to visualise what it was like to live in an era in which imprisonment accompanied by disgrace was a possibility which could at any time become a reality. I was regularly committing acts ("abominations against nature" etc.) which were punishable by imprisonment. In the middle of a Christmas party for example, when everyone was in festive mood I would feel a sudden cold clutch of fear at the heart at the thought that I might be spending the following Christmas in prison. (Quoted in Hall 1995: 136)

As a military officer he was doubly at risk, but a conviction, even if only leading to a fine, would also have been a social and professional disaster for many respectable civilians, particularly those in sensitive professions or living in small communities. Even prejudiced individuals are usually willing to ignore and discount gossip about or even quite strong circumstantial evidence against a homosexual colleague or neighbor, but there is certain obstinacy about a criminal conviction, particularly if it is reported in the newspapers. Even an account of a trial ending in an acquittal could ruin a person's standing and reputation. All the mutually negotiated evasions and deceptions and the generous obtuseness, unwillingness to pass judgment and resort to off-stage humor by others that make living with stigma possible, tolerable, and even entertaining are of no account when the law metes out public degradation. The very existence of such a law is a cause of anxiety and fear.

Where there is fear of exposure there is the possibility of blackmail and in the case of an activity that is against the criminal law there is no legal remedy available to the victim. A blackmailed homosexual could not complain to the police lest he be arrested and charged with gross indecency or even sodomy. In 1921, after a public scandal involving prominent lesbians, the House of Commons voted to make the sexual interactions of lesbians a criminal offense, but the House of Lords rejected the suggestion on the grounds that such a law would provide enormous opportunities for blackmailers (Grey 1992: 19). Those who said this clearly knew that the laws impinging on male homosexuals were in and of themselves a blackmailer's charter and thought that female homosexual activities, not being a threat to the nation's existence, boundaries, and defenders (see chapter 4) did not justify the infliction of this degree of suffering. In 1954, when the suggestion that the Wolfenden Committee be set up was being debated in Parliament, Earl Jowitt recalled that when he became attorney general in 1929 he had been amazed both at how much blackmail there was in England and that a large proportion of it had to do with homosexuality (*Hansard*, House of Lords 1954, vol. 187, col. 745). Long before the Labouchere Amendment of 1885 had worsened the situation for homosexuals, accusations of sodomy had been a common way of extorting money and favors from vulnerable individuals in eighteenth- and nineteenth-century England (Goldsmith 1998: 93, 115; Trumbach 1986).

The realization that blackmail was so prevalent and so damaging led to a very significant change in the administration though not the content of the law in 1964. The Conservative MP, Sir Thomas Moore, who had been shocked by the savage impact of the law on one of his constituents, asked the then Home Secretary, Henry Brooke, in 1963 whether he proposed to implement the proposals of the

Wolfenden report on homosexual offenses. When he learned that the then Conservative government was not taking any action, he tabled a motion in April 1964, calling on the government to decriminalize homosexual acts on the grounds that this "would tend to prevent much blackmail and many personal tragedies." In July 1964, it was stated that the Director of Public Prosecutions had asked the heads of local police forces to consult him before prosecuting men for homosexual offenses revealed because of blackmail complaints. From this point on, there were no further prosecutions for homosexual acts committed in private (Grey 1992: 85). The law was no longer enforced.

When Parliament came to debate decriminalization at length in 1964-67, blackmail was the most frequently mentioned objection to the law that was cited and the emphasis throughout all the debates was on the fear and misery caused by the existence and exercise of the law. The entire case for reform rested on the causalist argument that if the criminal laws penalizing homosexual conduct in private were removed there would in aggregate be less individual suffering and unhappiness than if they were retained (see *Hansard*, House of Commons 1965, vol. 738, cols. 1073-1089. and vol. 738, cols. 1073-1089; House of Lords 1957, vol. 206, col. 765; 1965, vol. 206, 90-99, 206, vol. 266, col. 693). There was little discussion of rights; they were unimportant. The arguments used were those propounded in 1785 (though not published at the time) by the leading British utilitarian Jeremy Bentham who, despite thinking homosexuals were preposterous, saw no useful purpose in inflicting penalties on those whose activities caused no pain to any other specific individual (Bentham 1978 [1785], Goldsmith 1998: 19, 94). Yet Bentham would not have approved of the care taken by legislators in the 1960s to avoid suggesting that homosexuals gained pleasure from their activities. In 1967, as in 1785, it was not permissible publicly to approve of sexual pleasures of an unnatural kind. Even at the end of the twentieth century there was an unwillingness to concede officially the legality let alone the validity of some of the more exotic forms of sexual activity merely on the grounds that they gave pleasure to someone or indeed to many. The pursuit of pleasure is still not an argument that is accepted by judges or politicians in Britain as justification for private consensual sexual activity that they think should be forbidden (Davies and Trivizas 2000; Grey 1993: 40).

Some of the MPs voting in favor of decriminalization no doubt did think to themselves that the pleasure obtained by homosexuals from their activities was a valid reason for changing the law. A few of them were themselves secret practitioners and more of them would have been during their younger days when closeted in one of Britain's all-male elite boarding schools. Most MPs with even a modicum of imagination and humanity would have understood the nature of homosexual desire by empathy or analogy. Yet all had to pretend that they disapproved of homosexual behavior. Pleasure could only be alluded to indirectly, for causalism, the dominant acceptable form of argument at this time, was about minimizing harm; it was not a form of hedonism or a pleasure embracing utilitarianism. Some of those in favor of reform probably were hedonists tolerant of differences of taste and choice, but all had to pretend that homosexual activities were at the very least unacceptable. It was also a tactic designed to avoid stirring up the violent opposition that a direct or indirect expression even of indifference to homosexual conduct would have caused.

Divorce: From Moralism to Causalism

The 1857 Divorce Act, which substituted secular divorce in the law courts for the previous ecclesiastical and political procedures, is a convenient point to begin an account of divorce in that part of moral Britain known as England and Wales. While the new Act gave those who could afford it greater freedom of action, the new procedures it introduced have been described as a moralist instrument of "character building" (Wiener 1990: 72) intended to strengthen morally the institution of marriage by making the dissolution of marriage depend on the public proof of fault for all to see. The purpose of the new legislation was not to end marriages that had broken down but to give the victims of gross marital misconduct a means of escape and to punish those who had offended. The divorce court was a civil court, but, as with the bankruptcy court, the proceedings in some respects resembled those of the criminal courts (Wiener 1990: 73). In either case, the purpose was to identify blame, and accurately to denounce an individual who had broken the rules and been responsible for the failure of a business or a marriage; in order to obtain a divorce there had to be an innocent as well as a guilty party. If there was an absence of clear guilt or if only guilt that was manifestly shared guilt could be demonstrated, then no divorce could be granted. The only grounds for divorce were adultery on the part of the wife and adultery aggravated by some other matrimonial offense on the part of the husband. It was a narrow and moralist test that permitted only a very low incidence of divorce. The number of divorces in England and Wales had risen to only 800 per year by 1914. The turning point came in 1912 with the *Report of the Royal Commission on Divorce and Matrimonial Causes* (1912), for a majority of the Commission's members were prepared to allow divorce on grounds of desertion, cruelty, and incurable insanity. The last of these was the most revolutionary since it was not the deliberate act of a responsible and blame-worthy individual choosing to break a rule but was an involuntary accident that could not be fitted into a moralist framework. There had to be a guilty party, one who had *freely chosen* that which was morally wrong (Wiener 1990: 211).

The proposals not only split the members of the Commission but also opinion in Parliament and no major change in this direction took place until 1937 in England and Wales (1938 in Scotland and 1939 in Northern Ireland), by which time the bishops of the Church of England were less powerful than they had been in 1912 and were now also badly divided on the question of civil divorce (Stone 1990: 395, 399-400). The other upholders of moral and moralist Britain, the judges, were very much in favor of the reforms because so many of the divorces being sought on the grounds of adultery involved collusion between the parties and deception of the courts. The couple agreed to divorce, the husband committed or pretended to commit an act of adultery and the wife then obtained an uncontested divorce based on the evidence of pre-arranged witnesses (Phillips 1988: 527; Stone 1990: 397-98). The entire moral intention of the law was being subverted. The 1937 Matrimonial Causes Act, though it broadened the grounds for divorce, remained based on the petitioner demonstrating fault on the part of the other party in court, usually adultery, cruelty, or desertion. Without proven fault there could be no divorce and there was no divorce by consent. If an application for a divorce was contested, the person accused of a matrimonial offense was still described as defending the action. The accusatorial procedure with its two clearly separate and conflicting teams of lawyers and witnesses ranged against each other, the recriminations and counter accusations, the testimony of private detectives and inquiry agents were still an unforgettable reminder that the purpose of the court was to determine guilt and innocence. Someone had to carry the blame or there was no divorce and an innocent party could not be divorced against his or her will, however severe the difficulties facing a guilty party who wanted to remarry. By the 1950s, there were 200,000 couples, often with illegitimate children, in this position.

In 1956, another Royal Commission that had discussed marriage and divorce reported and its members were once again badly divided. Some of its members wanted "irretrievable breakdown of marriage" to be an additional ground for divorce, such that divorce no longer be simply a response to a particular matrimonial offense that had been committed. They were willing to permit divorce by consent and to allow divorce after seven years separation (in certain circumstances even against the wishes of the other spouse). Nine of its members strongly opposed these proposals on moralist grounds and the Commission was deadlocked. *(Royal Commission on Marriage and Divorce, Report 1951-1955, 1956: paras. 64-8)*

One of the points that concerned causalists at this time was the position of the children of a guilty party who had entered a new irregular union but who could not remarry if the innocent party of the old marriage was obdurately opposed to divorce. Such children were, in fact, permanently illegitimate at a time when being so still carried a significant degree of social stigma. In most cases, parents could at this time legitimize children born out of wedlock by subsequent marriage, but this was not possible if one of the parents had been married to a third party at the time of their birth. Thus, even if the original spouse relented and granted a divorce or died and the parents were able to marry the children remained bastards, excluded forever like, and indeed in a sense as, *mamzerim.* Causalist reformers sought to remedy this situation by introducing the Legitimacy Bill into Parliament in 1959, but were strongly opposed by the more moralist MPs despite the innocence of the children concerned. The flavor of their objections is well conveyed by the speech of Philip Bell:

It is interesting to note that the real point behind our discussions is not the happiness or welfare of an individual, but how far it contributes to the solidarity of family life. The point is whether it makes the family a better unit. The point is not whether it makes it easier or more comfortable for people to live together, but whether it makes the family with its vow of faithfulness and honour, a better unit. Does it encourage people more to carry out their vows?... In our affairs there is often a desire prompted by hard cases and by irritation to take short cuts. We see it in all forms of legislation. It is attractive in that it remedies a particular pain. We may think that it is a good thing, but I fear that we miss the ultimate object which, in this case, as the Hon. Member said, is the holding together of family life. (*Hansard,* House of Commons 1959, vol. 605, cols. 768, 770)

We can see here the familiar moralist rhetoric of character development emphasizing the need to penalize those who broke vows and promises and contracts and to encourage prudence and self-control that had characterized the high moralist Britain of the mid-to-late nineteenth century described by Martin Wiener. For Phillip Bell, the preservation and betterment of the family were important ends in themselves and society ought not to be deflected from defending them merely because of causalist objections that in consequence a society's pursuit of such ends increased harm and suffering were being imposed on particular individuals.

Between 1964 and 1969 such views were largely swept away. The House of Lords ruled in *Williams v Williams* (1964) that cruelty did not require any intention on the respondent's part. It was enough that he or she caused it regardless of questions of autonomy or volition; the action could not, for example, be defended by pleading mental illness and thus an absence of personal responsibility. In effect, this ruling greatly extended the range of the notion of divorce without fault, first suggested in 1912 and first made part of the law in 1937, when divorce on the grounds of incurable insanity was introduced. In 1966, a church-based committee appointed by the Archbishop of Canterbury in 1964 (*Putting Asunder* 1966: 33, 67) and the Law Commission both suggested that the basis of divorce should no longer be matrimonial fault but irretrievable breakdown of marriage. The divorce court should decide on a fact not a fault. The Law Commission urged that the "empty legal shell" of the marriage should be destroyed with "minimum bitterness, distress, and humiliation" (*Reform of the Grounds of Divorce: The Field of Choice* 1966: para. 15).

In 1969, Parliament put all these changes into practice for causalist reasons, and irretrievable breakdown became the *sole* grounds for divorce. Fault was abolished, divorce by consent after two years separation was permitted, and divorce against the wishes of an unwilling spouse allowed after five years separation. It was a major turning point in the shift towards causalism.

Yet the ghosts of the old moralist criteria remained, for proof of irretrievable breakdown required the demonstration of one of five facts; the two based on separation are given above but the other three—adultery, unreasonable behavior, and desertion—involved old faults in a new form. Yet they did differ. Adultery in itself was not a basis for divorce; it had to be shown that the knowledge of the adultery made it intolerable for the petitioner to continue living with the respondent (Passingham 1970: 5). Likewise, the test of behavior soon became not whether it was cruel or unreasonable but whether a right-thinking person would consider that the petitioner, given what was known of the circumstances and about the character and personalities of the parties, could be expected to go on living with the respondent (*Ash v Ash* 1972, *Livingstone-Stallard v Livingstone-Stallard* 1974). The old faults had become transmuted into measures of harm suffered by particular individuals. The courts were increasingly concerned with the welfare of particular persons and not with upholding morality, character, or the family as an institution.

Nonetheless, the causalists were determined to get rid of the last trace of the idea of fault being the basis of the divorce. It was claimed that the adversarial nature of the proceedings and the need to collect and enumerate the faults of the other party were still creating unnecessary acrimony, bitterness, and hostility even though by this time few divorces were defended. The causalists wanted to banish fault altogether and introduce forms of mediation that were not concerned with locating blame in the past but with minimizing trauma in the future (*Report of the Matrimonial Causes Procedure Committee* 1985, Law Commission, *Family Law: The Ground for Divorce* 1990).

These reports and documents led to the Conservative government introducing a Family Law Bill into Parliament in 1995, which introduced no-fault divorce in its pure form. The moralists fought a vigorous but doomed rearguard action. The causalists argued that apportioning blame was difficult, even impossible, and pointless; it had no place in their forward-looking project of reducing harm irrespective of dessert. Indeed, the very idea of blame was anathema to them; it belonged to the moralist worldview that they had discarded, in which autonomous individuals chose to behave in an approved or in a wilful fashion. For the ideal-type causalist the behavior of individuals was *caused* by external circumstances and so attempting to allocate blame was meaningless.

However, the causalists did not in the end enjoy their final victory. The Family Law Act was passed by both Houses of Parliament in 1996, but the proposed divorce law was not put into practice. At the end of the twentieth century, divorces were still being decided on the basis of the 1973 legislation, a consolidation of the 1969 Divorce Reform Act and the 1970 Matrimonial Proceedings and Property Act. The proposed law probably would have reduced the level of distress associated with an individual divorce, but many had by now come to regard with total distrust the reformers' assertion that yet further moves in a causalist direction would render families more stable. This had been the claim of successive Law Commission Reports and of the reformers in the 1960s, but after the 1969 Act the divorce rate rose extremely rapidly during the early 1970s and continued to rise in the years that followed (Stone 1990: 402). Remarriage after divorce produced even more divorce since second marriages tended to be less stable than first ones. Fatherlessness with the serious problems this created for children became even more widespread, a state of misery that greatly dwarfed any decrease in the amount of transitional distress that made one route to divorce preferable to another. Neither the Conservative Party in power in 1996 nor the Labour Party, which won the 1997 general election, wanted to be seen as the party that put the 1996 Act into practice and the party associated, however unfairly, with enhanced family breakdown. It is an irony of sorts that the beneficial legislation of 1996, eminently justifiable on causalist grounds as it was, should have run into such difficulties because of the growth of an uneasy sense that some of the causalist victories of the twentieth century had produced more harm than they had prevented and failed on their own terms.

Why the Causalists Won

It could be argued that the moralists lost for the same reasons that respectable Britain had first faltered and then declined, namely that Britain became in the course of the twentieth century a society of large, impersonal institutions with an increasingly secular culture; indeed, the former change may well also have accelerated the latter. Causalism by contrast is a way of thinking that is integral to the working of large and complex institutions. Characteristically, such institutions work within a framework of rules that instead of asking the question "who is to blame?" asks "who is to pay if something goes wrong?" We can detect this in the spread of the enforcement of strict liability, such that an injured party may be compensated even where there has been no proven fault or negligence; indeed, it is usual to spread the risk involved by taking out insurance, and in many cases insurance is compulsory. Thus, the distance between fault and penalty becomes ever greater and the link between them attenuated, a situation that does not fit well with moralist perceptions of how society should be ordered. Likewise, in this new world of strict liability, when a regulation is broken, a penalty is automatically incurred regardless of intention or whether it was wilfulness or an innocent fault, and a company may be fined for a breach of the regulations by one of its agents even where he or she had been strictly ordered not to act in this way. The purpose of the law in such cases is not as in the criminal law to blame and punish but simply to make sure that the regulations are observed and that those harmed for whatever reason are compensated as effectively as possible. Regulations to do with safety or trading standards are typically of this nature. Anyone engaged in business or commerce or indeed driving an automobile will have direct experience both of strict liability and the necessity of insurance. Investigating and determining blame is lengthy, expensive, and uncertain and conflicts with the need for settlements and resolutions that are speedy and predictable. We can see such a system developing at the end of the nineteenth century (Durkheim 1933 [1893]; Wiener 1990: 262-63), and by the middle of the twentieth century it was ubiquitous (Devlin 1965: 27-34). The purpose of the law is no longer to allocate blame but to minimize harm, which is the essence of causalism. Yet once this had become the predominant way of thinking about laws and regulations in general it was almost inevitable that it should be extended into the area of the regulation of personal morality.

Once the allocation of blame ceases to be the governing principle in that large area of social life where large institutions impinge on the individual, it is inevitable that it should also decline in importance as a factor in the assessment of the conduct of individuals. We have seen how this happened in the case of homosexuality, abortion, capital punishment, and divorce, but it also has implications for our understanding of the death of respectable Britain. In a causalist world dominated by large institutions it becomes difficult to make simple moral judgments because the line between the harm that is the result of miscalculation or accident and that which is maliciously inflicted is blurred. The chain of causality is too long. Also in judging the actions of someone who has made a difficult decision within a complex system that he or she knows will directly harm others, we know that we have to balance this outcome against the possibly worse consequences of inaction or of an apparently more benign action. Causalism is far more appropriate in assessing such situations than trying to reduce them to simple tales of good and evil and imputing bad motives to people we do not know, in the manner of buffoons with placards protesting in the street. However, once we get used to thinking in this way we lose our ability to condemn those who commit simple, traditional crimes where the infliction of harm is deliberate and malicious and the consequences of the crime clear to perpetrator and observer alike. For a mugger or a burglar or the perpetrator of a violent or sexual attack on a stranger the pay-off is excitement, aggressive self-assertion, and possibly dishonest gain and the alternative course of action simply self-restraint. From a moral point of view there is nothing more to be said; to seek further explanations is merely to generate excuses. To try to understand is to pardon in advance. The very existence of these excuses becomes the cause of the increase in crime, or in other contexts of illegitimacy or drug or alcohol abuse. Most delinquents are not thoroughly evil people and they share in large measure the same patterns of disapproval and even of guilt and remorse as respectable people; in order to harm others they have to neutralize their own guilt and inner restraint, they have to silence their own doubts about their delinquent behavior with excuses and special pleading that make it look half justifiable. In a causalist society that denies individual autonomy and sees the magnitude of a harm inflicted as overwhelmingly more important than the malice or blameworthiness of the perpetrator, such excuses are ever more easily available to the would-be delinquents and allow them to deny their wickedness even to themselves. They are able to absorb and rotate the confusions of those unable to see that the uncertainty appropriate to assessing the functioning of decision-makers in complex systems is entirely inappropriate when applied to the straightforward wickedness of obviously deviant conduct. In addition, the decline of moralism and of the corresponding willingness to be judgmental has meant that those who are delinquent are no longer subjected to the powerful and certain scorn and disapproval of others backed up with opprobrium and even social exclusion. Instead there is a collusion in doubt between the clearly delinquent and those nervous of passing judgment.

The rise of causalism as a moral outlook with its emphasis on minimizing harm also has links with two of the great obsessions of the late twentieth century and early twenty-first century: health and risk. Individuals have always sought to prolong their lives, preserve their health, stave off ageing, or at least the appearance of ageing, and dull pain but without really understanding how to do so. Then in the course of the nineteenth century it became possible to provide new remedies for pain and ones that improved over time—notably anesthesia and painkillers that were neither addictive nor intoxicating. Because it was possible to quell physical pain in ways and to a degree that had been unknown to their ancestors, attitudes towards pain and suffering changed in the late nineteenth century. Pain became something to be avoided and palliated rather than endured with fortitude and there was also an increasing reluctance by those in positions of authority to inflict it or to allow it to be inflicted. It was more acceptable then to inflict legitimate pain than it is in Britain today, but far less than it had been in an earlier more brutal era. Although pain was still legitimately inflicted in prisons or schools or families, it had become a subject of criticism and controversy. It was part of a long-term trend in Britain that continued without interruption throughout the twentieth century. It even affected perceptions of the after-life as otherwise orthodox Christians gave up believing in Hell (Carroll 1965 [1895]: 110-17); by the late nineteenth century, as Gladstone put it, Hell had been removed to the "far-flung corners of the Christian mind there to sleep in deep shadow as a thing needless in our enlightened and progressive age" (Gladstone 1898, quoted in Rowell 1974: 212). Likewise, when spiritualists contacted the other world they found not Hell but Summerland, a place where the wicked were not punished or exposed to "cleansing" suffering but given opportunities for upward moral mobility through spiritual growth (Davies 1999: 352). Suffering was becoming the ultimate evil and we can perhaps see here one of the other major sources of causalism; at the very least both were part of the same broad pattern of change.

Equally important, public health was becoming the subject of government policy notably in regard to the disposal of sewage, the provision of a supply of clean drinking water, and compulsory vaccination. Such policies benefited the grubby and the well-scrubbed alike and had more affect on health and longevity than any amount of individual prudence or self-control. Individuals who objected were subject to coercion not for any moral failing on their part but as an exercise in harm reduction. It was a model of what causalism could achieve. The moralists were increasingly inclined to use arguments based on health as a means of reinforcing their message of self-restraint, character development, and the distribution of rewards and penalties according to dessert, but when they did so they both undermined the purity of their original morality and gave a hostage to fortune. To campaign for teetotalism mainly on health grounds is, to some extent, to concede the inadequacy of arguments based on the value of sobriety and self-control as aspects of a good character. It is also to render oneself vulnerable to changes in medical opinion.

The line taken by the moralists at the beginning of the twentieth century was that "THAT WHICH IS MORALLY WRONG CANNOT BE PHYSICALLY RIGHT" (Marchant 1909: 113, in capitals in original). The leader of the social purity movement, the Reverend James Marchant, expounded this proposition in a series of items he wrote for the magazine *Health and Strength*, "Great Britain's organ of physical fitness." The example he seems to have had in mind was the morally shocking but popular and widespread habit of self-abuse, though he never said directly what he was talking about. The problem for the moralist who employs such an argument is that it is apt to reverse itself and the impact of an activity on health becomes the determinant of whether or not it is moral. The argument from health then displaces all other moral considerations such as duty or self-sacrifice. Duty can seriously damage your health says the causalist health-warning. When moralists choose to enlist the support of doctors, they are yielding power to a profession for whom causalism is a tempting ideology. Doctors can easily change sides, as happened over the law relating to abortion.

Even at the beginning of the twentieth century when the moral reformers were busily adding health warnings to their moral exhortations and indeed asking the state to enforce morality in the name of health, the more perceptive among them saw that this would lead to the victory of causalism and their own demise. In 1902, Frances Power Cobbe[6] (1902: 251) wrote in relation to the moralists' attempt to employ causalist arguments about public health in their crusade against the "social evil" of prostitution:

I think I can trace the steps which have led to the present disastrous state of things.... The rise of utilitarian, dependent, morality—duty regarded as dependent on expediency, conscience no longer recognized as the voice of God or as revealing an eternal and immutable moral law. The logically consequent adoption of the principle that whatever action is conducive to bodily health is *ipso facto* morally and lawfully right.

In the moral, respectable moralist Britain of 1902 such a comment was prophetic; it was a recognition of the close relationship between the promotion of health and the rise of causalism, both of which were central to the politics and indeed the public awareness of the twentieth century.

What was missing in causalist Britain, in marked contrast to the experience of the United States, was any discussion of rights. The questions of capital punishment, abortion, and the decriminalizing of homosexuality were all decided by the British Parliament; it alone had the power to do so. Parliament was sovereign in these matters in contrast to the United States where such laws were enacted by the individual states but subject to constitutional scrutiny both by each state's own courts and ultimately by the Supreme Court, the interpreter and upholder of American constitutional rights. It was only in the late 1960s, as we shall see in chapter 4, that *individual citizens* of the United Kingdom began to use the European Court of Human Rights to bring about important changes in the laws relating to personal morality. Before 1966 individuals could not petition the E.C.H.R. in this way. Whereas causalism was part of a distinctive and indigenous pattern of law reform suited to British constitutional tradition, the recourse to judges and to the language of rights was to prove an alien intrusion that represented not just another alternative to moralism but the undermining of the very national integrity of moral and post-moral Britain.

Notes

1. This is only true of the debates in Parliament. The arguments employed outside were far more varied in this respect.
2. Also treason, piracy with violence, and arson in a naval dockyard, but apart from murder only treason in wartime was of any importance. The others were odd anachronisms. The last execution for treason was in 1946.
3. In 1948, the House of Commons voted in favor of the suspension and in effect abolition of capital punishment after a Labour backbencher proposed adding an additional clause to this effect to the Labour government's Criminal Justice Bill. The Conservative majority in the House of Lords, knowing they had the support of the people, rejected this and sent the bill back to the House of Commons. Because they did not want the Criminal Justice Bill delayed, the Labour government instructed

members of the government in the House of Commons to vote against the additional clause and help to defeat it, so that the main Bill would pass the House of Lords without being contested and provoke a constitutional crisis that might well have led to new elections and the defeat of the government. However, this was a matter of procedure and priorities and not of policy.

4.   Lord Parker, speaking on the Third Reading of the Murder/Abolition of the Death Penalty Bill in October 1965, deliberately and consciously recapitulated what he had said on the second reading on 19 July 1965, which is why I have placed the two extracts together. See also the speech by Lord Morris of Borth-y-Gest, Hansard, House of Lords, vol. 268, cols. 535-8 on the earlier occasion.

5.   There have been many attempts since by statisticians to measure this (see, for example, Bedau 1983; Ehrlich 1975; Phillips 1980; Yunker 1976; Zeisel 1983), but their conclusions all depend on arbitrary assumptions that can be disputed. It is fair to say that the acceptance or rebuttal of any particular set of calculations by an individual observer depends largely on whether he or she is in favor of or opposed to capital punishment. In any case, the Parliamentarians largely depended on intuition and anecdote. (See also Davies and Trivizas 1994.)

6.   She was an enthusiastic, if somewhat unorthodox writer on theology, and also, a point very relevant in the light of her denunciation of the new morality of health promotion, an ardent anti-vivisectionist.

3

The Death of the Death Penalty and the Decline of the Sacred Hierarchies

Thus far, the history of the death penalty has been treated in terms of the shift from moralism to causalism that has underlain most changes in British legislation on contentious moral issues. It is the most important of the stories that can be told and one that is part of a very broad change in British society, but it is not the whole story. In relation to the death penalty there is another significant story to be told, that of the decline of the influence of the sacred hierarchies of church and state, the Church of England and the armed forces, that of the strange death of conservative Britain, and the strange death of a Conservative party whose ideology was tied to the idealization and maintenance of a particular traditional, hierarchical order. The Conservative party itself survived and even flourished, but only by diluting that ideology to an almost homoeopathic extent and becoming the party of free trade, free enterprise, and deregulation, the sales pitch of Classical Liberalism not of establishment conservatism; the latter and the moral outlook associated with it are dead. Let us first, however, look at the attitude of the established church, the Church of England, towards capital punishment.

The Death Penalty and the Church of England

For the Church of England, both murder and suicide were offenses against the sanctity of life, the human life that God had created; it was a sinful act of rebellion for any individual wantonly to destroy his or her own life or that of another. Only the state, which, together with the established church was the embodiment of society, could justly take life whether by execution after trial for wrongdoing or for neglect of duty in wartime.

107

Historically, execution by the state for a great variety of crimes was, from the point of view of the church, permissible as a matter of expediency, but after 1837 only murderers were hanged and this was not merely permissible and expedient, but just and necessary. When a murderer took the life of another it so disturbed the sacred moral order that equilibrium could only be restored by the taking of the life of the murderer by society. Execution for murder was retribution for the crime against God of deliberately taking away a life given by and belonging to God. Executing a murderer was a religious duty, the carrying out of God's commandment to Noah, the ancestor of all mankind, that:

> Whoso sheddeth man's blood, by man shall his
> blood be shed: for in the image of God made He man.
> (Genesis 9: 6, *King James Bible*)

The text was a particular favorite of Christian defenders of capital punishment, from the nineteenth-century evangelical philanthropist Anthony Ashley Cooper, later Earl of Shaftesbury, to the Bishop of Truro in 1948 (*Hansard*, House of Lords 1948, vol. 155, col. 481). Trial judges would often quote this text when sentencing a murderer to death (Potter 1993: 55-63), sometimes adding "The land cannot be cleansed of the blood that is shed therein but by the blood of him that shed it" (Numbers: 35:33: *King James Bible*). Death by hanging for murder was expiation and atonement.

After the abolition of public executions in 1868 it was possible to treat executions "as a religious ceremony and by a clergyman of the state church." They had become a "solemn act of religion, a human sacrifice conducted in an inner sanctum, beheld only by the high priests of hanging and a select congregation" (Potter 1993: 75-6).[1] Archdeacon Christopher Wordsworth, later to become Bishop of Lincoln, preached in Westminster Abbey of the "sanguinary code, engraven on men's heart and uttered by his conscience, which is the voice of God" (cited in Potter 1993: 98). Until 1901, a bell was tolled before an execution and until 1902 a black flag hoisted in the prison afterwards, signals indicating that a ritual sacrifice was taking place within, which conveyed a sense of solemnity, awe, and mystery to those outside. Until 1927, the chaplain took the condemned man to his fate audibly reciting prayers from the form of service for the dead. A further religious aspect of executions in late nineteenth- and early twentieth-century Britain was noted by the former prison chaplain Harry Potter:

One other motive was equally potent: the evangelical opportunity, the unique setting that hanging provided for the sacrament of God's grace. It was precisely among the most religious clergy, not the most arrogant or the least sensitive, both Evangelical and Anglo-Catholic, that the opportunities afforded by the imminence of death was so valued (Potter 1993: 111).... Edward King, Bishop of Lincoln spent much time counselling the condemned in Lincoln Castle but never once did he condemn the punishment. The records of his involvement are moving and show how powerful and effective such ministry could be; they also reveal complete satisfaction with the existence of the death penalty.... In a letter to Archdeacon Stow who had asked him to see an unrepentant murderer, King wrote that when confronted with such a life so "very dead to spiritual things, perhaps this sharp knife is the only pruning that could save the little life that remains from complete death." (Potter 1993: 112-13)

Central to these ministrations was the acceptance by the condemned murderer that his or her sentence was just; the feelings expected from them were ones of submission, resignation, and penitence. When, from time to time, a murderer evaded execution by committing suicide this greatly upset the ministers of the church in charge of his or her moral and spiritual welfare. The nature of the person's death had been transformed from an act to be carried out as a statement of the principle of the sanctity of life to one that indicated a total repudiation of this principle. Resignation and submission had become defiance, penitence had become wilfulness, an ordered death under Christian auspices, a pagan choice of death contrary to God's order. The chaplain of Lancaster prison wrote in his diary of his horror at the suicide of the murderer Walker Moore in 1862. Moore had misled the earnest and hardworking chaplain into thinking he was waiting for his execution in a mood of thoughtful religious seriousness, but on the day before his execution he drowned himself in the cistern of a water closet in the chapel yard. Potter wrote of this event:

Self-murder had compounded rather than a judicial sacrifice expiated his sin. The distraught chaplain could "not describe the pain which this calamity to the gaol caused" him. He did not "recollect a more painful day in [his] lifetime." (Potter 1993: 50)

The contrast, so well described by Potter, is one that continued to carry considerable weight in the early 1950s and received mention in the *Report of the Royal Commission on Capital Punishment* 1949-53 (1953), 266-67, para.769:

We ought to mention here a suggestion—though only to dismiss it—that the prisoner ought to be offered some lethal dose the night before his execution and allowed to escape the gallows by drinking it if he so chooses. The suggestion is prompted by feelings of humanity, but the objections to it are manifest. The purpose of capital punishment is not just to rid the community of an unwanted member; it is to mark the community's denunciation of the gravest of all crimes by subjecting the perpetrator in due form of law, to the severest of all punishments. Moreover, so long as suicide is condemned in England by the law as a crime and by the Church as a sin, the proposal could be represented as one to make murderers a privileged class in whom alone this act was condoned. The Archbishop of Canterbury said:

"I think if society demands this penalty, it must itself inflict it, and quite clearly inflict it itself, and not invite the victim to do it for himself. I think that even in those grave and serious conditions a man should stand for his own responsibilities and meet them and at that point it is not wise to invite him—I even think it would not be kind to invite him—to seek his own way out.... It is always a sin to commit suicide; to take one's own life is a form of self-murder.... It is a dilemma he should not be faced with."

The leaders of the Church of England were the great upholders of the state's prerogative to execute those who threatened society whether by murder or by desertion from the army in wartime. The bishops of the Church of England who sat in the House of Lords said nothing during the debates on the use of the death penalty for military offenses, which divided Parliament in the 1920s and early 1930s. It was an issue they felt forced to avoid discussing and they seem to have treated it as a technical military matter for their counterparts in the military hierarchy to decide. The shooting of deserters was not a moral issue but a legitimate exercise of power by the state in wartime. The Church of England had helped turn World War I into a righteous crusade (Marrin 1974; Wilkinson 1978) and been an enthusiastic recruiter of volunteers for the army; its leaders were not in a position to criticize the actions of their military cousins even if they had wished to do so. They were two hierarchies too close to one another to quarrel; the only serious disagreement between them came over the army's wish to regulate and even facilitate the soldiers' access to female prostitutes so as to prevent venereal disease. It was not just that the bishops and their Church owed their position to the state or that the validity of capital punishment was written into the very constitution of the Church of England, for their Roman Catholic counterparts agreed with them; they both drew on a common tradition and a common hierarchical view of the lawful powers of a properly constituted state.[2] The Church of England is a Protestant church, but it also sees itself as a Catholic church and as part of a continuous tradition and of an apostolic succession of bishops that stretches back before the Reformation to the time when Britain was still a Roman Catholic country. It is this sense of continuity that periodically leads to Anglican defections to Roman Catholicism when action by the Church of England, such as the appointing of a Bishop of Jerusalem (a former rabbi) jointly with the German Lutherans in the nineteenth century or the ordination of women in more recent times, seems to betray its Catholic roots.

The bishops of the Church of England in the 1930s were, with one exception, disinclined to question the morality of capital punishment for murder. The Bishop of Durham, Herbert Hensley, made it quite clear in a letter to Mrs. Violet Van der Elst, a vigorous campaigner against the death penalty, in 1937, that he had "always been of the opinion that capital punishment as administered in this country is wholesome and indeed on many grounds requisite" (Van der Elst 1937: 270; the underlining in his handwritten letter is the bishop's own).

However, there was a marked division between the Christian denominations in their attitudes toward capital punishment. The leading figures in the Church of England and in the Roman Catholic Church believed that the state had, as a power given to it by God, the right and duty to execute murderers. The Church of England, the established church, was closely tied to the state. It gave the British state and its actions a sacred character and provided a religious legitimation for capital punishment, as an important expression of the power and meaning of the state. The Church of England and the armed forces were the two hierarchies of the state: a spiritual hierarchy and a hierarchy for the exercise of force. There were close relations between the two hierarchies and both were set apart from the mundane world of the market place that was the focus of most people's lives. The even more hierarchical Roman Catholic Church, though the church of a minority, had always taken the same view of the rights and duties of any legitimate state to inflict capital punishment. By contrast, many of the leaders of the Free Churches, the Nonconformist Protestant churches, who lacked a hierarchical internal structure of government and were locked into opposition to the Conservative and Church of England establishment doubted whether it was right for the state to execute murderers (Potter 1993: 106-8). It contradicted their peaceable and sometimes pacifist outlook (Martin 1997: 73-101), and some of its leaders saw the taking of life by the state in this way as morally wrong and un-Christian. They believed in the value of each full particular person rather than in the sanctity of life as such and rejected the more abstract and corporate view held by the Church of England, which, in its own terms, was, of course, a Catholic institution.

In 1931, a House of Commons Select Committee chaired by a Presbyterian minister reported in favor of the suspension and in effect abolition of capital punishment (*Report of the Select Committee on Capital Punishment* 1931) and the assemblies of the Congregational Union urged the government to implement the Report, saying it regarded capital punishment as "inconsistent with the Christian belief in mercy, redemption and the value of human personality"; the General Assembly of the Presbyterian church took a similar view. The Baptist and Methodist press concurred (Potter 1993: 135). It was a division of opinion and outlook between the churches that was to endure. In 1956, the abolitionists sought the support of religious leaders whom they asked to sign a Memorial against capital punishment. One hundred and fifty leading Nonconformist Protestants signed the Memorial, no Roman Catholic leaders did so, and only five out of the forty-three diocesan bishops of the Church of England signed it (Potter 1993: 178). The strong division of opinion between the leaders of the Free Churches and those of the hierarchical corporate churches was still very evident indeed.

When capital punishment was debated in Parliament in 1948 the bishops of the Church of England in the House of Lords spoke up three to one in favor of retaining it. The clearest statement of the hierarchical outlook of its leaders came from Dr. Mervyn Haigh, the Bishop of Winchester, who spoke at length of the religious quality of this unique retributive penalty:

> But it has never been a characteristic of Christian belief to say there is nothing sufficiently sacred to allow of life being surrendered or taken for its sake. If anyone is interested in the *official* view of the Church of England on this subject, I may recall the modest language of the Thirty-Seventh Article of Religion, which says that for sufficiently heinous offences Christian men may be put to death.... The death penalty has about it a vertical dimension and, therefore, in my view is capable of arousing, and does in fact, arouse among an immense number of people, what I can only describe as a quasi-religious sense of awe.... I urge that the question to be considered is not simply whether there will be a few more murders or a few less, but the whole attitude of the British people to what I have described as the criminality of crime and to the majesty of the whole system of law from the top to the bottom. (*Hansard*, House of Lords 1948, vol. 155, cols. 424-25, 427-28)

Potter further quotes Haigh as saying,

> The execution of a murderer is a solemn ritual act and its object is not only to demonstrate that murder does not pay but that it is shameful. The penalty is not only death but

death with ignominy. The death penalty fulfils this role in an unequalled way because of this quasi-religious sense of awe which attaches to it. In wantonly taking a life, the murderer is felt somehow to have invaded the sphere of the sacred and to be guilty of profanity. His impious act can only be countered by imposing on him a penalty which also has a "numinous" character. This is a deeply rooted belief which cannot be wholly rationalized but should not be summarily dismissed. (1993: 147)

Geoffrey Fisher, Archbishop of Canterbury, as always, sought a compromise that distinguished between degrees of murder with only the most wicked being subject to capital punishment; but he also used the occasion to emphasize the sanctity of life:

Christian belief is that human life is to be treated as a sacred thing, as a trust from God, and not, save in utmost need, to be wittingly ended by man. That belief is being assaulted from many different directions. It must be asserted against suicide; it must be asserted against ideas for legalizing euthanasia. (*Hansard*, House of Lords 1948, vol. 156, col. 48, emphasis added; see also Fisher Papers, 1949, vol. 55; Tuttle 1961: 72-73).

Only George Bell, the Bishop of Chichester, felt that capital punishment was contrary to Christian teaching; his view was consistent with his courageous and unpopular criticism of the deliberate, planned terror bombing of German cities by the R.A.F. during World War II, in which as many as 100,000 civilians could be killed in a single night. His outspokenness may well have prevented him from becoming Archbishop of Canterbury in 1945 (Lloyd 1966: 463-64). In each case, Bell broke with the Church of England's tradition that the conduct of war and the execution of traitors and murderers were the just prerogative of the state acting within a framework of law and that it was the duty of the Church of England's leaders to uphold this and refrain from criticism.

In 1956, members of the House of Commons, on a free vote on a Private Member's Bill, again voted in favor of the abolition of capital punishment and the matter was once again debated in the House of Lords. The Archbishop of Canterbury Geoffrey Fisher drafted a new speech that he proposed to make in the House of Lords, once again advocating the use of the death penalty as a way of upholding the sanctity of life:

There are only two moments at which society says to every one of its members—"take note of the dignity of life." One is in war when society says to itself "members, you have this precious possession of life—we ask you to sacrifice it for us all." The other occasion is murder where society says to a murderer "you have deprived a fellow man of his life; that is such an indignity that you must pay for it with your own life." In both these occasions society is recognizing that life is a matter of tremendous importance and responsibility. To call for its sacrifice is one way of showing it. Abolish war—abolish the death penalty and society is left with no single manner in which it declares its witness to the dignity and solemn responsibility of life. It is treated as one of the trivial things and the death toll on the roads becomes a measure of how it is valued. Thus I defend the death penalty on the grounds that it stands for the dignity of human life. (Fisher's Papers 1956, vol. 167: 201)

Fisher's linking of war and capital punishment in this way reveals that for him society was sacred. Society had the right to call for and indeed compel its members to risk sacrificing their lives in war. Society had the right to take the lives of enemies, rebels, and traitors. A murderer was a rebel who infringed the state's monopoly of taking life and who undermined the majesty of society. The community, acting through its representatives, the jury and the judge, must reassert its primacy by executing the murderer. Vengeance belongs to God, but it has been delegated to society, a society represented by the leaders of its political, legal, military, and religious hierarchies. The soldier killed in battle is a hero worthy of praise, the murderer who is executed is a villain to be execrated. Yet they both died for England; their deaths ensured that the social order would endure. They are opposites, yet part of a single perception of the meaning of life and death. Hierarchical churches and armies are curiously similar institutions with their clearly demarcated ranks and titles and the uniforms that indicate these. There is a sharp boundary between them and the rest of the world indicated in the very words used in English to distinguish between those inside and those without, between priests and laity, soldiers and civilians. Hierarchical churches and armies have a common rhetoric of service, sacrifice, and subordination, of loyalty, steadfastness, and obedience. On matters of life and death, the two hierarchies had a symbiotic relationship. The memorial tablets of stone and brass that dominate the walls of so many Anglican churches speak of war with pride as well as sorrow. The sure hope of the Resurrection and the glory and survival of Britain both in their different ways deny the grave its victory.

Fisher's draft speech remained a mere draft, preserved by chance in his private papers, for his personal chaplain could see in 1956 that these sentiments already belonged to an earlier era and advised him to rewrite his speech completely (Fisher's Papers 1956, vol. 167: 204). Today that never-to-be-delivered draft is a reminder of an aspect of a hierarchical moral Britain that now seems strange and remote. The late 1950s had once again proved to be a turning point, not just in the decline of moralist Britain but also in the hierarchical version of the belief in the sacredness of life. It was to receive a further blow in 1961 when suicide, which had been a criminal offense in England for a thousand years, indeed since the reign of the Anglo-Saxon King Edgar, ceased to be a crime. Until 1824, persons who had committed suicide were buried ignominiously at a crossroads with a stake through the body and a stone on the face, and as late as 1882 had to be buried at night (see also Beloff 1989: 164). Even in 1961, according to the rules of the Church of England, such a person was not entitled to a Christian burial. However, by 1961, causalism was establishing its dominant position. The same Lord Chancellor, Viscount Kilmuir, who had justified the Conservative Government's Homicide Act of 1957 in entirely causalist terms, now in 1961, on behalf of the same government, argued in favor of the decriminalizing of suicide on the grounds that the existing law did "nothing but add to the stress and pain of the relatives and friends of the deceased" (*Hansard*, House of Lords 1961, vol. 229, col. 248). Likewise he was concerned for those whose suicide attempts failed, "that the stigma of having been subject to the criminal law does sometimes cause real harm and distress; and here is not infrequently added the stigma of having been in prison" (*Hansard*, House of Lords 1961, vol. 229, col. 249). There was little opposition to the change.[3] In the past, the use of criminal penalties had been justified as a way of stating that suicide was morally wrong, a denial of the gift of life, and a form of rebellion against both God and society. Accordingly, those who tried and failed had been punished for much the same reason as murderers were hanged, namely to uphold a hierarchical view of what constituted the sanctity of life. Now the legal penalties for suicide were being removed as a way of reducing the aggregate suffering of individuals, regardless of whether or not their actions were wrong. The individual had become more important than God's will and more important than duty to society. In the House of Lords, the Bishop of Carlisle found it difficult to argue against this compassionate reform, but he wanted to retain some kind of condemnation in the law, so that suicide would remain a crime even when it no longer was one. The Bishop felt that "It may be very difficult but I sometimes think all things are possible to lawyers" (*Hansard*, House of Lords 1961, vol. 229, col. 259). He declared:

I am not satisfied that it (Clause 2) is sufficiently strong to uphold the sanctity of life.... I want to be assured that there is in this Bill something of law that secures and makes very clear to everyone the sanctity of human life. To abrogate the rule of law whereby suicide is a crime is right; but in doing so there must, in my judgement, be enough left in the law to convey to everyone that to take life, one's own life, is literally a dreadful thing, contrary to natural instinct and contrary to natural law.... I want the Bill amended to make it crystal clear that suicide, even when legally permissible, is still a dreadful offence against nature.... I cannot help but think that natural law would determine the taking of one's life as unlawful. (*Hansard*, House of Lords 1961, vol. 229, col. 258-9)

The bishop's language with its evocation of natural instinct and natural law was as outdated in 1961 as Archbishop Fisher's proposed defense of war and execution had been in 1957. It had become an obsolete world view. By 1967, during the debates on homosexual law reform the bishops no longer felt able to denounce sodomy as a form of unnatural vice. The word *natural* had ceased to refer to the design and purpose of human life and action by the Creator; it has since been annexed by those whose secular superstitions have made them fearful of scientists' increasing ability to manipulate the world. Godly America is happy to accept GM (genetically modified) crops, but the Godless green Europeans accuse the scientists of playing God and going against nature. The world has been laterally inverted.

Most people in Britain had long felt sympathy rather than moral disapproval for those individuals who had come to find life so unworthwhile as to seek to end it, regardless of what the law said. For a long time prior to 1961, it had been common for a verdict of suicide to carry the rider, "while the balance of mind was disturbed," often on the flimsiest of grounds, in order to spare the relatives further grief. Most attempted suicides never came to the attention of the police and doctors tended not to report them; there is a parallel here with the case of abortion. Indeed, one of the causalist arguments used by the Lord Chancellor in favor of the removal of the criminal status of suicide was that it would permit a new openness that would improve the chances of effective medical intervention. It is possible that this was one of the causes of the marked fall in the suicide rate in England and Wales later in the 1960s, though probably a very minor one. By contrast, the incidence of parasuicides (suicide attempts not intended to succeed but to attract sympathy) rose very sharply. Before 1961 attempted suicide had been discouraged by the condemnation it attracted; now the promise of sympathy encouraged it, particularly among young women. In Britain, suicide had finally ceased to be regarded by the state in terms of guilt and innocence and as a fit subject for punishment, and the entire discourse about it now concerned the minimizing of suffering.

However, as we have already seen, the Archbishop of Canterbury, had in 1956, shifted the basis of his support for capital punishment from the need to bear witness to the sanctity of life to the unique efficacy of capital punishment as a deterrent. The two views are not incompatible, but by the time of the debates on the 1957 Homicide Act the Archbishop was emphatic that the question of whether to employ capital punishment was one of expediency. In doing so, he had abandoned moralism but he had not abandoned the traditions of the hierarchical social order to which he was so strongly attached. He had merely moved closer to another hierarchical view of capital punishment, one associated with those who held or had held senior positions in the armed services.

The Death Penalty and the Army

The history of the death penalty in Britain in the late nineteenth century and the first half of the twentieth century has so far been discussed mainly in relation to murder, with those in favor of the death penalty and in particular church leaders speaking of retribution and atonement and the emphatic denunciation of the murderer who has taken innocent life. However, the highest frequency of executions in the twentieth century in Britain occurred in quite different circumstances under the auspices of the armed forces, an institution whose purpose was, when required, to take life on behalf of the state. Military executions, most of them for desertion, were not part of the great drama of guilt and innocence involved in the trial, conviction, sentence, and hanging of a murderer. Yet, the execution by hanging of a murderer and the execution by firing squad of a deserter are in many crucial respects the same phenomenon, namely, the state exercising its monopoly of legitimate force deliberately and directly to take the life of an individual according to an accepted set of procedures for what are considered to be valid and sufficient reasons. Here they will be studied together for the first time, since criminologists have only studied capital punishment for murder and only military historians have discussed the execution of deserters. The study of capital punishment for desertion will enable us to cast further light on the politics of capital punishment for murder and also to understand better the moral outlook and standards of two highly important and influential institutions in British society, the armed forces and the Conservative party.

Between 1900 and 1964, the year when capital punishment for murder was discontinued, only about eleven to twelve civilians were on average hanged for murder in any one year, a total of only 737 executions in all; this in a country with a population of about thirty million people aged 18 or older. During this same period of time, 278 men were shot for *purely military* offenses, mainly for desertion, while serving in the British armed forces. Most of these executions took place during World War I when, on average, there was an execution every week; this in an army at its peak of between four and five million men and in the early years of the war much smaller (*Statistics of the Military Effort* 1922: 29-32, 62, 739). It would not be unreasonable to argue that trial by court-martial and death by firing squad was a more frequent phenomenon in Britain in the twentieth century than trial by jury for murder and hanging, and that the abolition of capital punishment for purely military offenses was as significant as the ending of capital punishment for murder. Both abolitions may be seen as turning points in the strange death of conservative Britain. An exploration of the strangely neglected processes that led to the abolition of military capital punishment enables us to perceive more clearly a further dimension of capital punishment for murder and provides an additional explanation of why Conservatives and Anglicans were so strongly in favor of executing murderers. Those twelve British hangings of murderers per year were not simply an exercise in retribution and deterrence they were also an expression of the power and moral confidence of a hierarchical British establishment and of the leaders of conservative Britain who constituted a very powerful force in British politics.

In the years before World War I, capital punishment was rarely employed by the British army. During the Boer War (1899-1902), four military executions occurred, but three of these were for murder. Only one deserter was executed, even though cases of "willful missing" (see Kipling 1990: 181-82) were probably rather common. The army had the power to impose capital punishment for a wide range of purely military offenses in wartime but it rarely exercised it.

During World War I, the "contemptibly small" British army consisting of professional soldiers was transformed into a mass army of several million men, initially by the vigorous recruitment of volunteers and from 1917 by conscription, something quite alien to Britain's national tradition. For the British people it was a new kind of war; its nearest predecessor was the American Civil War, another conflict into which large numbers of volunteers were enticed by crusading rhetoric, and in which masses of conscripts were compelled to fight, another war that dragged on for several years and was mainly fought on a relatively narrow front with enormous casualties. Over 700,000 British servicemen were killed in World War I, a large number of casualties for a country of between forty and fifty million people (*Statistics of the Military Effort* 1922: 237). The long, grim lists of names of those who fought for King and country and made the "supreme sacrifice" on war memorials in villages, towns, and churches throughout the United Kingdom have written these losses into the very architecture of Britain. It is a war that is still remembered and commemorated throughout the United Kingdom at the beginning of the twenty-first century for its heroism and comradeship and for its pain and loss.

During the war, over 3,000 men were tried by court-martial and condemned to death and 346 men under British command were executed, of whom 291 were British, the others being from the colonies and dominions. Of the 346 executions, 266 were for desertion, eighteen for cowardice, seven for quitting one's post without orders, six for striking a superior officer, five for disobeying orders, two for sleeping at one's post, and two for casting away one's weapons in the face of the enemy (*Statistics of the Military Effort 1922*: 648-49). They were all acts of disobedience punished with death for the sake of example and purely in order to deter other similar acts of disobedience. They expressed the fear of the leaders of the army, not that the soldiers would conspire and mutiny and shoot their officers but that increasing numbers of individuals would come to disregard orders or even slip away from the stress of battle altogether. It was not the qualities of a particular deserter or act of desertion or even the number of desertions at the time that decided whether the death penalty was imposed or inflicted but the degree to which senior officers felt jittery about the possibility of mass desertion. In the winter of 1916-17, there were very few desertions, but the leadership's fear of desertions was high and one Brigade Commander declared, "offences of this kind are now prevalent and ought to be dealt with severely to discourage others" (Babington 1983: 110). In order to achieve maximum deterrent effect there would be a special parade of the condemned man's unit the evening before the execution with the prisoner present under guard and the adjutant would read out the evidence, finding, decision, and sentence of the court-martial and the official confirmation. It was felt that as many men as possible should be present to listen (Babington 1983: 17).

Politicians and many senior army officers knew that these executions would be unacceptable to public opinion in Britain and where the civilians back home were concerned they tried to minimize knowledge of and publicity about these very executions whose significance they were trying to bring home firmly to as large a number of soldiers at the front as possible. The next of kin of the executed man were frequently deceived as to the nature of his death (Putkowski and Sykes 1992: 217, 224, 229, 257; *Hansard*, House of Commons 1928, vol. 216, col. 52) and this deception was extended to reports in the local press and to the casualty records of the regiment (Putkowski and Sykes 1992: 229, 258-59). It was a way of staving off local anger, resentment, and controversy. During and after the war, individual MPs often asked for details of the number of men executed and what their families had been told, but the official answers to these questions were evasive (*Hansard,* House of Commons 1919, vol. 80, col. 1553; vol. 81, col. 30 and cols. 128-29; vol. 82, cols. 128-30, and cols. 656-57; see also Moore 1974: 75-83, 121-24). In November 1917, it became *official* policy to use ambiguous terms such as "died in service" or "died" without giving any cause or context in the formal notifications sent to next of kin (Putkowski and Sykes 1992: 83; see also Moore 1974: 124). The government wished to avoid any kind of disagreeable political row over the execution of a particular individual, to avoid being pressed about the degree of his guilt, and to avoid having to admit that he had been shot merely to encourage the others. It was also decided in November 1917 that the dependents of those executed should receive war pensions on the same basis as those killed in action and this was made retrospective. When details of executions did emerge it caused a great deal of disquiet. Philip Morell, MP, said in the House of Commons:

The stories that come to one of these death penalties and sentences are quite poignant. Of all the horrors of war, I think nothing is more horrible than that men are condemned to be shot, and are actually shot by their comrades, in many cases for failure of nerves or it may be sleeping at their posts —something which does not necessarily show moral delinquency but only grave neglect of duty. (*Hansard*, House of Commons 1918, vol. 103, col. 847. See also cols. 846-55)

As soon as the war ended the executions stopped. Those in command were unsure about whether to execute men who had been sentenced to death for deliberate desertion during the last weeks of the war but the War Office made it clear that these sentences should not be carried out. No action was taken against returning prisoners who had committed serious military offenses before being captured. There was no further need for deterrence, the only reason for imposing the death penalty for such offenses. We may contrast this with the postwar execution of Private Theodore Schurch in 1946, sentenced to death by court-martial for having treasonably assisted the enemy during World War II, which like the executions for treason of the civilians Amery and Joyce in the same year was an act of pure retribution. These latter sentences looked backwards at the actual offense and condemned its wickedness. The same point may be made even more strongly about the execution of collaborators with the enemy at the end of World War II in countries such as Norway, Denmark, the Netherlands, and Belgium, countries that had abolished capital punishment or not made use of it for many decades. After 1945, capital punishment was restored and applied retrospectively and sleeping death penalties were reactivated (*Hansard*, House of Commons 1948, vol. 449, col. 1934; Amnesty International 1979: 111-122). The rules of due process were often ignored, particularly in France where many of those executed had been officials of the entirely legitimate, if repellent, Vichy government and had had no direct involvement in war-time atrocities. The purpose was not to deter potential collaborators in the wars and occupations of the future but purely to denounce and suitably punish those found guilty of betrayal. By contrast, to execute deserters or men found sleeping at their post in Britain after the end of World War I was unthinkable; these were not hated traitors convicted of a detestable offense but ordinary men who had failed or been negligent under conditions of prolonged and considerable stress.

On the contrary, everyone in Britain, for a variety of reasons wanted to erase the past and remove any taint or stigma that might have been attached to the memory of those who had been shot. This was made clear by Colonel Lambert Ward in a speech in the House of Commons in 1919 in which he even advocated the destruction or falsification of the relevant historical record, though as a man in favor of the death penalty for military offenses who had experience of sitting on wartime courts martial that sentenced men to death he may have had many reasons for taking this line. Colonel Ward said:

> I should like to obtain an assurance from the Secretary of State for War that there shall be no difference made between the graves of those men who were killed in action or died of wounds, or disease, and those unfortunate men who paid the penalty of their lives under Sections 4 and 12 of the Army Act, or who, in other words, were tried by court-martial and shot for cowardice or desertion in face of the enemy. I bring this forward because it has been on my conscience for some time…. I ask the House not to dismiss this petition by the remark that these men were cowards and deserved their fate. They were not cowards in the accepted meaning of the word…. These men, many of them, volunteered in the early days of the war to serve their country. They tried and they failed…. In many cases they were the victims of circumstances…. I should like to ask him (the Secretary of State for War) for a further assurance, and that is that all the records of these trials shall be destroyed and not kept permanently as records of the War Office. Now that the war is over and we have got peace, I do not want people in this country to think that tucked away, stored in some dusty corner of the War Office is a record of how their husband, their father, their brother or their son was tried by court-martial and shot for cowardice or desertion in the face of the enemy. (*Hansard,* House of Commons 1919, vol. 118, cols. 2090-2)

When someone seeks to change the past by destroying the records, it is a sign that an unresolvable contradiction exists. The British government had, for propaganda reasons, turned the war into a crusade against "Prussian militarism" and yet more British than German soldiers had been executed for military offenses. The war had been stubbornly continued for four years despite huge casualties because it was the "war to end war" and yet in 1919 the regulations that prescribed the death penalty for military offenses in wartime remained in place ready for the next war. Those executed did not deserve their fate, but the same fate awaited their equally undeserving successors in the next war. It was as if those in command were saying, "We have a bad conscience about those whom we executed but it was necessary and if necessary we shall do it again." Their attitude was not arrogant but stoical, but it did not fit easily with the outlook of moral Britain in peacetime. Predictably, it led to political conflict.

The first indication of this was the creation of a Committee to Enquire into the Law and Rules of Procedure Regulating Military

Courts-Martial by the Army Council. It reported in 1919 that most courts-martial had been held in an impeccable fashion and that no major changes were needed. It was probably a whitewash, but the evidence examined by the committee has never been published so we cannot accurately gauge the thickness of the coat. It took the standard line of the military leadership that they must have the power to inflict severe penalties in wartime on active service for "unless discipline in armies be preserved, such forces are but a mob—dangerous to all but their country's enemies" (*Report of the Committee to Enquire* 1919: 108), and was signed by the three military members of the committee, by the army's Judge Advocate, by the chairman Sir Charles Darling, and by two of the five Members of Parliament serving on the committee, both of them Conservatives; the other three MPs refused to sign the report (*Report of the Committee to Enquire* 1919: 110). There followed ten years of low intensity parliamentary conflict between the parties in which the Conservatives, who, together with the military leadership wished to retain capital punishment for military offenses, were forced into a steady though orderly retreat, conceding one position after another up to their final defeat in 1930. The Conservatives were bound to lose. Public opinion was against capital punishment for offenses whose moral turpitude it could not discern; even the proponents of execution could not and did not claim that it was the just punishment of the wicked. In the 1920s, there was no threat or prospect of another war and many deluded themselves into thinking that perpetual peace was about to be achieved through disarmament and collective security through the League of Nations. It was not a good time to be arguing in favor of capital punishment as a way of inducing reluctant warriors to fight.

In 1924, the Labour government referred a list of proposed changes in relation to military capital punishment to an Inter-Departmental Committee. However, the Conservatives won the general election of November 1924 and appointed one of their own MPs, Captain King, as chairman. The Committee, most of whose members were military men, predictably reported that the death penalty was necessary to protect morale and discipline and that it "enforced on the troops the lesson that complete self-sacrifice is demanded by military duty in war" (*Report of the Interdepartmental Committee* 1925: 5, para. 13). The report once again stressed that the sole purpose of military capital punishment was deterrence and not moral condemnation. However, the Committee conceded that the death penalty should be abolished in peacetime except for mutiny and for certain minor military offenses where it had been exercised only rarely. In 1925, attempts were made with the official support of the Labour party to remove the death penalty for most military offenses by means of amendments to the annual Army Act (Moore 1974: 207; Thurtle 1945: 93). In 1928, the Conservative government, with the support of the Army Council, abolished the death penalty for eight offenses including sleeping on post, disobeying an order, and striking a superior officer (*Hansard,* House of Commons 1928, vol. 216, col. 34; Moore 1974: 209-10).

The Labour party countered with an unsuccessful proposal that the death penalty be done away with for all military offenses except mutiny, treachery, and desertion (*Hansard,* House of Commons 1928, vol. 216, cols. 32-82; Moore 1974: 210-11). In 1929, the Conservatives lost the general election and there was once again a minority Labour government dependent on Liberal support. In 1930, the Labour government abolished the death penalty for cowardice and for leaving one's post without orders despite the opposition of the military members of the Army Council (*Hansard,* House of Commons 1930, vol. 237, cols. 1577-80; Babington 1983: 211; Moore 1974: 212). When the annual Army and Air Force Bill came to be debated, Ernest Thurtle, MP, with the almost unanimous support of the Labour MPs proposed an amendment removing capital punishment for desertion on active service in wartime. The Labour government's Secretary of State for War opposed this on behalf of the government, asking for time to consult the leaders of the military, but the government then decided to allow a free vote on the amendment and capital punishment for desertion was abolished by 219 votes to 135 (*Hansard,* House of Commons 1930, vol. 237, cols. 1226-30; Moore 1974: 212-13; Thurtle 1945: 110). There was strong opposition in the House of Lords to the abolition of the death penalty for cowardice, desertion, and leaving one's post, especially from those army commanders in World War I who had been given peerages in recognition of their achievements (*Hansard,* House of Lords 1930, vol. 27, cols. 151-71; Babington 1983: 211; Moore 1974: 214-16). The House of Commons refused to compromise and the peers gave way rather than provoke a constitutional crisis, for they knew full well that the changes had the support of the public. During World War II, some senior military commanders, particularly during the campaigns in North Africa, wanted the return of the death penalty for military offenses but realized that it would be futile to pursue the matter due to the intense opposition it would have generated both in Parliament and outside (Moore 1974: 224-25; Thurtle 1945: 111). The death penalty was only retained for the military offenses of treachery, mutiny, and deliberate desertion to the enemy, that is, for those that clearly demonstrated a reprehensible disloyalty to one's country rather than mere weakness under pressure. The events of 1930 marked a key turning point in the strange death of military Britain for the wishes and advice of the army's leaders had been deliberately disregarded by the legislature.

It was also a stage in the strange death of conservative Britain, the other being the abolition of capital punishment for murder in 1965. The retention of capital punishment, whether for desertion or for murder, was a key part of conservative and Conservative party ideology, but by tacit agreement between the various political parties it was never used as an electoral issue. If we consider the strange death of moral Britain in terms of its central dimension, the rewarding of the virtuous and the penalizing of the wicked, then the turning point in relation to capital punishment came with the 1957 Homicide Act when causalist criteria replaced moralist ones in determining who should be executed. In effect, moral Britain was sacrificed in order to extend for a time the life of a doomed conservative Britain. The heart of moral Britain was stopped in order to preserve for a time the strength of its conservative arm. Predictably the arm itself ceased to function in 1965 when capital punishment was finally abolished. What was finally lost in 1965 was what had been already partially eclipsed in 1930, namely the right of the state to take the life of individuals according to due process in defense of the preservation of order and in the interests of the nation as a whole. For this purpose it is not necessary to execute every individual who commits a capital offense nor is it necessary to single out for execution those whose moral guilt is most flagrant. However, as we have already seen (and as is even more apparent from the American experience) this view of the world clashed with what was a more central tradition of moral Britain, namely that each person should be treated as an individual and receive their just desserts. It is quite clear that this did not happen during World War I. During that war, 266,784 British officers and soldiers were tried by court-martial. Seven thousand, three hundred sixty-one were found guilty of desertion, a capital offense, but only 2,675 were sentenced to death, and only 240 were executed for desertion. Just over 10 percent of those sentenced to death ended up being shot by firing squad and the vast majority of those convicted of a military offense, which could attract the death penalty, received more lenient sentences. Often those in command deliberately substituted a lesser charge such as absence rather than press charges of desertion (*Statistics of the Military Effort of the British Empire* 1922: 649, *Hansard,* House of Commons 1923, vol. 162, col. 1509-10; 1930, vol. 237, col. 1611-12). Those few men who were executed were drawn from an enormously greater pool of offenders and there was no way of justifying why they had been singled out. Had the details of their cases ever been reviewed by the U.S. Supreme Court, Justice Stewart would no doubt have commented that their execution was "cruel and unusual in the same way that being struck by lightning is cruel and unusual...(and that they were) a capriciously selected handful upon whom the sentence of death (had) been...wantonly and so freakishly imposed" (*Furman v Georgia* (1972), 408 U.S. 238, 92 S Ct 2726; 33 P. Ed. 2d. 346 [at 390]. See also comments of Justice White [at 392] and Huie 1954). It was a totally different situation from the trial by civilian courts and execution for murder in Britain described earlier. The Conservatives in the British Parliament in the 1920s and in 1930 found themselves in the uncomfortable position of having to defend the continuation of this process in the face of political dissent from the Labour and Liberal members of parliament who could for once quite reasonably claim to be representing the conscience of moral Britain and thus depict the Conservatives as oppressive.

Why then did the Conservatives continue to fight a losing cause? Indeed it was a triple loser, for the Conservatives not only lost in Parliament but had no support among the electorate and were faced with opponents employing a set of moral principles that by now were almost universally held and which in other contexts they themselves accepted. If we can answer this question it will enable us to understand the distinctive nature of British conservative ideology, the social bases of the British Conservative party, and the nature of the affinity between ideology, party, and support for capital punishment among British conservatives.

In 1930, capital punishment for desertion in wartime was abolished on what was, in principle, a free vote by the members of Parliament; speakers on both sides of the question claimed that it was an issue that cut across party lines. Nonetheless, the Conservatives voted overwhelmingly in favor of retention and the non-Conservatives voted equally unanimously for abolition.

What is very striking when the list of Conservative MPs voting for retention in 1930 is examined is how many of them used their military titles in Parliament; they had either been professional military officers or were proud of the commissions they had held while serving in World War I and were still using this mark of their rank. By contrast, few Liberal and Labour MPs used such titles, either because they did not possess them or because they chose not to use them. The Conservatives alone were drawn from and identified with "the officer class," those who saw it as their right and duty to exercise command, to make binding decisions about the use of force by the state, and, hence, about life and death. It is this experience of power and commitment to hierarchical order that links conservatism and capital punishment in a way that the mere possession of wealth

Table 3.1
Voting on Capital Punishment for Desertion by Party in 1930

	Conservative	Labour	Liberal	Other	Total
Abolish capital punishment for desertion	2	195	20	2	219
Retain capital punishment for desertion	129	2	4	0	135
Total number voting	131	197	24	2	354
Total number of MPs by party	260	287	59	9	615

(Based on data in *Hansard*, House of Commons 1930, vol. 237, cols. 1625-30.)

or a strong position in the market place does not and cannot. It is an expression of the consciousness of those who give orders and expect them to be obeyed automatically in a world where moral duty and coercion are fused together, a world whose ethos is in marked contrast to that of the everyday capitalist market place of contract, calculation, and negotiation. The Conservative party was the political expression of this hierarchical establishment. The Labour and Liberal parties represented those who for one reason or another found themselves or chose to place themselves outside that establishment and in opposition to it; they were people defined not by their liability to be shot for desertion but by the impossibility of their ever taking part in a decision to shoot someone else for desertion. This is the nature of the similarity between the Labour and the Liberal parties prior to 1931 and also in the last decades of the twentieth century; they were both defined in terms of their opposition to a traditional conservative, social, and political order. In the late nineteenth and early twentieth centuries, the Conservatives were the party of empire whereas the Liberal and Labour parties contained substantial numbers of middle-class pacifists and unilateral disarmers and even vegetarians. At the beginning of the twenty-first century the two camps of the forceful and the feeble were even divided over whether fox hunting with dogs should be permitted.

In a society where socialism has become an established force due to the total overthrow of the old order, socialists are enthusiastic supporters of capital punishment for all manner of offenses against the state including property crimes. Those who run a command economy, without the benefit of market forces and incentives are, like the leaders of an army, fearful as to what will happen if their commands are not obeyed.

Socialism is the extension of the military principle throughout the whole of society, reducing everything to commands, and permeating all relationships with a mixture of ideology and coercion. Most of Britain's Labour politicians never aspired to such heights; rather, like the Liberals they remained in a state of permanent opposition, even when their party enjoyed power in Parliament. This opposition reflects a dimension of the way in which not only British society but any social order is stratified, which is quite different from the differentiation of society into economic classes according to systematic differences in the market position of individuals, even though the two may be correlated. We may call this dimension "dominion."

In Britain and other complex and consolidated societies in which the state has achieved a monopoly over the use of legitimate force there exists a stratum of men (and increasingly today, but not in the past, women) who exercise and administer this force or sense that they may be called upon to do so: the actual and potential officers of the army, navy, and air force, senior police officers and civil servants in the relevant departments of state, and in the past the members of the colonial service. They constitute the category of the "dominant" and they exercise authority in relation to those we may term the "subordinate," whose duty it is to support them and carry out their instructions. In a stable, long-established democratic society like Britain the members of the dominant category only exercise delegated power and ultimately they take their instructions from the elected politicians. Nonetheless, by reason of their experience, expertise, and social position they constitute an influential group and one that is conscious of its own identity, distinctiveness, and importance and to an extent of having its own distinctive ideology and morality. It is a group whose members have a sense of close affinity to the Conservative party; indeed, their commitment to traditional conservatism was probably stronger than is or was the case with elites defined in purely social or economic terms. Its members exercise or could be called upon to exercise a particular kind of power, the disciplined use of force. They have been a core group for British conservatism and the Conservative party has been the party of dominion calling upon popular support for policies of national unity and assertiveness. The moral values they espoused were those of duty and discipline, loyalty and honor, fortitude and sacrifice. Such values are essential to any society and were held in general respect in Britain, but at times they coexist uneasily with the values of individualism and of popular sovereignty that make Britain distinctive. The Labour and Liberal parties have upheld, in one form or another, an ideology of "underdoggery" and of qualified opposition to the ethos and ambitions of those I have termed the "dominant." It was this that led them to oppose strongly British rearmament in the 1930s (Fry 2001: 35-46). They were the super-appeasers who opposed even acquiring the means that would make resistance to aggression possible.

The debate over the abolition of capital punishment for desertion in 1930 was an ideal opportunity for Labour and Liberal MPs to express their particular ideology and moral values, ideal because they could claim the support of moral Britain and put the Conservatives in the wrong as "the nasty party," a hard-hearted and hard-faced entity lacking public support. The Labour government did not want a direct and open clash with its own military advisers (no government would) but it knew exactly what would happen when it allowed a free vote to its own MPs. The curious case of the abolition of the death penalty for desertion gives us a rare insight into one of the major moral and ideological divisions within Britain here revealed in its pure form unclouded by other considerations.

The proof of the argument advanced here lies in an examination of an important group that is usually badly neglected by scholars, namely those who failed to vote at all. How did the Conservative MPs who failed to vote differ from those Conservatives who voted for retaining capital punishment? Even on a free vote, the pressures of habitual party loyalties are such that individual MPs are reluctant to offend their party colleagues by voting the wrong way. It is easier for those who have doubts or who dissent simply not to turn up, a form of behavior that is ambiguous and may be covered by a variety of acceptable individual excuses which we cannot know and which are of no real interest to us. It is the aggregate pattern that counts and dividing the Conservatives into those making habitual use of military titles and those not doing so reveals the very clear pattern shown in Table 3.2 (based on data from *Hansard,* House of Commons 1930, vol. 237, cols. 1625-30, and *The Times' House of Commons* 1929).

It is clear that although there was an even division of Conservative MPs between retentionists and abstainers, the retentionists were significantly more likely to be using a military title than the abstainers and those using a military title were more likely to be retentionists than those not possessing or using such a title. There was a substantial difference in outlook between those who were officers and gentlemen and those who were merely gentlemen. I am willing to predict that a more detailed examination of those Conservatives without military titles who abstained (in contrast to the untitled retentionists) would reveal most of them to be men of high social status and from a prosperous business or professional background but who were

Table 3.2
Conservative Voting on Capital Punishment for Desertion by
Military Title in 1930

	Voting to Retain Capital Punishment for Desertion	Not Voting or Voting to Abolish Capital Punishment for Desertion	Total
Conservative MPs using a military title	55	26	81
Conservative MPs not possessing or not using a military title	74	105	179
Total	129	131	260

(Chi-square = 15.72, p< 0.001; Tschuprow's T = 0.15)

lacking in indirect as well as direct connections with the military or with the other coercive hierarchies of the state.

But for the acute economic crisis of 1931, which led to the splitting of the Labour party then in government and to its loss of office (Fry, 2001: 4-11), an attempt to abolish capital punishment for murder would probably have followed its abolition for desertion as a result of a free vote in which the Labour and Liberal MPs would have outvoted the less numerous Conservatives. It would also have been an occasion in which the disagreement on this issue between Anglicans linked to the Conservative party as the spiritual wing of a hierarchical traditional establishment and Protestant Nonconformists, a group self-defined by their opposition to that establishment, would have been manifest. In 1929, a Select Committee on Capital Punishment had been appointed by Parliament, which took evidence in 1929-30 and reported unanimously in favor of the suspension and (in effect after a decent interval) the abolition of capital punishment, but only after all six of its Conservative members had resigned (*Report from the Select Committee* 1931; Tuttle 1961: 40). If the abolitionists had gained the day in the House of Commons, the Conservatives would have used their majority in the House of Lords to reject it (as they were to do in 1948), and then might well have broken with convention and appealed to public opinion knowing that this time they would have had moral Britain on their side. So far as the voters were concerned, murderers *deserve* to be executed but deserters do not. Most men can imagine themselves being deserters in a moment of fear and weakness and most women can empathize with this; by contrast, while everyone can imagine themselves as the victims of murder they perceive murder as a horrid crime that only other people commit. In subsequent decades, opinion polls have consistently shown strong public support for the execution of murderers (Cameron 2002: 139; Christoph 1962: 44; Erskine 1970; Tuttle 1961: 71) and there is no reason to think that views were any different in the 1930s. An appeal to the ideology that opposed "dominion" would have mobilized a majority in support of the abolition of capital punishment for murder among Labour and Liberal MPs in Parliament as it had done in the case of the deserters but not among the public for whom both instances were assessed in terms of guilt and innocence and just dessert. That is what moralist Britain believed in and those politicians who lumped the two cases together, whatever their ideological persuasion, would have been out of step with moral Britain.

We are now in a position to understand a further aspect of that peculiar tangle, the Conservative government's Homicide Act of 1957, which divided murder into capital murder and non-capital murder in a way that undermined moral Britain. It is worth briefly recapitulating its provisions and looking at them again from another point of view. The capital murders were killing in the course of theft, killing policemen and prison officers, killing by shooting or an explosion, and committing murders on separate occasions. Thus far, emphasis has been placed on the importance of deterrence in deciding which murders should be capital offenses and indicating that the existing code of moral Britain was giving way to the causalist program of minimizing harm regardless of dessert. However, the distinction as stated by the Lord Chancellor, Viscount Kilmuir, in 1957, was a dual one:

> The death penalty is to be retained for those cases where murder is most dangerous for the preservation of law and order and where the death penalty is likely to be a particularly effective deterrent. (*Hansard*, House of Lords 1957, vol. 268, cols. 1168-9)

Here we can see once again the pronounced Conservative concern with public order and with preserving the state's monopoly over the use of force (and the associated protection of those who exercise force on behalf of the state), and monopoly over the right to take life whether by execution after trial or through the use of guns and explosives by the armed forces. Just as the possibility of the British army collapsing through cumulative desertion in 1914-18 was remote and the execution of fewer than 300 men during a war in which more than 700,000 men died in action futile, so, too, it is difficult to see why anyone could have thought it necessary to execute six or seven murderers every year between 1957 and 1964 in order to prevent the undermining of British political and public order. Even in the relatively violent and disorderly Britain of the early twenty-first century, murder is a rare crime and the possibility of the political system being seriously threatened by forces indigenous to Britain is extremely unlikely. Indeed there has been no possibility whatsoever of serious and violent political disorder at any time in the one hundred and fifty years before the millennium. The only serious violence during that entire period occurred within or about Ireland and its secession from the United Kingdom. From time to time, agitators have spoken of revolution, or there has been a petty escalation of the routine political or economic conflict that is inevitable in any free society. Conservatives have responded to their words with the rhetoric of alarm, and radical historians, fantasizing about revolution, have seized on these ritual statements and used them as evidence of an instability that never existed.

Even a small degree of public disorder in Britain has at times provoked some of those in charge of protecting order to predict disaster and to demand extra powers to deal with it in exactly the same way that those in charge of protecting health and safety grossly overestimate the risks involved and take absurd precautions that not only curtail individual liberty but may even indirectly lead to higher mortality and morbidity overall (Neal and Davies 1998). The politicians and administrators of the late twentieth century lurched from one techno-moral panic to another—the heterosexual AIDS epidemic that never happened, the "beef-on-the-bone" panic, the panic over the miniscule exposure of school children to asbestos used as fire-proofing in school laboratories, the paranoia about GM (genetically modified) food. Such fears have led to nonsensical bureaucratic policies aimed at attaining zero risk and even to the absurd demands that commercial products be *proven* to be safe, the ultra-precautionary principle (Neal and Davies 1998). It has been a re-run of the generals' fear that their armies would run or melt away or of the upholders of law and order that the entire social and political system might be overturned if there were no capital punishment. In some cases, the two sets of fears have coalesced to induce anxiety throughout the entire political elite and, correspondingly, draconian regulations, as seen in the steady tightening up of the pointless and ineffective restrictions on the ownership and use of guns in Britain (Malcolm 2002). However, our task here is not to deride such fears as irrational but rather to understand the reason why those who express and act on them see their fears as rational and their responses to them as necessary. In the face of a catastrophic disaster such as losing a war, a complete breakdown of law and order or a massive increase in disease or accidental death and disablement, those decision-makers who will be blamed if counter-measures fail always seek maximum caution and control; the costs of these excessive precautions are borne by someone else. It was the misfortune of those in favor of capital punishment that the cost was borne by particular, identifiable individuals rather than being widely diffused throughout the society through increased costs, taxes, and restrictions on liberty.

Perhaps the Conservatives' concern that a tide of murder would follow the abolition of capital punishment is best related not to their fear of the breakdown of order but to a fear of disobedience. In the view of Geoffrey Fisher, Archbishop of Canterbury, murder was disobedience to God and in the eyes of those who exercised "dominion," murder was disobedience to their state and themselves and an infringement of their monopoly. Even if only a few murderers were executed it affirmed that monopoly, denounced disobedience, and showed who was in charge.

An acknowledgement of the importance of the connection between the assertion of authority and the employment of capital punishment means that we must also reconsider the condemnation on religious grounds of suicide by those condemned to death, which was discussed earlier. Suicide by the condemned is also a form of defiance of the exercisers of the monopoly of the use of legitimate force and more immediately of those imposing the execution, for the person who takes his or her own life chooses how and when to die and is no longer an object in the hands of the state, entirely subject to the decisions of others. We can see this from the way in which those guarding prisoners condemned to death deprive their charges of any item of clothing, such as ties, belts, or laces, that could be used to commit suicide and watch them continuously (Baechler 1979: 96) lest they "cheat the gallows." If condemned prisoners manage to evade these precautions, as the murderer Dr. Crippen did by breaking the lenses of his eyeglasses and cutting open a blood vessel, they are remorselessly resuscitated. Either way the prisoner dies, but that is beside the point; the question is who is to be master.

So long as the Conservative justification of capital punishment was fused with the main "moralist" tradition of moral Britain prior to 1957 the case for capital punishment could be upheld, but capital punishment could not survive on the basis of deterrence and the preserving of order alone. It should though be stressed that there is a moral argument underlying the expedient view of capital punishment, much as there is a moral underpinning to causalism. The Conservatives genuinely believed in the legitimacy and merit of the society I have termed moral Britain and saw capital punishment as a necessary part of the defense of that society as a whole. Indeed, on this issue the Conservatives were close to the increasingly causalist ethos of British society, not just in relation to the protection of the ordinary citizen from murder but also to the harm done when law and order breaks down even in part and gives way to chaos even if only locally.

The point can be seen more clearly if we examine the British political elite's obsession with ever-tighter controls over the private ownership of guns (Malcolm 2002), an obsession which in different ways affects all the political parties. It is now almost impossible for a private individual legally to own a gun in Britain, except for certain sporting guns used for hunting in rural areas. The right to bear arms once seen as a necessary protection against tyranny has long since been abandoned and forgotten. For the people to own their own guns is for Conservatives a disobedient infringement of a state monopoly exercised by the "dominant" through the institutions they control. Their Liberal and Labour opponents simply do not like guns and the very thought of the legitimate ownership of guns by the people is apt to set off their deep dislike and fear of the use of force. In the twenty-first century, the restrictions are an irrelevance since criminals can easily obtain and increasingly frequently use illegal guns, but, like the executing of deserters or the hanging of a handful of murderers once were, the restrictions on gun ownership are fiercely defended.

The weakness of the hierarchical Conservative tradition in Britain after 1965 is shown not by the abolition of capital punishment, which can be explained as a mere consequence of the Conservatives losing the election in 1964, but by its irreversibility. It never proved possible to restore capital punishment in any form despite the Conservative electoral victories in 1970, 1979, 1983, 1987, and 1992. The Conservative party was now badly divided on the issue and even in 1964 a quarter of all Conservative MPs voted for abolition and only just over a half voting for retention on a free vote. We may contrast this with the solidarity of the anti-Conservatives. In 1964, only one Labour MP and only one Liberal MP voted for retaining capital punishment and between 80 percent and 90 percent of their members turned up to vote for abolition (*Hansard,* 1964, vol. 704, cols. 1002-10; Richards 1970: 186). It was a symbolic triumph for those ideologically opposed to traditional conservatism. The Conservative party was itself ceasing to be the party of the traditional hierarchies in which the men who had exercised dominion were influential. The latter continued to adhere to a belief in capital punishment, but their numbers and influence were dwindling. Of those Conservative MPs who had been educated at services establishments to be career officers in the armed forces three-quarters voted to retain capital punishment and less than a fifth for abolition in 1965 (Richards 1970: 185; see also 190-91). As the proportion of Conservative MPs who had any kind of experience of the armed forces fell, so, too, the proportion of Conservative MPs who supported capital punishment declined. By the 1990s there was a new generation of politicians ,most of whom had never served in the army, even as pre-1960 National Service conscripts and had never "heard a gunshot in anger—off the grouse moor" (Coker 1998: 22). By 1997, there would be only sixty-three MPs in Parliament, less than a tenth, who had ever served in the armed forces and among those under 55 there were only twenty-one, or less than 5 percent of that age group of MPs (Brazier 1998: 63). There were thirteen attempts to restore capital punishment between 1969 and 1994, but in 1994 only 159 MPs voted in favor of bringing back hanging for murder and 403 voted against. There were substantial majorities against its restoration for any type or category of murder. The Conservative party had become a party of free enterprise "emancipated" from tradition. One critic of this trend wrote of the damage done to the armed forces by a new kind of Conservative government with a radical free market ideology "determined to transform the great nineteenth century professions into trades" (Coker 1998: 24), in which any sense of vocation or moral commitment would become an anachronism and the "ethos of risking one's life for an ethical ideal" obsolete (Coker 1998: 25).

The end came in 1998 when Parliament effectively removed its own power to debate and decide the issue by voting in favor of Protocol 6 of the European Convention on Human Rights that completely outlawed capital punishment for murder in peacetime. The United Kingdom signed Protocol 6 in 1999. Treason and piracy also now ceased to be capital crimes; the last executions for treason had been in 1946. Previous governments had declined to sign the Protocol on the grounds that such issues were a matter for the British Parliament to decide and that no Parliament could bind its successors. Such a transfer of sovereignty was a further symbolic defeat for a traditional conservatism based on a confidence in Britain's special destiny—only the United States now retains that kind of imperial confidence. However, the loss of the nation's autonomy in deciding a moral question of this kind meant the death of moral Britain as a whole. If an individual should sign away his right to make moral decisions, he or she ceases to be a moral agent; it is a point that also has an implication for nations. No one in Britain is any less likely to be executed as a result of the signing of the Protocol; its sole significance lies in the way in which British power over internal moral issues has been depleted.

Notes

1.   This was the view of those who, at a time when executions were held in public, wanted hanging to be carried out in seclusion.

2.   It has been suggested that the Roman Catholic Church has turned against capital punishment on principle (Toscano 1999: 100), possibly to reinforce its pro-life stance on abortion. Rather it has taken up the causalist stance that capital punishment is unnecessary in modern societies even though the state retains the right to inflict it (Dulles 2001).

3.   This was one point in a long linear process of change throughout the nineteenth and twentieth centuries. There was no U-curve in attitudes to suicide.

4

The Queer Death of the Laws Prohibiting Homosexual Behavior

Until 1967, those indulging in male homosexual acts could be prosecuted and severely punished in Britain. Well into the nineteenth century sodomy was punished by death, and even though prosecutions were rare and pardons common, in 1806, six men were hanged for sodomy and only five for murder (Harvey 2001: 125-26). The last execution for sodomy took place in 1835 and in 1861 the death penalty was replaced by a minimum sentence of ten years penal servitude and possible life imprisonment. There were also prosecutions for attempted sodomy. In 1885, an extra clause was added to the Criminal Law Amendment Act at the instigation of Henry Labouchere, MP, making any kind of sexual behavior between two men a criminal offense punishable by up to two years imprisonment. It was under the Labouchere amendment that Oscar Wilde was convicted and given the maximum sentence in 1895. All these offenses could be prosecuted and punished, even if they took place in private between two consenting male adults.

Prosecutions for the latter were not frequent. There were at most only about a hundred convictions each year in England and Wales and proportionately fewer in Scotland where the official prosecutor, the Procurator Fiscal, would only take a case to court if he thought it was in the public interest.[1]

Given that there were probably somewhere between 180,000 and 360,000 adult males who were inclined by preference to homosexual activities (estimates based on data in Wellings et al. 1994: 185-90), most of whom will have occasionally or even frequently indulged in such acts, the law was obviously arbitrary and capricious in its operation. It imposed not only criminal penalties but unwanted expo-

139

sure and publicity and social obloquy on an unlucky and sometimes trapped or betrayed tiny section of a substantial minority. For those arrested, some of whom committed suicide, the law struck like lightning, randomly and without warning, except that sometimes malice sparked it off. Even for the majority of homosexuals who were not caught the law was a source of fear (Grey 1992) and a reinforcement and symbol of their stigmatized position in a hostile society.

Even if the law had never been enforced it would have remained a source of unease and insult since it defined male homosexuals as criminals. The law was a barrier to any major improvement in their social position. It was a public statement that homosexual activities and by extension homosexuals deserved to be regarded with intolerance, disgust, and contempt. Indeed, looking back from the twenty-first century, it is this aspect of the laws criminalizing homosexual behavior that is most obvious and most shocking to enlightened contemporary opinion. However, the *interesting* question and the subject of much of this chapter is why these laws were enacted in the first place and why they were maintained and enforced. Why did homosexual behavior between males attract such strong moral condemnation in Britain (and in many other societies), a condemnation that was expressed in and enforced by the criminal law? Why was there such horror at and even hatred of the behavior and by extension identity of a small and in the past not very conspicuous minority, behavior that rarely impinged on other members of society?

The author has shown elsewhere on the basis of a comprehensive comparative study (Davies 1982; Davies 1983c) that the main reason why male homosexual behavior is or was so savagely punished in many societies and institutions (in contrast to its toleration in others) is that in the intolerant societies it was perceived as a metaphor of and a threat to the fragility of important social boundaries. Comparative analysis shows that the groups most disturbed by the very existence of male homosexual behavior were those who both valued and feared for the stability of the boundaries of their nation, or institution; they saw homosexual acts as breaking down the boundaries of one of the most fundamental of natural categories: male and female. One of the two men committing a homosexual act was seen as taking on the role of a woman and thus behaving in an unnatural way. This was particularly true in the case of sodomy, an act in which one of the men penetrates the anal orifice of the other[2] and thus also violates the boundary of the body itself. Perhaps for this reason it was much more severely punished in Britain than other homosexual acts classified as "gross indecency"; these only became criminal as a result of the Labouchere amendment of 1885 and carried lesser penalties than sodomy.

In this chapter I will apply this thesis to Britain and to show how the abhorrence of homosexuality in males was linked to a sense of national boundaries and identity. Britain's national identity was, in the past, strongly linked to Protestant Christianity, and this was even more true of Wales and Scotland. It is here, too, that we must seek the origins of the vigorous rejection of male homosexuality in Roman Catholic Ireland. The thesis that a harshness towards male homosexual behavior expressed through law is rooted in the defense of identity, and particularly a threatened identity in countries with a strong Christian tradition whether Protestant, Roman Catholic, or Orthodox, can be further demonstrated by an examination of the persistence of the British laws penalizing male homosexual behavior in Ulster, the Republic of Ireland, the Channel Islands, the Isle of Man, Cyprus, Tasmania, and the Cayman Islands long after they had been abolished in England and Wales. In each case, these entities either enjoyed a degree of autonomy within the United Kingdom or else had become independent of British rule while retaining laws of English origin or ancestry. Britain was in most cases the original source of these laws, but the contemporary enthusiasm for them was entirely local. From the mid-1950s, Britain became a secular country with a much weakened sense of national identity, but these other islands were both far more religious and had a strong but threatened sense of identity.

First, however, it is necessary to look in detail at the religious and, by distant origin Jewish, roots of the link between British identity and boundaries and the severity with which male homosexual behavior was regarded.

National Boundaries and Sexual Taboos: The Biblical Roots of the British Laws against Homosexual Behavior

The clear connection between the defense of national and ethnic boundaries and the condemnation of homosexuality for the Jews of the Old Testament and later for Christians also can be demonstrated by a careful examination of the passages in the Book of Leviticus in the Old Testament that condemn homosexuality:

> You shall not lie with a man as with a woman: that is an abomination. You shall not have sexual intercourse with any beast to make yourself unclean with it, nor shall a woman submit herself to intercourse with a beast: that is a violation of nature. (*New English Bible*, Leviticus 18, 22-24)

> If a man has intercourse with a man as with a woman, they both commit an abomination. They shall be put to death, their blood shall be on their own heads. (*New English Bible*, Leviticus 20: 13-14)

> A man who has sexual intercourse with any beast shall be put to death and you shall kill the beast. If a woman approaches any animal to have intercourse with it you shall kill both woman and beast. (*New English Bible*, Leviticus 20: 15-16)

The passages quoted indicate that the prohibitions are there in order to set the Jewish people, the chosen people of God, apart from the heathen, the people outside their ethnic and religious boundaries. The prohibitions are part of an elaborate code of rules and taboos that serve to maintain and protect the boundaries of the Jews and to ensure that they will maintain that identity and integrity, even under adverse conditions such as exile (Davies 1982; Davies 1983c; Davies 1987a). This is made quite explicit later in the law of holiness in connection with the Jewish dietary rules that separate the clean animals that may be eaten from unclean animals that it is forbidden to eat:

> I am the Lord your God: I have made a clear separation between you and the nations, and you shall make a clear separation between clean beasts and unclean beasts and between unclean and clean birds. You shall not make yourselves vile through beast or bird or anything that creeps on the ground for I have made a clear separation between them and you, declaring them unclean. You shall be holy to me because I the LORD am holy. I have made a clear separation between you and the heathen that you may belong to me. (*New English Bible*, Leviticus 20: 24-27)

These rules work at many different levels. In the first place, they insist that the Jews should conduct the details of their everyday lives in ways that are radically different from their neighbors and which are clearly designed to keep the two groups apart. The Jews obtained no direct practical or material benefits from observing these rules and the very arbitrariness and strictness of enforcement of such a code set the Jews apart from their more pragmatic heathen neighbors, who did not possess and obey a similar detailed set of rules given to them by God. Secondly, the very structure of the rules,

which insist on the preservation of pure categories and strict boundaries in everyday life, is a perpetual reminder to the Jews, keeping
them aware of the need to preserve the boundaries and identity of
the Jewish people as a holy people. The dietary rules that stress the
separation of blood (the life of the animal, which belongs to God
and may not be eaten) from meat, and the separation of meat from
milk dishes illustrate this pattern. Only the meat of animals that chew
the cud and have a cloven hoof, such as cattle, sheep, and goats
may be eaten (others are *traife* and forbidden). Fish must have fins
and scales and swim and birds must have wings and feathers and
fly to be fit for consumption. Everything must be a proper example
of its class and things that are ambiguous are forbidden. Likewise
the Jews observed the rule of *shatnes*, which forbade, for instance,
the sowing of a field with two kinds of grain or the making of a
garment from both wool and linen (Leviticus 19: 19). The Jews
were also forbidden to breed mules by crossing horses and donkeys
(Leighton 1967: 46); they could buy this sterile but useful hybrid
from other peoples but not breed it for themselves, because to do so
would have involved the breaking of categories and boundaries.
By the same token, transvestism was forbidden:

> No woman shall wear an article of man's clothing, nor shall a man put on woman's
> dress; for those who do these things are abominable to the LORD your God. (*New
> English Bible,* Deuteronomy, 22: 5)

It is now possible to see why the prohibition of homosexuality in
Leviticus (18: 22-24) is to be found immediately next to the prohibition of bestiality, whether committed by men or women. In either
case, the forbidden sexual behavior breaks a boundary and disrupts
a distinction that preserves a category, whether it be that between
humans and animals or that between male and female. The linking
of these two forms of behavior in this way may be upsetting and
offensive to homosexuals, or indeed to shepherds, but it is quite
clearly present in the scriptures. In the past, the same link was to be
found in the laws of England and Wales for the single term "buggery" embraced both sodomy and bestiality. Not only male homosexuals but also rustics caught seeking consolation with a sheep or a
cow could be very severely punished. In the distant past, they could
be and were executed and even in the nineteenth (Phillips 1977:
269) and twentieth centuries those convicted of bestiality in Britain
could be and often were sentenced to several years in prison.

All these rules have a common framework and a common purpose that is rooted in a particular national-religious morality. There is no universal reason for penalizing homosexuals or transvestites, or come to that those who commit bestiality. These rules were devised, whether by God or by man, to ensure the continued existence of one particular, small but holy nation. The framework of Jewish thought within which the prohibitions occur has been well stated by Mary Douglas (1966: 53):

> We can conclude that holiness is exemplified by completeness. Holiness requires that individuals shall conform to the class to which they belong. And holiness requires that different classes of things shall not be confused.
>
> Another set of precepts refines on this last point. Holiness means keeping distinct the categories of creation. It, therefore, involves correct definition, discrimination and order.

The Jewish prohibitions of homosexuality and bestiality, unlike the Jewish food rules, which were explicitly repudiated in the New Testament (Acts 10: 9-16; 11: 5-10), became part of the Christian moral tradition (Coleman 1980: 88-101, 207-8), because they fitted the sexual asceticism of a church which revered celibacy and virginity and regarded marriage as a concession to those lacking in self-control (Bullough 1976: 172, 182; West 1977: 120, 126). Later, as we have shown elsewhere (Davies 1982; Davies 1983c), the prohibition of homosexuality was intensified by the policies of senior Roman Catholic ecclesiastics who wanted to create a centralized and disciplined all-male, celibate church hierarchy.

Preserving the Categories and Boundaries of the British: A Special People and Their Bible

In Britain those forms of sexual behavior that broke down natural categories, together with sexual relations that took place across valued but threatened social boundaries were, from an early time, condemned alongside one another in a way that indicates that they were seen as related phenomena. The treatise on English law, *Fleta*, composed towards the end of the thirteenth century stated:

> FLETA xxxvii.3 Those who have (sexual) dealings with Jews or Jewesses, those who commit bestiality and sodomists are to be buried alive, after legal proof that they were taken in the act and public conviction. (Cited in Bailey 1975 [1955]: 145)

This explicit linking together of homosexuality, bestiality, and having sexual connection with non-Christians also existed in France where in Paris in the thirteenth century "one Jean Alard found guilty of cohabiting with a Jewess was burned as was she, since coition with a Jewess is precisely the same as if a man should copulate with a dog.... the crime for which Alard was convicted was described formally as sodomy...sexual relations with Turks and Saracens have also been held to constitute bestiality" (Masters 1962: 286). In the face of these explicit statements, it can hardly be said that the thesis advanced here linking sexual prohibitions and communal boundaries is being imposed on reluctant data.

Until the Reformation those accused of homosexual behavior were dealt with by the church courts in Britain, but under Henry VIII jurisdiction moved to the secular courts and new statutes were passed that punished "the detestable and abominable crime of Buggery committed with mankind or beast" with the death penalty (25 Hen VIII, c.6, Bailey 1955: 147; West 1977: 280). It was at about this time that a separate and distinctive British identity rooted in Protestantism began to emerge. The new Protestant Church of England that emerged from the Reformation was not an international church; it was the established church of one particular people. The Reformation took an even more radical form in Scotland and again led to the formation of a national church, the Church of Scotland, Calvinist in theology, Presbyterian in government. The Bible was now widely available in English and Welsh translations and became the basis of popular discourse about religion in those countries. The sense of identification with the Jews of the Old Testament and the feeling the British had that they as a people enjoyed a special relationship with God, which led to the strict observance of the Sabbath in Britain, also underlay the legal prohibition of and hostility towards homosexuality to be found both in England and Wales and in Scotland.

However, the national sense of being a special nation with a moral mission rooted in biblical Protestantism was in decline after World War II with the loss of Empire and the secularization of British society. In 1954, the Church of England Moral Welfare Council produced a pamphlet, *The Problem of Homosexuality* (1954), supporting the legalization of "homosexualism" between adults for essentially causalist reasons aimed at the minimizing of harm and claiming that "homosexualism" as a social problem was not, as a rule, so far reaching and devastating in its consequences as ordinary premarital or extra-marital sexual relations (Church of England Moral Welfare Council 1954).

Homosexuality for Lords and Bishops:
Defilement and Contagion

This Church of England publication was strongly condemned by Earl Winterton, a traditionalist, in the House of Lords in May 1954 in a debate on the setting up of the Committee on Homosexual Offences and Prostitution. The Earl stated that, on the contrary, the "filthy, disgusting, unnatural vice of homosexuality is more evil and more harmful to the individual and community." He denounced the causalism of the Moral Welfare Council as "an astonishing doctrine to emanate from an organization of the Church of England" (*Hansard,* House of Lords 1954, vol. 187, col. 739).

The Bishop of Southwell, Frank Russell Barry, speaking in the House of Lords, and responding to the Earl Winterton's comments condemning homosexual practices, noted that "Society—our society, at any rate—reacts very violently against it (homosexuality) because it feels, and rightly feels, that such practices are injecting poison into the bloodstream" (*Hansard,* House of Lords 1954, vol. 187, col. 752). The Bishop used here the strong language of pollution and defilement as a metaphor of the need to defend national boundaries and identity, language fitting to a nation with a sacred collective identity. The Bishop of Southwell went on to expand on this theme in an unclear and apprehensive way characteristic of the 1950s, a time of transition between the moralist Britain of the first half of the twentieth century and the causalist Britain that succeeded it:

Public opinion at the present is deeply stirred about the whole matter, and well it may be, because the increase in unnatural offences is an ominous warning of something going radically wrong in the moral foundations of the social order. And historically as Earl Winterton pointed out in his opening speech, this always seems to be a sign of a demoralized or decadent culture. Where people cease to believe effectively in what has hitherto been the *communal* religion, and when there is scepticism and cynicism about the meaning and value of life itself, people get driven back upon themselves, and introversion very easily brings perversion with it. It is a warning which cannot be ignored, and it is one more bit of evidence to show that once *a people* lets its ultimate convictions go, then there can be no stopping halfway and the *whole moral bottom* is in danger of falling out of *a society.* As St. Paul said about this very point a long time ago, once the creature is *confused* with the Creator, once people cease to believe in God and, therefore, in ultimate moral obligations, everything begins to go bad on us, and natural instincts and affections become unnatural and perverted. (*Hansard,* House of Lords 1954, vol. 187, col. 751) (Emphasis added)

A further major controversy over homosexuality occurred in 1957 following the publication of the *Report of the Committee on Homosexual Offences and Prostitution* (1957). The authors of the report, with one exception, took the view that there were some matters that were issues of private morality and none of the law's business and that male homosexual acts in private should cease to be criminal (*Report of the Committee on Homosexual Offences and Prostitution* 1957: 9-10).

The bishops of the Church of England were divided on the recommendations of the Wolfenden report. The Bishop of St. Albans, Edward Michael Gresford Jones, chairman of the Church of England Moral Welfare Council, was pleased that the recommendations of the Report were similar to the proposals of his own Council's Report (see above) of 1954 (*Hansard,* House of Lords 1957, vol. 206, col.766), but the Bishop of Rochester, Christopher Chavasse, again used the language of *pollution* to oppose decriminalization:

There is no more baneful or *contagious* an influence in the world than that which emanates from homosexual practice. It makes a life of *leprosy.* The most reverend Primate was quite right: there are such things as sodomy clubs. There was one in Oxford between the wars and I was informed that there was another in Cambridge which even shamelessly sported a tie. And these are plague-spots wherever they exist.... the emotion and moral indignation and horror which are aroused in the human heart by the thought and contemplation of unnatural vice and which find expression in the Holy Scriptures, both in the Old and in the New Testaments, are probably more right in teaching us our attitude toward unnatural vice than academic discussion divorced from reality. (*Hansard,* House of Lords, 4 December 1957, vol. 206, col. 797 and 798) (Emphasis added)

Leprosy is not, in fact, particularly contagious, but it is believed to be so and *leper* is a common metaphor for members of an utterly excluded group. In the middle ages, lepers were at times forced to live outside the towns and villages of the healthy and to ring a bell to warn others of their approach; like Jews and homosexuals, they were excluded from Christian society and on occasion persecuted as feared outsiders thought to be plotting against society (Barber 1981). Leprosy like homosexuality was perceived as threatening, outraging, and violating the boundaries of the body whose normal outline is marred as a toe, finger, or nose rots away; both leprosy and homosexuality can thus act as a metaphor for the decay of the social body and of the boundaries of society.

Sodomy as an Especial Threat to Boundaries

As always, Geoffrey Fisher, the Archbishop of Canterbury, tried to find a viable if saponaceous compromise between the traditional view expounded by the Bishop of Rochester and the concern for the individual homosexual expressed by the Bishop of St. Albans. The nature of the compromise he offered is truly revealing. The Archbishop said:

> ...if it proved legally possible—I do not know whether it is—to separate what the noble Lord, Lord Pakenham, called the extreme offence (sodomy), and to leave that still a crime, I should wish to leave it as a crime still.... I believe that this crime does stand in a class by itself and is almost different in kind from other homosexual offences. I believe personally that that opinion can be upheld on moral grounds. (*Hansard,* House of Lords 1957, vol. 206, col. 757)

Why should sodomy have horrified the Archbishop so much more than the other forms of homosexual behavior, known in English law as gross indecency, which had only been rendered crimes as late as 1885 by the Labouchere amendment? The answer lies in part in the strong hold that the Old Testament story of God's destruction of Sodom and Gomorrah, the wicked cities of the plain, where homosexual sodomy was practiced (Genesis 19:1-29) had on the British and Christian imagination. Before the destruction, God sent two angels of male appearance as his messengers to the house of Abraham's kinsman Lot, who was living in Sodom, to warn him of the fate of the city. Lot made them welcome:

> Before they (the visitors) lay down to sleep, the men of Sodom, both young and old, surrounded the house—everyone without exception. They called to Lot and asked him where the men were who had entered his house that night. "Bring them out," they shouted, "so that we may have intercourse with them." (*New English Bible,* Genesis 19:3-5)

When the evil and predatory Sodomites clamored at Lot's door demanding that he produce these handsome angelic visitors, so that they could bugger them,[3] the embarrassed and desperate Lot offered the mob his two virgin daughters, who had not known man, as sexual substitutes for the angels. At this point God intervened and *confused* and blinded the mob. While homosexuality might not have been the only crime of the generally sinful and idolatrous cities of

Sodom and Gomorrah, there can be no doubt at all that the story of the angels' visit to Lot is a condemnation of homosexual sodomy and that the traditional interpretation of the story in this way is correct. The importance of the narrative in generating popular prejudice against homosexuality is shown by the peculiar lengths to which commentators such as Derrick Sherwin Bailey (1975) and John Boswell (1980) have gone in claiming that the sin of the Sodomites lay merely in their infringement of the rules of Middle Eastern hospitality. According to the earlier translations of Genesis (19: 5), the mob outside Lot's house demanded that Lot produce his visitors so that they might "know" them. The verb *to know*, in the Hebrew of the Old Testament as in English, can mean either "to become acquainted with" or "to have sex with." Bailey (1975 [1955]: 2-3), and following him Boswell (1980: 94), used the very dubious statistical argument that the verb is used in the former sense in the Old Testament far more often than the latter is and that therefore it is more likely that the Sodomites merely wished to know who Lot's visitors were, a violation of the rules of hospitality not of sexuality. In that case, why Lot should offer them his daughters to buy them off and stress that his daughters were virgins who had "not *known* man" is left unexplained. The close proximity of these two sentences that include the verb "to know," one about angels and Sodomites and one about the virginity of Lot's daughters clearly indicates that the writer was referring to sex in both cases.

The Conservative government of the time did not take up what Archbishop Fisher liked to call his "wise and expedient" suggestions (the Archbishop's favorite choice of moral language) and all forms of male homosexual behavior remained illegal until 1967. In 1965, when it was clear that there would soon be a complete decriminalization of all male homosexual acts committed in private, Viscount Dilhorne, a senior lawyer of traditionalist views, tried to revive the former Archbishop Fisher's distinction between the extreme offence of sodomy and less flagrant homosexual crimes (*Hansard,* House of Lords 1957, vol. 206, cols. 757, and 1965, vol. 267, col. 290-91, and 1965, vol. 269, col. 719). But by now the boundaries of moral Britain were fast eroding. Viscount Dilhorne failed to get any support whatsoever from the bishops of the Church of England who sat in the House of Lords, none of whom was willing to make a sharp moral and legal distinction between different kinds of homosexual acts. Dilhorne's attempt to retain the law prohibiting sodomy while decriminalizing other homosexual acts was defeated in the House of Lords by 86 votes to 52. Geoffrey Fisher's successor as Archbishop of Canterbury, Michael Ramsey, together with the Bishops of Chichester, Lincoln, and Manchester, voted against Dilhorne's proposal (*Hansard*, House of Lords 1965, vol. 267, cols. 315-8). The new Archbishop of Canterbury argued:

> ...it is impossible to distinguish between the abominableness of various kinds of homosexual actions, and I do not really think it makes for morality when there is embodied in the criminal law a distinction that is not really a rational moral distinction. (*Hansard*, House of Lords 1965, vol. 267, cols. 302-3)

Unnatural Vice Ceases to be Unnatural

The Bishop of Worcester, Mervyn Charles-Edwards, was even more indifferent to these ancient questions. Speaking of his pastoral work among homosexuals he declared:

> I must put completely on one side any feelings of repulsion at conduct which I personally find disgusting. I must indeed beware of assuming that I am normal and he is abnormal, for in the *artificial* life we live *today* it is extremely difficult to define what actually is the normal and what is the abnormal. (*Hansard*, House of Lords 1965, vol. 266, col. 134) (Emphasis added)

The willingness of the Bishops to ignore the *social* basis of the traditional moralists' view that homosexual behavior was abominable and a threat to the social and moral order of their people and nation and to regard and reduce this view to a mere expression of personal distaste was a further indication of the slow death of moral Britain. Tradition and national community had been replaced by the fragmented modernity of "the artificial life we live today," in which all categories and boundaries are uncertain.

The Bishop of Chichester, Roger Wilson, however, was greeted with a degree of scorn by the few remaining traditionalists in the House of Lords when he somewhat recklessly attacked their favorite argument about homosexuality undermining the nation:

> *Bishop of Chichester*: We should be inclined to say that the moral fibre of the nation may be just as much undermined by heterosexual misconduct as by homosexual misconduct.

> *Noble Lords*: "Nonsense." (*Hansard*, House of Lords 1965, vol. 266 col. 660)

Although the bishops of the Church of England were by no means unanimously in favor of reform, none of them voted against any of the Bills to decriminalize homosexuality in the years 1965-67. Those bishops who disagreed with decriminalization either abstained or stayed away from the debate or were not sufficiently senior to be members of the House of Lords. Only one bishop, the Bishop of Leicester, R. R. Williams, spoke out against the reforms in the House of Lords.

From 1964 onward, those who saw themselves as the upholders of the old national-religious tradition felt betrayed by the established Church of England on this issue. Lord Rathcavan who, significantly enough, was not an Englishman but an Ulsterman, spoke for them when he said:

> ...I cannot believe that the attitude which they (the bishops) are adopting will be adopted by the great mass of the decent, honest, clean-living members of the Church of England.... I wonder what is going to become of the Church, when we see the attitude of the Bishops on this Bill. (*Hansard*, House of Lords 1965, vol. 267, col. 309)

By the late 1960s, the very boundaries and identity of the nation were dissolving. Anglicanism had ceased not only to be the dominant religion of England but also through expansion abroad was ceasing to be a predominantly English cluster of churches. Some found these changes threatening, but a substantial section of Britain's upper-middle-class elite was indifferent; the old moral Britain could, for all they cared, die and give way to a formless, shapeless, androgynous, looser kind of society. For them boundaries were simply obstructions and categories were merely cages. The world had been turned inside out.

By the late 1960s the British people were no longer at the center of an Empire and had lost any sense of being a special people favored by God; they had also, to a large extent, lost their religion, which had been a key element in sustaining that worldview. It was no accident that this was the stage in their history at which the British decriminalized homosexuality. One of the opponents of the change was the World War II military hero, Field Marshall Lord Montgomery of Alamein, a representative of that other traditional pillar of the established national order and source of severity towards homosexuality, the armed forces. He declared in the House of Lords:

> Far from helping these unnatural practices along, surely our task is to build a bulwark which will defy evil influences which are seeking to undermine the very foundations of our national character—defy them; do not help them. I have heard some say— and

indeed the noble Earl said so himself—that such practices are allowed in France and in other NATO countries. We are not French and we are not other nationals. We are British, thank God!... I would appeal to all noble Lords who have at heart the best interests of the young men of Britain to go with me into the Not-Content lobby and knock this Bill for six right out of the House. (*Hansard*, House of Lords 1965. vol. 266, col.647)

Here we have a clear statement of the *particular* and *national* character of Britain's former moral and legal condemnation of homosexual practices. The ban on homosexuality was for Lord Montgomery not a universal moral rule that applied to the French and other Natoese peoples but one which only pertained to those who are "British, thank God"! The British have a particular national character that must be protected by a "bulwark." British cricket-loving peers must take up their bats and "knock for six" this attempt to damage their nation, hitting it over and landing it outside the very boundaries of their ground. The bulwark metaphor was also frequently used by the Sabbatarian defenders of Sunday, the Lord's Day, the proper observation of which was often described by them as a *bulwark* protecting the nation. The strict keeping of the Sabbath and an abhorrence of homosexuality were for these upholders of a national morality two key aspects of national righteousness and national character that had to be defended, both as ends in themselves and as part of an implicit covenant with the God whose favor the British had enjoyed in the past and would need in the future.

By 1967 such arguments carried little weight and both the House of Commons and the House of Lords voted by substantial majorities to decriminalize, at least in England and Wales, consensual homosexual behavior undertaken in private by two men over the age of 21, for the straightforward causalist reason that the existing laws badly harmed individual homosexuals. The protection of a Christian and British identity and boundaries was no longer the key focus of concern.

The Slower Case of Scotland

The decriminalization of homosexual acts in 1967 only applied to England and Wales and was not extended to Scotland until thirteen years later in 1980. There was from the start far more opposition to change in Scotland. The one Scottish member of the Wolfenden Committee (1957) James Adair had disagreed with its conclusions and written his own dissenting report (*Report of the Committee on Homosexual Offences and Prostitution* 1957: 117-23).

Opinion polls at the time showed that less than half of the English, but 85 percent of Scots, were opposed to reform (Miller 1995: 284; see also Jeffrey-Poulter 1991: 33, 48, 74, 141). Secularization came later to Scotland than to England, and the myth of faith and nation was particularly strong in Scotland. The Church of Scotland, Scotland's national church, almost alone of the main British denominations, consistently opposed decriminalization (*Hansard,* House of Commons 1966, vol. 724, cols. 846-7, 860). Opinion in the main English denominations was divided, but in general they were willing to accept that the criminal law could no longer be used to enforce their morality for them; also the secularization of English society and indeed the inner secularization of many English Protestant denominations had left them in a weaker position than the Church of Scotland when it came to upholding tradition and the fiercer propositions of the Bible. It was only in 1973 that the Lord Advocate agreed that he would cease to prosecute in cases where homosexual acts had been committed in private and, as late as 1976, the Scottish laws against homosexuality were once again reaffirmed. An attempt at reform in 1977 did not succeed and it was only in 1980 that an opportunistic amendment to the Criminal Justice (Scotland) Bill extended decriminalization to Scotland. The British Conservative government took a neutral view and it passed by a large majority of mainly English MPs; every single Scottish Conservative MP voted against the amendment (Grey 1992: 227-28; Jeffrey-Poulter 1991: 121, 137, 143-45). As in the case of the decline of the Scottish Sabbath, Scotland had ceased to be a country defined by restrictions on everyday behavior rooted in national and religious tradition.

The Special Case of Northern Ireland

Attempts to extend decriminalization to Northern Ireland by political means failed. Police raids on the homes of leading members of the Northern Ireland Gay Rights Association led one of them, Geoffrey Dudgeon, to go outside the system to the European Court of Human Rights, claiming that the British government's refusal to extend decriminalization to Northern Ireland was a denial of his right to respect for his private life, and in 1978 the court agreed to hear his case. The British government had stated in 1978 that it proposed to extend the 1967 Sexual Offences Act to Ulster, but then delayed taking action indefinitely because of the strong protests against it within Ulster itself (Grey 1992: 228; Jeffrey-Poulter 1991: 148-50).

The Democratic Unionist party unanimously denounced any move towards decriminalization and its leader the Rev. Dr. Ian Paisley, MP, declared:

> The crime of sodomy is a crime against God and man and its practice is a terrible step to the total demoralization of any country and must inevitably lead to the breakdown of all decency within the province. (Rev. Dr. Ian Paisley quoted by Jeffrey-Poulter 1991: 149-50)

Paisley also launched his campaign to "Save Ulster from Sodomy" (Bruce 1986: 150-51) and collected signatures to a petition from both Protestants and Roman Catholics. The Roman Catholic bishops sent a written statement to the British government also objecting to decriminalization. They were united against the homosexuals (Jeffrey-Poulter 1991: 150-53).

However, in 1981, the European Court of Human Rights ruled in the case of Mr. Geoffrey Dudgeon that the (unenforced) laws in Northern Ireland penalizing homosexual behavior between adults in private were an unjustified interference with Mr. Dudgeon's right to respect for his private life and in breach of Article 8 of the European Convention for the Protection of Human Rights and Fundamental Freedoms signed by Britain as a member of the Council of Europe. Clause 1 of Article 8 states, "Everyone has the right to respect for his private and family life, his home and his correspondence." A majority of the judges, by fifteen votes to four (*Dudgeon v United Kingdom* 1982, 4; E.H.R.R. 149 at para. 72), refused to accept that the interference in the private lives of homosexuals complained of by Mr. Dudgeon was justified by Clause 2 of Article 8:

> There shall be no interference by a public authority with the exercise of this right except such as is in accordance with the law and is necessary in a democratic society in the interests of national security, public safety or the economic well-being of the country, for the prevention of disorder and crime, for the *protection of health and morals* and for the protection of the rights and freedoms of others. (Emphasis added)

A majority of the judges in the Dudgeon case took the view that in the great majority of countries that had signed the Convention, including most of the rest of the United Kingdom, it was no longer found necessary or appropriate to use the law to penalize male homosexual acts (*Dudgeon v United Kingdom* 1982; E.H.R.R. 149 at para. 60). They deduced from this that the "protection of morals" achieved by making adult homosexual behavior a criminal offense was not important enough to justify such a serious interference with so intimate an act of private life and infringing the rights of the individual. The right to privacy as laid out in the European Convention and in Article 8 Clause 2, cited above, is so hedged around with exceptions as to be almost vacuous and meaningless. Whether an exception is upheld or not depends largely on the prejudices of the clutch of judges from many countries assembled to hear that particular case. The Court's ruling was based on the view that had been taken previously by the legislatures of most of *the other* Council of Europe countries. In effect, the Court took the view that the moral and religious sentiments of a particular individual nation or province can be set aside if these do not conform with the view taken in a majority of the states belonging to the Council of Europe. Thus, a supposed human right to privacy was upheld in the Dudgeon case because the test of what was necessary for the protection of morals applied was a foreign and *political* one based on the previous decisions of other European governments. This politically based European test of what was "necessary" now supplanted any previous explicit or implicit preferences of *particular* national moral and religious convictions of the people of the specific state or province in question (in this case Northern Ireland), even if these had been very strongly held. It was as if the U.S. Supreme Court had struck down the law against sodomy in Texas, not as an extension of the principles of *Griswold v Connecticut* 1965 or *Roe v Wade* 1973 but on the grounds that most other states did not have such laws.

The British government now brought the law in Northern Ireland into line with the law in mainland Britain by executive act, by an Order in Council (Bruce 1986: 150). There was strong opposition to this in Ulster from both Protestants and Roman Catholics; however, the British government claimed that it had no option but to enforce the ruling of the European Court of Human Rights, regardless of local public opinion in Ulster.

Boundaries and Constitution

Enoch Powell, the Ulster Unionist MP for South Down was one of those who led the campaign against the British government's willingness to concede. He was not an Ulsterman but an Englishman of Welsh ancestry who had formerly been a Conservative MP in England. He was a very strong British patriot who had left and denounced the Conservative party in 1974 in protest against the decision by the Conservative party to join what in time became the European Union; he told the British people to vote Labour. He later joined the Ulster Unionists, which was consistent with his British nationalism. In England, he had always voted in favor of homosexual law reform (*Hansard*: 1966, vol. 738, col. 1130) and held tolerant views and he was not the sort of person to trim his views to gain favor in Ulster. Rather his objections were to the loss of sovereignty involved. He said that the European court was

> ...not acting as a court of law but as a sovereign legislature making laws at its own discretion.... I would sooner receive injustice in the Queen's courts than justice in a foreign court. And I hold that man or woman to be a scoundrel who goes abroad to a foreign court to have the judgements of the Queen's courts overturned. (Jeffrey-Poulter 1991: 152, citing *Belfast Telegraph*, 15 March 1982)

Enoch Powell was entirely right in principle; the European Court had acted as a sovereign legislature and diminished the United Kingdom's independence and autonomy. It is perhaps fitting that the issue on which the European Court should have infringed and invaded British sovereignty on a moral question was the law relating to male homosexual acts. However, Professor Powell had got his details wrong. The matter had never been before the Queen's courts and Mr. Dudgeon had never been charged or convicted. The Court of European Human Rights had not invented a new law at its own discretion; it had merely insisted that the United Kingdom extend the laws applying in England and Wales to Northern Ireland, which has no separate legal system, and in 1982 Northern Ireland's political autonomy had been suspended because of the intense ethnic and religious conflict there. The point rather is that a foreign *legal* institution had usurped the powers of the British Parliament, thus undermining the key British constitutional tradition of parliamentary sovereignty. The Convention to which Britain had signed up did not justify the court's decisions and the criteria used to bridge the gap were quite explicitly political and referred to decisions made by the legislatures of other Council of Europe countries. The United Kingdom was diminished by having the decisions of foreign parliaments forced upon it and Northern Ireland was diminished by being forced to accept a law based on the preferences of England and Wales and not its own.

Why Ulster Was Different

As was the case with Sabbath observance, Ulster proved to be once again the last stronghold of moral Britain. In Ulster, a distinctive British identity is both more valued and also more fragile than is the case in mainland Britain. These are exactly the circumstances under which one would expect tough measures against homosexuality to be favored. The Ulster Protestants who desire continued union with Britain are less than 60 percent of the population of Northern Ireland, and the Roman Catholic minority until very recently had a much higher birth rate. Should the British government decide to rid themselves of a political and economic burden, and unilaterally quit Northern Ireland, the Ulster Protestants might well find themselves a 20 percent minority in a strongly disunited united Ireland. The Roman Catholics of southern Ireland, after the Irish Free State was set up in 1922, made Ireland a monolithically Catholic state in which Protestant views and sensibilities over matters such as divorce or contraception or censorship were totally disregarded. The Roman Catholic Church had a moral monopoly (Blanshard 1954; Inglis 1987) in Ireland and this was strengthened when Ireland adopted a new constitution in 1937 that explicitly gave the Roman Catholic Church a special and privileged position in the state. In 1911, when the whole of Ireland was still part of the United Kingdom, there were 330,000 Protestants in the twenty-six (southern) counties that today constitute the Republic of Ireland, that is, they were about a tenth of the population. By 1971, there were only 130,000 Protestants or 4 percent of the population and, by 1981, the Protestants constituted only 3.5 percent of the Irish Republic's population (Bruce 1986: 152; Inglis 1998: 18-20). The fear of the Ulster Protestants that a united Ireland with a single unchallengeable myth of faith and nation (see Martin 1978: 107) would undermine their traditions and crush the vitality out of their community was not an unreasonable one. As with the Jews of ancient Israel, the Ulster Protestants responded to their precarious position by punishing the boundary-blurring sin of homosexuality, a metaphor of their own predicament.

The conflict between Protestants and Catholics in Ulster and the close connection between religion and ethnic and national identity have led to enhanced religious fervor on both sides of the divide. During the Protestant marches that take place in Northern Ireland every summer, the members of the Protestant Orange lodges carry huge banners through the streets of Northern Ireland, some of which have woven into them pictures of their sacred book, the Bible, with the heading "The Secret of Britain's Greatness." The Bible is, of course, the book that condemns homosexuality. The younger generation in secularized mainland Britain tends to be grossly ignorant of the contents of the Bible, but in Northern Ireland the scriptures are still revered. The fears of the Ulster Protestants are not shared by the British political elite of the mainland of today, who no longer strongly value, nor fear for, Britain's national identity. The people of Ulster's fear for their national existence is a feeling that could not even be understood, let alone considered, by most of the judges in the multinational European Court of Human Rights which, by definition, is not very interested in questions of national identity.

However, the Roman Catholics in Northern Ireland had also strongly supported the campaign of the Protestant leader, Rev. Dr. Ian Paisley, to "save Ulster from sodomy" (Bruce 1986: 150-51) and signed his petition in large numbers. They did so because their own predicament was the mirror image of that of the Protestants. The Roman Catholics are an Irish Catholic minority in Protestant Ulster and its capital city Belfast and also in the United Kingdom as a whole. Northern Ireland's Catholics, fearful of the Protestant British connection, have retreated into a separate and sectarian social world with its own segregated schools (at the demand of the Roman Catholic hierarchy), institutions, and even sports and a concern to maintain its boundaries and separate identity at all costs. The very nature of the conflict between the two national-religious groups over the allegiance of Northern Ireland has made the members of both groups terrified of the possibility of implosion and of a total loss of identity; hence both groups were happy to persecute the homosexuals, who were the very symbol of these fears and a group whose moral condemnation is sanctioned by *both* the religious traditions in Ulster.

Senator Norris Derails Ireland in the European Court of Human Rights

For much of their history, the Roman Catholics of the Irish Free State, later the Republic of Ireland, also felt that their national identity was threatened by their larger, more powerful and economically and culturally dominant neighbor the Protestant United Kingdom, whose language they speak, many of whose pastimes they share, whose abortion clinics and divorce courts they use and whose citizenship they have always been able to enjoy immediately for the price of a ferry ticket. Irish national morality and Irish national identity have been defined in opposition to that of their British neighbor.

It is curious then, but not surprising in terms of the thesis advanced here, that after independence in 1922 the Irish retained the English laws[4] that penalized male adult homosexual behavior (*Norris v Ireland* 1991, E.C.H.R. 186, paras. 12-13). Indeed, the commitment to these laws would have been strengthened by the Roman Catholic views and values built into the constitution in 1937, a proclamation of De Valera's ideal of an autarchic homogenous Ireland (Hanafin 2000: 58) and rooted in a distinctive philosophy of law. In 1983, the Irish Supreme Court ruled that the Irish laws against homosexual acts, though unenforced in practice, were still valid (*Norris v Ireland* 1991, E.H.R.R. at paras. 21-4), even though the Irish government had, like that of the United Kingdom, ratified the European Convention on Human Rights and despite the European Court's findings in favor of the right to privacy of homosexuals in the Dudgeon case from Northern Ireland (*Norris v Ireland* 1991, E.H.R.R. at para. 23). The Irish judges held that "Homosexuality has always been condemned in Christian teaching as morally wrong. It has equally been regarded by society for many centuries as an offence against nature and a very serious crime" (*Norris v Ireland* 1991, E.H.R.R., 186, para. 24). Senator Norris of Trinity College, one of the representatives of the Dublin universities in the second chamber of the Irish Parliment, Seanad Ëireann, having lost his case in the Irish Supreme Court, took it to the European Court of Human Rights in 1988. The Court ruled that:

> Such justifications as there are for retaining the law in force unamended are outweighed by the detrimental effects which the very existence of the legislative provisions in question can have on the life of a person like the applicant. Although members of the public who regard homosexuality as immoral may be shocked, offended or disturbed by the commission by others of homosexual acts, this cannot on its own warrant the application of penal sanctions when it is consenting adults alone who are involved. (*Norris v Ireland* 1991, E.C.H.R., 186, para. 46)

This is a judgment that makes no concessions to the *special and particular* requirements of Irish identity and morality, or to the Christian and Catholic views expressed by the judges of the Irish Supreme Court in 1983. Indeed, the Court crassly reduced the collective morality of the Irish people to the shock and offense felt by a collection of unconnected individuals, thus imposing an alien ideology on Ireland.

The Irish government was now trapped. It could in theory derogate from the judgment, but in practice it would eventually have to abolish the laws that made homosexual acts criminal, a change that was against the wishes of the Irish Roman Catholic Church and Irish public opinion (Holden 1994: 197-98). In June 1993, the Irish Parliament decided that homosexual acts should be decriminalized, despite strong opposition from the clergy (Holden 1994: 197). External forces had triumphed over internal tradition and the moral identity, and boundaries of Ireland had dissolved. Devout Irish Roman Catholics saw this and other similar changes "as a frightening decline into the moral quagmire of Europe" (Holden 1994: 198). The changes cannot be described as an aspect of globalization for they were purely legal and political and were in no way connected with questions of trade, economic inter-dependence, or the migration of people. Quite simply, the Irish government had previously assigned part of its sovereignty to the European Court of Human Rights because it thought it would be good for Ireland's international standing and prestige. To be fully part of the Council of Europe meant that Ireland could appear important, progressive, and part of the modern Western democratic world. It did not occur to Ireland's political leaders that the political rights guaranteed by the Convention might one day have implications for homosexuality or abortion. When the Convention was originally drafted, many other neighboring democratic countries such as Britain and West Germany still had laws condemning and punishing homosexual behavior, but by 1988 most West European countries had abolished any such laws. The test applied in practice by the European Court of Human Rights in deciding whether a violation of the right to privacy by a particular country should be upheld or struck down is to look at the relevant laws in the majority of the signatory countries, which left Ireland isolated and vulnerable. In the De Valerian past, an Irish government might well have repudiated the Convention after such a defeat on a moral issue. By 1988 Ireland was too entangled with the other Western European countries. In 1993, homosexual behavior was legalized in Ireland with the age of consent set at 17, lower than in many other European countries (Inglis 1998: 221), and measures were taken to mitigate hostility towards and discrimination against gay men and lesbians. The new Irish political elite was more concerned not to appear "backward" to "modern" liberal Europe than to appease the local Roman Catholic Church or to respond to the democratic wishes of its own people. The Roman Catholic Church in Ireland now retreated into the position taken by most of the Protestant churches in England and Wales some decades before, namely that although homosexuality was morally sinful it was not necessary for the state to treat it as a crime (Inglis 1998: 221). As we shall see in chapter 5, moral Ireland was to lose further decisive cases in the European Court of Human Rights and this forced its guardians to dismantle much of the legal framework enforcing Ireland's moral traditions. The alternative was to suffer an intolerable loss of face and to be excluded from being regarded as fully European by the more liberal nations at the heart of modern Europe. The periphery cannot hold; things fall together.

The Final Defeats of the Moral Periphery

Meanwhile the British government forced the local parliaments of the Channel Islands (self-governing off-shore islands that are associated with the United Kingdom but which have their own legislatures) to repeal their laws penalizing male homosexuality, by putting financial and legal pressure on them. When it came to a choice between traditional morality and privileged off-shore banking, they chose banking. The wallet has its reasons as well as the heart. The British government did not want to have to defend and lose another case in the European Court of Human Rights. The islanders were in each case small, compact, God-fearing communities with a strong sense of local identity that they wished to defend in an increasingly and threateningly cosmopolitan world; their laws against homosexual behavior were and were seen by them as one way of doing this. However, the world outside in the form of the British government, and behind the British government, the even more impersonal and implacable European Court of Human Rights, was able to force them to change their laws.

The last of the cases rooted in English law to come before the European Court of Human Rights related to Cyprus, a Commonwealth country that wished to retain the laws against homosexual behavior inherited from the time when it was under British colonial rule. A naïve person might have expected that the Cypriots would have wished to rid themselves of this remnant of colonial tradition now that they were fully independent. However, the *reasons for wishing to retain a law to enforce private morality are not necessarily the same as those for introducing it in the first place.* The ethnic conflicts in Cyprus between Orthodox Christian Greeks and Muslim Turks that have led to the partition of the island with a great deal of violence, including the rape of Greek women by Turkish soldiers, have made the Greek Cypriots fearful for their identity and boundaries. As our theory suggests, this fear has made them keen to retain the existing laws imposing penalties on sexual practices that break boundaries and threaten categories. The Cypriots' anti-homosexual laws were only struck down as a result of a decision in the European Court of Human Rights (*Modinos v Cyprus* 1993, 16, E.C.H.R., 149), along essentially the same lines as the decisions the Court made in the case of Ulster and the Republic of Ireland.

There are two very clear patterns to be discerned in the collapse of the laws against homosexual behavior in the United Kingdom and Ireland. The first was produced by secularization, and a loss of distinctive identity such that those who held power in the legislature ceased to be concerned with the maintenance of clear categories and strong boundaries. In essence, this is what happened in Great Britain. In the rest of the United Kingdom and in Ireland there had persisted a strong sense of identity and boundaries often rooted in a fusion of faith and nation and a commitment to preserve the laws against homosexuality that could not be shaken. Yet change occurred, a change imposed from the outside by an alien multinational court, a change derived from decisions made by legislatures in other countries.

An Antipodean Confirmation of the British and Irish Model

The nature of the pattern of events within the United Kingdom may be seen even more clearly if we look at the parallel case of Australia. It is clearer because the participants in the conflict over the decriminalization of homosexual acts in Tasmania were even more direct and *explicit* about it being essentially a question of preserving boundaries and identities than had been the case in the United Kingdom. In Tasmania, the implicit conflict over identity and boundaries that underlay the conflict over the decriminalization of homosexual acts in Tasmania between 1988 and 1997 was deliberately exacerbated by those Tasmanians who wanted homosexual law reform. They turned their cause into a general attack on the distinctive identity and separateness of Tasmania and then took the issue to a remote and alien judicial body outside Australia and used its ruling to force a conflict between the federal Commonwealth of Australia and the off-shore island state of Tasmania.

By 1988, Tasmania was the only Australian state to render male homosexual behavior criminal, though the law was no longer enforced; all the other states, together with the Australian federal government, had abolished such laws. Tasmanians had a very strong local identity, they were "Tasmanian not Australian," and their connection with their state was in many ways more important to them than their national citizenship (Henderson 2000: 97). Tasmania was an island with a homogeneous population that was unhappy about the invasion of their territory by big-city Australians going there in search of a quiet place to live out an alternative lifestyle. The invasion provoked a sense of the need to defend and maintain the borders of Tasmanian society (Henderson 2000: 38). Opposition to the pressure for homosexual law reform within Tasmania led to the formation of the Concerned Residents Against Moral Pollution (CRAMP) group to oppose outside intrusions (Henderson 2000: 41). The Tasmanian Attorney General John Bennett declared, "Hell can freeze over before they get homosexual acts legalized in this state" (Morris 1995: 49). The reformers by contrast openly said that they wanted to break with the tradition of a homogeneous Tasmania to create what they called "an interesting, diverse, colorful" place (cited in Henderson 2000: 35). For most Tasmanians the idea of living in colorful, "interesting times" was quite abhorrent and the reformers not only lost their case locally but enraged the local politicians and people to the point where the editor of a local newspaper *The Examiner* (4 July 1991) could speak of "the beginning of a new era of poofter bashing" (Morris 1995: 99).

The reformers now further inflamed local fears of their culture being penetrated by powerful outsiders by taking their case to the federal level, to the government and judiciary of Australia and to the United Nations Human Rights Committee (UNHRC) and by helping to organize a trade boycott of their own state (Henderson 2000: 39). In 1991, the reformers were able to go directly to the UN committee because Australia had by this time signed the first optional protocol to the International Covenant on Civil and Political Rights. A Mr. Nick Toonan lodged a complaint that his rights had been violated and, in 1993, the Australian government sent its response to the UN Committee, putting forward both the Tasmanian state government's case and its own point of view, which totally contradicted that of the Tasmanians, saying:

> The Australian government does not accept that a complete prohibition on sexual activity between men is necessary to sustain the moral fabric of Australian society. (*Government of Australia Submission to United Nations Human Rights Committee,* 27 September 1993, cited in Morris 1995: 111)

Unsurprisingly, the UN Committee ruled unanimously in April 1994 that Tasmania's laws prohibiting homosexual behavior were contrary to international standards of human rights to privacy and to equality before the law. The Tasmanians must have expected to lose, for even before the UN decision, George Brookes, a member of the Tasmanian Legislative Council, had told a pomatose visiting journalist "I would hope that the state government would tell the United Nations to go to buggery" (Morris 1995: 104).

What particularly outraged the Tasmanians was that the power of their own democratically elected and accountable legislature had been over-ridden by a body, UNHRC, which "does not meet in public, is not required to publish the reasons for its decisions, and was at that time made up of a number of members who came from non-democratic countries or countries that retain criminal laws against homosexuality" (Henderson 2000: 45). The UNHRC seems to have taken the ECHR decisions in the cases of Northern Ireland, Ireland, and Cyprus as precedents so that ultimately the law was changed in Tasmania to fit the arbitrary priorities of the legislatures of European countries (albeit democratic ones) on the other side of the globe. A few months later, the Australian federal government passed the 1994 Human Rights (Sexual Conduct) Act, which was in effect a federal privacy act. In 1997, the Tasmanians gave way and their legislature agreed by one vote to decriminalize homosexual acts. The reformers had won, not by persuasion as they had in the other Australian states, but by force. In England and Wales, the reformers, as we saw in chapter 2, had succeeded in achieving decriminalization as early as 1967 by limiting their argument to the causalist question of the harm done to individual homosexuals by the operation and indeed

existence of the criminal law. In Tasmania, the reformers deliberately sought a confrontation with the central values and concerns of
the people over the preservation of their boundaries and community. In doing so they rendered Tasmania the most obvious and explicit version of the theory advanced here about Britain. The not
very strange death of moral Tasmania provides a better-focused picture of what happened in the strange death of moral Britain.

The Sudden and Unexpected Emergence of Family Values

It should now be clear that the severity with which male homosexual behavior was punished in moral Britain was because such
actions were seen as a threat to an entire society with a distinctive
national identity and religious tradition. The threat was greatest for
the two institutions that were the pillars of that identity and tradition,
the churches and the armed forces, and it was here that hostility to
homosexuals was and remains strongest. As the power and influence of these institutions has declined, so have the taboos against
homosexuality.

However, two of Britain's central institutions, its market economy
and its family life, do not and cannot play any part whatsoever in the
explanation of the strange birth and death of the condemnation of
homosexuality. It is important to stress this point since muddled think-
ers are apt to assume that because in general these institutions shape
our everyday experience, our life chances, and our perceptions of
the world so strongly then they must also determine society's reac-
tion to homosexuality. This is not the case, nor is there any evidence
that it ever was the case. The absurd idea that there is any connection one way or the other between capitalism and hostility to homosexuality is not even worth taking time to refute. In an impersonal market place, neither buyers nor sellers, neither producers nor
consumers, neither capitalists nor workers, nor rentiers care or need
to care what a person's sexual inclinations are. A pink pound is as
good as any other. Who cares if a banker, a mathematician, a machine minder, a manufacturer, a farmer, a bricklayer, an attorney, or
even an interior decorator, an actor, or a ladies' hairdresser is gay so
long as he pays his way and does his job? Neither a laissez-faire
libertarian nor a Benthamite aggregator of individual pleasures less
pains (Bentham 1978 [1785]) has or had any reason to join in the
once widespread condemnation of homosexuality. Homosexual ac-

tivities neither create problems for the accumulation of property nor for its security, nor in practice for its transmission. If Britain is more tolerant of homosexuals at the start of the twenty-first century than it was at the end of the nineteenth it is not because of the evolution of capitalism in a particular direction nor because of its long-term triumph punctuated by episodes of crisis. Capitalism is an economic system that is remarkably flexible and provided that norms of honesty, commercial trust and fair-dealing are maintained it can coexist with most systems of personal morality. Whether homosexuals are cherished or mistreated has little effect on profits. The general tendency of capitalist enterprise is to ignore and even to subvert boundaries of all kinds, a tendency which is hardly likely to lead to a negative perception of homosexuals and their behavior. Indeed, in socialist countries such as the Soviet Union, the People's Republic of China, or Cuba homosexuals were treated far more harshly than in Christian democratic capitalist countries (Miller 1995: 483-493) because their social and economic order was so strongly bounded and hierarchical. Homosexuality creates no problems for a system as open, fluid, and flexible as capitalism, a system based on spontaneous order (Barry 1982). When homosexuals have been persecuted in capitalist societies, it has been by the least capitalist institutions in the society, institutions that often pre-date capitalism, and institutions that seek to maintain closed boundaries in the face of pressures from the market place. Purely economic categories and boundaries such as property, professional qualifications, and restrictive practices are not threatened by homosexuality.

Likewise there was *no* significant link between the forces seeking to uphold and preserve marriage and the family and the persecution of male homosexuals or the punishment of those detected in homosexual acts in the past. The latter have always been perceived as a threat to society as a whole rather than to particular institutions. The one institution that has been singled out in Britain as in need of protection from homosexuality is the armed forces, the institution most closely tied to the defense of national boundary and identity, *not* the family. Marriage, family and kinship are irrelevant to any discussion of the *origins* of the taboos against homosexuality. It is important to make this point because at a very late stage in the death of moral Britain, Section 28 of The Local Government Act 1988 was passed prohibiting local authorities (municipalities, counties) from "promoting" homosexuality, and the debate about homosexuality came for the first time to be centred on family values. The concern with family values was a product of a widespread concern over the unprecedented and disturbing collapse of the family, discussed in chapter 1, a collapse caused by the marked rise in illegitimacy, separation, and divorce and not in any sense caused by homosexuality. The appeal to family values in this new attack on homosexuals was a piece of opportunism; secularization and a declining concern with national identity had forced those hostile to homosexuality on religious grounds or in the interests of maintaining boundaries to seek new arguments and so homosexuals were made a scapegoat for the decay of the nuclear family. It has also to be said that the new indignation was to some extent provoked by verbal attacks on the family by radical homosexual activists, which had dismayed most homosexuals who, above all, wanted social acceptance.

The censure of homosexual acts in the Bible and in the medieval period consistently links them to bestiality, whether committed by men or women, which is hardly a family issue. There was no consistent, persisting, or strong perception among the moralists of homosexuals as a distinct group of men with settled preferences and even a distinct way of life that could prove a threat to the family. Lesbians who could have been cast in this role were rarely mentioned. Male homosexual behavior like sex with animals was perceived as a set of random acts of wanton wickedness that anyone could commit, but which were most likely to be committed by those unable to marry or who were temporarily or permanently deprived of the company of women, such as monks, the secular clergy (Richards 1991: 135, 138), or sailors. For them it might become a habit and a preference rather as a shepherd on a lonely mountainside might come to be habituated to sexual relations with sheep, but it was not usually seen as an innate predisposition. In Roman Catholic Europe (of which Britain was a part until the Reformation) there was a sizeable and in theory non-procreative rival to family life for men, for they could become priests, monks, friars, or members of other celibate orders. These organizations took more men away from family life than the refusal to marry by that small minority of homosexuals who found women sexually repellent could have done. However, the institutions of the church were attacked by secular opinion not because of their impact on the birth rate but because of their wealth and power.

Besides, it is the failure of women to marry or re-marry, as with the ban on widow remarriage in India, or to have children whether legitimate or illegitimate that determines the birth rate (Davies 1976); men, from this point of view, are relatively unimportant. Likewise a man who becomes a priest or a religious against the interests of his family, kin, or lineage creates far more problems, and is often seen as creating problems by the family concerned (Maritain 1948: 6; Martin 2002: 24-26), than those males with a preference for homosexual acts possibly could. Many a royal dynasty has died out because by chance the last heir to the throne was a religious celibate, but most kings with a taste or even a preference for homosexual relationships have also married and either had children or at least sought to have children through their own natural insemination of the queen. The bottom of the page does not mean the end of the line.

The institution in which committed homosexuals were and remain a problem is the Roman Catholic Church itself and not the family, and the persecution of homosexual behavior has always been stepped up at times of church reform. Church reform means in practice the consolidation of power at the center and increased control over priests, bishops, benefices, and resources by the Pope and his advisers. One manifestation of this in the past was the periodic sudden tightening up of the rules on celibacy to ensure that priests do not have families and in particular sons who may inherit office within the church or make off with church property. The priest must be entirely subject to church control with no rivals for his loyalty and affection (Coser 1974), and so reform means a strengthening of the boundary between priests and laity and also of the hierarchical boundaries within the church itself between deacons, priests, and bishops and within religious orders (Brooke 1964; Heer 1962; Lambert 1977; Lea 1932). But as has already been demonstrated, when social boundaries are being strengthened and defended, homosexual activities come to be regarded as a threatening metaphor for institutional disorder. Relations of a homosexual kind are particularly threatening to a closed and rigid all-male hierarchy for another reason, namely, that they can cut across boundaries of rank as well as external boundaries and undermine control from the center. This is why at the time of church reform between the middle of the eleventh and the thirteenth centuries and after the tightening up of the rules on celibacy, the attitude of the church towards those detected in homosexual acts became much more hostile and the punishments far more severe (Boswell 1980: 277; Davies 1983c; Goodich 1979: 43-45, 71). Since the church was the guardian of the morals of the wider society the persecution of those detected in or suspected of sodomy was intensified in the society at large and when the boundaries of the secular world itself came under threat, homosexuals like Jews, lepers, and other ambiguous groups were defined as suitable cases for elimination. It was this tradition that was eventually taken over by the state in England at the time of the Reformation, though without the paranoid zeal found in other countries; few sodomites were executed in fifteenth- and sixteenth-century England and just as there was no widespread hunt for witches in England, neither was there a witch hunt for homosexuals.

Throughout the medieval period and subsequently, there had been a steady, if at times muted, condemnation of non-procreative sexual behavior culminating in orgasm as contrary to God's design and purpose; far more important is the fact that such acts were arranged in a hierarchy of wickedness and only some of them attracted severe penalties. Those detected in bestiality or homosexual sodomy, or homosexual acts construed as attempted sodomy or preparation for sodomy, might well be executed or at the very least have to undergo the most rigorous of penances. Non-procreative sex between men and women, even if it included unorthodox forms of penetration, was not regarded with this degree of condemnation, nor was it treated as harshly, nor was self-abuse, nor were sexual relations between women. Non-procreation was only one of the accusations leveled against those indulging in homosexual practices and not in any sense the most important one. The preservation of marriage and the family was, of course, a vital objective for both church and society, but it was of no importance as a factor in generating hostility to homosexuality.

Marriage and the family have been just as important in societies such as some of the small states of ancient Greece at certain times, or parts of Arab North Africa today where homosexual practices were and are common even among the predominantly heterosexual, and in Japan where male homosexuality is tolerated, as in the countries where homosexuals are persecuted. Such activities were and are permitted provided that their practitioners marry and establish families. There was and is no conflict in these societies between the demands of family and the pursuit of homosexual practices. The Muslim communities of North Africa from Tangiers to Tunisia have long been the playground of homosexuals from Europe as diverse as John Maynard Keynes, Joe Orton, Oscar Wilde, André Gide, and Kenneth Williams seeking a place in which they could go public about their proclivities and have sex with local boys and young men without incurring savage disapproval (Lahr 1980; Sheridan 1998: 95-99, 118-121; Skidelsky 1983; Miller 1995: 301-3; Williams 1993). Nonetheless, family and kinship ties are strong in the Maghreb and the very basis of the local social order.

We must, therefore, utterly reject theories like those of John Boswell (1980: 32-34) who suggests that gay people seem "dangerous in kinship (based) societies" and that the wish to maintain and exalt extended family ties and lineage is the basis of hostility to homosexuals or homosexual behavior.[5]

The same error can be seen in Jeffrey Weeks' claim that the Labouchere clause in the Criminal Law Amendment Act of 1885 penalizing acts of "gross indecency" between men was derived from the contemporary perception of homosexuality "as a threat to stable sexual relations within the bourgeois family" (Weeks 2000: 25). This would have been news to Labouchere, a quirky left-wing radical who had lived openly and adulterously with his mistress, the actress Henrietta Hobson, wife of a Bristol solicitor called Pigeon (Pearson 1936: 63). The irregularity of his domestic arrangements was often mentioned when he addressed the electors, and the crowds would shout, "Ow's 'Enrietta?" To forestall this, he took to opening meetings by stating, "I wish to convey to you all the gratifying intelligence that Henrietta is quite well" (Pearson 1936: 67). The very use of the phrase "bourgeois family" reveals the purely ideological basis of Weeks' assertion and he provides no empirical evidence to support it. There is none and the same objections may be made to the views of the otherwise reliable Antony Grey (1992: 18). It is completely wrong to assert and worse still to *assume* that the defense of family values was an important source of hostility to male homosexuality in Britain before the 1980s.

Perhaps the most decisive piece of evidence demonstrating that homosexuality is not a family issue is that men are consistently more hostile to homosexuals and to male homosexual behavior than women. Even in an attitude survey carried out in Britain in 1990-91 it was revealed that over 70 percent of British men believed sex between two men to be always or mostly wrong but only 58 percent of women felt this way. A similar gap between the sexes was found for all age groups and categories of marital status. By contrast, on issues to do with sexual behavior that might impinge on the family, women were far more censorious than men. British women had a greater commitment to the ideal of monogamy than men and were more likely to see casual sex as always wrong (Wellings et al. 1994: 245-56). These findings are consistent with those from surveys done in other similar societies and with those from earlier British surveys such as the survey *Television and Religion* (1964: 82) conducted in 1964. The views expressed about same sex relations between men are consistent between surveys done at different times with different kinds of sample. They match all the other information we have and are most likely reliable.

The protection of the family is an issue for women and male homosexuality is an issue for men. Women are indifferent to male homosexuals because their behavior does not threaten the family and because they are not likely to be a source of unwanted or threatening sexual approaches to females. Men in Britain, by contrast, may well perceive male homosexuals as predatory sodomites to be feared or else as contemptible catamites. Homosexuals are not rejected because men are concerned about the disruption of families but because men see them as undermining the security of the relationships between men in all-male groups based on solidarity, comradeship, and male friendship and as confusing the hierarchies of masculinity within which men place one another. Neither of these are important to women and indeed women may at times find these relationships between men in groups incomprehensible, alien, ridiculous, or even exclusive and oppressive. Institutionalized all-male groups can be both a rival to family life and the place in which male power and status in society is celebrated and reinforced.

In the early debates about homosexual conduct and about homosexuals in the British Parliament in the 1950s and 1960s, it was men not women who expressed total revulsion and even hatred towards male homosexuals:

> I am wholly against the Bill. I cannot stand homosexuals. They are the most disgusting people in the world, and they are, unfortunately, on the increase. I loathe them. Prison

is much too good for them; in fact that is the place where many of them like to go, for obvious reasons. If noble Lords will only consider for one moment the filthy habits these people have in private, I do not believe they will vote in favour of the Bill. (Earl of Dudley, *Hansard*, House of Lords 1966, vol. 275, col. 158-9)

Those who have preceded me have been experts but I am not. I know nothing or very little about what is called buggery but from what I do know about it I hate it and I dislike it. (Sir Cyril Osbourne, *Hansard*, House of Commons 1966, vol. 724, col. 829)

If I had my way I'd castrate every single one of the dirty buggers. (Conservative MP, cited in Grey 1992: 46)

By contrast it was the women in the House of Lords such as Baroness Gaitskell or Baroness Wooton who were scornful of the intensity of their male colleagues' rejection of homosexuals and their horror at their conduct (Grey 1992: 124-25, *Hansard*, House of Lords 1965, vol. 266, col. 126-9; vol. 267, cols. 305-6; vol. 269, cols. 697-8).

Indeed the men who hated homosexuals were often indignant at the women's tendency to tolerate that which these men saw as the "filthy, disgusting, unnatural vice of homosexuality" and "corrosive and corrupting immorality" (Earl of Winterton, *Hansard*, House of Lords 1954, vol. 187, cols. 739, 745).

...When we were young this thing was never mentioned in decent mixed society. In male society, its votaries were contemptuously described by a good old English cognomen which I cannot use in your Lordships' house. Today, at any rate, to my disgust, you hear young ladies, themselves of irreproachable morality, say, half pityingly, half facetiously, "Of course, he is a 'pansy': he cannot help it." Hostesses have been known to say: "If we ask Bill, we must ask Joe. You see, he is peculiar and they are inseparable, like two lovers." (Earl of Winterton, *Hansard*, House of Lords 1965, vol. 187 col. 744)

In the 1950s and 1960s, those who defended the laws that rendered male homosexual behavior criminal rarely mentioned the defense of family life as a reason for their hostile position; homosexuality was not a family issue in the way that say divorce or illegitimacy were. Curiously it was the reformers who spoke most about the family[6] when they declared that forms of heterosexual behavior such as adultery or fornication were more harmful to third parties or to family life than homosexuality (Church of England Moral Welfare Committee 1954; *Hansard*, House of Commons 1966, vol. 724, col. 850-1; vol. 738, cols. 1068, 1079, 1104; House of Lords 1965, vol. 206, 97). The reformers ascribed rational arguments based on their own priorities to their opponents and then refuted them to their own satisfaction and in doing so failed to understand what motivated their opponents' hostility.[6]

It was *only* in the 1980s that homosexuality did become a family issue and when it did it involved, as the author would have predicted, lesbians as much as, if not more than male homosexuals. A different kind of conflict had arisen and in many respects it was one generated by homosexual activists rather than the defenders of the family.

The 1967 legislation had made male homosexual behavior in private legal, or at least permissible under restrictive conditions, and that set in motion an irreversible trend towards liberalization that continues in the twenty-first century. It has only ever been interrupted by hiccups, never by a serious backlash. As opponents of the legislation feared at the time, the implications and consequences of the 1967 act have proved to be far more radical than might be inferred from its content. Norman St. John Stevas stressed at the time that although male homosexual behavior was now legal it was still "contrary to public policy" and that homosexual relationships in contrast to the family had no recognized status and gave rise neither to rights nor duties (Norman St. John Stevas, *Hansard,* House of Commons 1966, vol. 738, cols. 1120-1). St. John Stevas was in favor of the reform, but he was a mollifier. He wanted the opponents of reform to feel that in law very little had been changed and that it would not lead to further major social changes. He was wrong on the latter point, however, and one suspects that a man as intelligent as Dr. St. John Stevas, a future master of Emmanuel College, must have had some inkling as to what would happen in the long term. There was bound to be trouble later, when, as an inevitable consequence of the 1967 Act, homosexuals were freer to campaign openly and social attitudes to them had ameliorated. While homosexuality is not a threat to marriage and the family, for many gays and lesbians these were a key source of problems in their own personal lives. Their families of origin were often pressing them to marry, to create a new nuclear family and provide grandchildren, and had difficulty in comprehending or accepting both their reluctance to do so and the sexual orientation that lay behind this reluctance. Indeed in the late 1960s and early 1970s, these pressures may have been more intense than in the past. It was the norm in Britain in the late 1960s that people would get married and have children. Over a thirty-year period, peaking in 1972, marriage had become more popular and couples had married younger (Coleman 2000: 55-8). There were fewer accepted social niches and bolt-holes in which confirmed bachelors not of the marrying kind could hide and avoid the pressure to marry, particularly the pressure from their own families. In this way, the family was experienced as the source and origin of their social embarrassment; this led them to assert without evidence that the family, the source of their immediate personal difficulties, must also be the place of orgin of the intense hostility towards homosexuals found in their society. We have no reason to accept the logic of any argument that is based only on such experiences. In modern Japan where there is *little* social hostility to homosexuality young Japanese male homosexuals also find the pressure to marry a major problem (Miller 1995: 522). The pressure is a general one and even stronger on women. In Japan, a women unmarried at twenty-five is called a Christmas cake because no one wants it after the 25th.

Radical activists among the homosexuals came to believe that the respect, regard, and recognition given to the nuclear family of father, mother, and children was the cause of their exclusion from social esteem and failure to be regarded as part of the normal and accepted institutional order. The most radical among them wanted to destroy the family altogether. They saw the family as the cause of "heteronormativity" and thus of homosexuals being regarded as an unfortunate oddity and even a suitable case for treatment. In the late 1960s and 1970s, they joined forces with all manner of revolutionaries who wanted to overthrow the "bourgeois family" in favor of a variety of amorphous living arrangements that would be part of a general overturning of capitalist society (Grey 1992: 183). In some mysterious way, this time it was not going to evolve along the violent and repressive lines of earlier socialistic experimenting, a violence and repression that was often explicitly extended to male homosexuals, that remnant or at least expression of bourgeois decadence, as happened in the Soviet Union, China, and Cuba (Miller 1995: 483-93). The anti-family movement was merely a rainbow coalition of radicals and like all rainbows it was wet and empty and had a crock of taxpayers' gold at the end of it.

In the 1980s this meant that homosexual activists became drawn into the numerous existing conflicts over money and policy between the Conservative central government and those local councils (municipalities) that were controlled by the extreme left wing of the Labour party. In the 1980s, the latter had begun to allocate facilities and indeed sums of money to gay political causes. This incensed free market libertarians in the Conservative party such as Teresa Gorman, MP. The strongly libertarian Mrs. Gorman was *not* unsympathetic to homosexual demands for freedom and she also wanted all restrictions on abortion abolished because she saw them as an illicit use of the power of the state against women. However, in her ideal world, no taxpayers' money should be spent on any kind of radical propaganda; the promotion of homosexuality was merely one example. The gay activists had foolishly managed to unite two quite antipathetic sections of the Conservative party, the libertarians and the traditionalists, and both were in favor of Section 28 that sought to stop local authorities sponsoring the activists' antics.

The 1980s, in any case, were not a good time in which to mount radical attacks on the family, nor even to argue for the sponsoring of new kinds of families in a world where there had already been a growth in diversity through dissolution and collapse through choice. By the 1980s, as we have seen, the nuclear family was experiencing serious problems for reasons that had nothing to do with the homosexuals. In the 1970s and 1980s, there was a massive rise both in illegitimacy and in the incidence of divorce, and from 1972 onward a marked decline in the popularity of marriage. By 1994, nearly a quarter of all households with dependent children would be lone-parent households and the proportion of children growing up in historically unconventional families would have become the highest in Europe (Coleman 2000: 79-80). It was this collapse of family life, which also had clear, obvious, and severe social and economic consequences, that led to Mrs. Thatcher's (the prime minister) pursuit of a return to family values. Due to the activists' clumsiness, homosexuality and lesbianism now become a family issue for the first time.

One indication of this is that many of the leaders of the new campaign against homosexuality in the name of the family were women, notably Dame Jill Knight, MP, and the life peers Baroness Cox, Baroness Young, Baroness Blatch, and later Baroness O'Cathain, all of them strong believers in the virtues and importance of the family. This new female leadership had nothing in common with the angry old men of the 1950s who had expressed so vigorously their total hatred of and disgust at male homosexuals and their activities. Rather they merely wished to prevent local authorities from intervening to undermine the special place that the family occupied in education, where it was held up to young people as an ideal and as the normal context in which children were brought up, in order to make gay *and* lesbian couples appear to be an alternative deserving of equal respect and esteem. They came to enjoy the support of the prime minister, Mrs. Thatcher (Jeffrey-Poulter 1991: 218). Mrs. Thatcher was not hostile to homosexuals (Grey 1992: 184; Jeffrey-Poulter 1991: 234) and had previously voted in favor of the decriminalization of homosexual behavior. Towards the end of 1987, Dame Jill Knight introduced a new clause, Clause 28, into the Local Government Bill (which was about other completely different issues such as compulsory tendering for contracts), and when the Bill was passed it became Section 28 of the 1988 Local Government Act stating that "A local authority shall not—(a) intentionally promote homosexuality or publish material with the intention of promoting homosexuality, (b) promote the teaching in any maintained school of the acceptability of homosexuality, as a pretended family relationship" (hmso.gov.uk/acts1988/UKpga_19880009_en). Section 28 had little impact on or significance for what happened in the real world, but it was to provoke a controversy that raged between the gay and Christian minorities well into the twenty-first century, somewhat to the surprise and embarrassment of the political parties who were concerned about losing the votes of one group or the other. It became a key symbolic issue out of all proportion to its actual effect. Section 28 was a constraint on local authorities, not on schoolteachers and so it could not have had and did not have the effect in the classroom that its proponents would like to have produced and which its opponents feared. Section 28 did not constrain the freedom of speech or of publishing of private individuals, organizations, or companies and in practice because there was a specific exemption within the section for publications about health, local authorities used this loophole to carry on as before. No one was ever prosecuted for breach of Section 28. The row about Section 28 was a row about who gets to make authoritative statements round here, particularly statements in some sense legitimized by democracy.

Gay men and lesbians, who had packed the public gallery of the House of Commons during the discussion of Clause 28 and repeatedly interrupted the debate, shouted in anger when it was passed. There followed a protest march and a minor scuffle with the police. Many well-known, reasonably well-known, and would-be well-known people wrote to the newspapers to protest when Clause 28 was also subsequently passed by the House of Lords and became law as Section 28. Three militant lesbians abseiled from the public gallery of the House of Lords, screaming slogans to the amazement of the assembled peers of the realm. There were further demonstrations in London. Four lesbians invaded the studios of the BBC as the six o'clock news was being broadcast. One chained herself to the leg of Sue Lawley, the newsreader. Another of the women had to be overpowered and literally sat upon by the newscaster Nicholas Witchell (Jeffrey Poulter 1991: 222, 228-33, 252).

It is important to note that many of the most militant protesters against Clause (later Section) 28 were women. Women were now for the first time prominent on *both* sides of a controversy about homosexuality, one that impinged equally on male and female homosexuals and possibly even more on lesbians than on their gay counterparts. For the *first time* same-sex relations had become a family issue and thus one that involved women more closely than men.

The protests against Section 28 were a piece of bad camp theater. The triumph over tragedy of 1967 had become the failed farce of 1988. Yet it was a farce on both sides. We can now see that the enacting of Section 28 did not and could not achieve what the promoters wanted, namely, the restoration of a family stability that had been destroyed by the activities of heterosexuals, leading to fatherless households. Gays and lesbians were a tiny and irrelevant minority singled out and attacked because they were both vociferous and unpopular in a way that the real culprits, these who had chosen to breed and quit and to divide and misrule were not.

Even at the beginning of the twenty-first century, Section 28 was still a major source of contention and in 2000 attempts by the Labour government to repeal it were on two separate occasions heavily defeated in the House of Lords after long and impassioned debates. Fifteen Labour peers, including five former ministers, defied their own party and government and voted to keep Section 28. A further prolonged "homosexuality versus the Christian family" issue erupted in 2002 when the Adoption of Children Bill was amended in the House of Commons that year to make unmarried couples including homosexuals and lesbians in Britain eligible to adopt children *as a couple*. Either one of the partners could already do so as an *individual*, but they could not do so together, taking *joint* responsibility for the adoption. The amendment was rejected by the House of Lords; acquiescence to such adoptions by the state would also have given weight to the campaign by gay and lesbian couples to obtain legal recognition for their partnerships from both church and state. Such a request, like the wish of gay men and lesbians to be allowed to serve quietly in the armed services, was, in fact, a very conservative road to acceptance but it was one very strongly resisted by those with religious objections to homosexuality.

Indeed, the lengths to which those employing the new vocabulary of family values were prepared to go to attack homosexuality (but not, for example, illegitimacy) indicate that the old concerns about social and religious boundaries had gone underground and become the love of order that dare not speak its name. For the orderly, Section 28 had been a symbolic victory over what they still thought of as the sins of the cities of the plain and the perversions denounced by St. Paul (Jeffrey-Poulter 1991: 205-211), and they were willing to defend Section 28 to the last ditch. It was no longer possible in a by now moribund moral Britain to run a campaign against homosexuality on the basis of an appeal to a single agreed and accepted national and Christian tradition, the defense of which had been at the core of the taboos against homosexuality. Those who were hostile to homosexuality by virtue of their religious convictions knew that they had no chance of succeeding in a counter-attack on the sons and daughters of Gomorrah in a secular society with an exiguous moral "majority," and so they took up the cause of family values.

Even though Christian leaders such as the then Archbishop of Canterbury, George Carey, and the Scottish Cardinal, Thomas Winning, were prominent supporters of the campaign to retain Section 28, the organizers of the campaign tried hard to prevent it being treated as an exclusively Christian issue and looked for Jewish, Muslim, Sikh, and Hindu support. Lord Ahmed and Lord Patel were among the Labour peers voting in the House of Lords against their own party and in favor of Section 28. The Christian Institute, Britain's leading evangelical Protestant think tank, even quoted the Koran in an appendix to its formal statement opposing gay marriage. Some rather obscure Talmudic discussions about the threat posed to family formation and stability by homosexual relations were also cited (www.christian.org.uk/html-publications/gaymarriage.htm [November 2002]). It was thus intimated that they were seeking support within the traditions of other religious minorities in Britain, many of which seen from a strictly orthodox, bible-believing Christian position should have been labeled heretics and heathens. The world of moral Britain had been turned upside down.

Thus, there were three quite different stages in the dismantling of the laws prohibiting male homosexual acts and constraining homosexuals in other ways that represent three distinct periods in and facets of the strange death of moral Britain. The first was the collapse in England and Wales of the morality of a nationally and religiously homogeneous society concerned with protecting its own particular traditions and social boundaries. The implications of the collapse were reflected in the changes in the law. No such moral collapse occurred in the autonomous peripheries of the United Kingdom, and the legal changes were imposed by an alien court on this periphery, and on a series of countries formerly under British rule or influence and still retaining for their own reasons an English legal system or at least the particular English laws penalizing homosexuality. In the latter countries and provinces, the moral autonomy of the society itself was undermined. This second stage was a double blow to the integrity of, say, moral Ulster or moral Ireland since the boundaries and identity of the society were directly assaulted as well as indirectly undermined. The third and least important stage in the collapse in the restrictions impinging on homosexuality occurred in a Britain where both of the given institutions into which an individual is born, namely family and nation, had already been fatally undermined and the religious tradition that had reinforced them had withered away. The decline of religion, nation, and family alike were autonomous changes; none were the result of the activities of the homosexuals but were products of quite separate sets of political events and of choices made by other individuals. Nonetheless, it provoked a new kind of conflict between homosexuals and a heterogeneous alliance of traditionalists over what purported to be a family issue. Restrictions that had their origins in the maintenance of a taken-for-granted strong national identity were now for the first time defended in the name of preserving a family unit that had been seriously weakened by heedless heterosexual parents. At each stage, it was, in the true sense of the word, a tragedy that a loyal minority should have been so harshly treated by the defenders of the most central and vital institutions of moral Britain, a society defined by and esteemed for its devotion to liberty.

Notes

1. In the 1950s, there were a further 1,200 prosecutions each year of those engaging in homosexual activities, but most of those involved having sex in a public place such as a park or lavatory accessible to the public or seeking to set up a sexual assignation in one of those places, in the street or at a railway station either for mutual enjoyment or as a form of prostitution. These remain criminal offenses, though in practice they are not pursued by the police with the same vigor and duplicity (such as entrapment) as in the past and are less likely to be prosecuted. Even so, at least two Anglican bishops (Dalrymple 1998) have been arrested for cottaging (activities in public lavatories) by the police and prominent politicians, including a minister, have had to resign after night time romps and cruising in London's parks and open spaces. In 2003, as a symbol of the legal equality of homosexuals, it was proposed that their having sex within public lavatories should be decriminalized provided the door is closed so that they are not visible to those in the building for reasons more closely related to its designated purpose.

2. In some states of the United States oral sex is also prosecuted as sodomy.

3. The Sodomites sought to break two sets of boundaries between categories at once, that between mortal human beings and angels and that between men and women (Davies 1999: 343).

4. Any English statutes passed before 1922 when Ireland became independent still apply in Ireland unless specifically repealed. The English common law also applied and applies in Ireland, but not in Scotland, which has always had a separate legal system.

5. Boswell pursues this point relentlessly even though the entire thrust of his own evidence is against it; indeed his evidence proves that the church *was* the key source of hostility. However, he was determined at all costs to avoid admitting that Christianity has been consistently hostile to homosexuality even though the degree of that hostility may have varied considerably over time (see Richards 1991: 32). This same fatal obsession also underlies his failed attempt to demonstrate the acceptance of same-sex unions in pre-modern Europe (Boswell 1994: 280-82). Homosexual unions were *not* accepted and blessed by the medieval church and the Christian religion was opposed to homosexual practices until it was weakened by secularization and modernism in the twentieth century.

6. A very large proportion of the Parliamentary references to the relationship between family difficulties and homosexuality refer either to theories that an individual's homosexuality is a product of a defective relationship with his parents, and particularly his mother, or to the sad fate of homosexuals who lack the pleasures of married and family life. See *Hansard,* House of Commons 1966, vol. 724, 806-838, vol. 738- 1070).

5

The Strange Death of Roman Catholic Britain and the Crisis of Moral Ireland

Abortion and Roman Catholicism in Britain and Ireland

The banning of abortion has throughout Europe been a distinctively Roman Catholic cause. Yet, curiously, the origins of the legislation prohibiting abortion in early nineteenth-century England were in no way Roman Catholic. The strongest support for anti-abortion legislation at that time came from the medical profession. At a time before aseptic surgery and anesthetics, abortion was perceived as a dangerous procedure, one often carried out by medically unqualified persons, and had to be eliminated. It should also be added that the doctors had a self-interest in driving unqualified rivals out of business in order to establish their own preeminence in and, if possible, monopoly over medical questions. Banning abortion was part of a broader strategy for raising the power and status of the profession.

However, the reasons why legislation is enacted and the reasons why it is subsequently upheld and maintained are not necessarily the same. When, from the 1930s onward, there was increasing pressure to liberalize the abortion laws in Britain, by far the strongest opposition to such a change came from Britain's Roman Catholic minority, perhaps a tenth of the population, most of whom were of Irish descent and many of whom had been born in Ireland (Hornsby-Smith 1987: 116, 162).

Prior to the secession of the Irish Free State in 1922, abortion had not been a matter of public controversy in the United Kingdom, though if it had been, it is possible that a large, well-organized, and combative Irish Party within the British Parliament would have blocked any attempt to liberalize the 1861 law on abortion. It is one of the curiosities of the history of Britain and Ireland that the attainment of Irish independence in 1922 made abortion law reform possible in England and Wales in 1967, which, in turn, led to unexpected controversies within the Irish Republic as the Irish government and the Irish courts sought to restrain Irish women from seeking abortions in Britain.

The political division between the two countries after 1922 meant that the Roman Catholic crusade to defend the restrictive abortion law of 1861 took two entirely different forms. In independent Ireland, national identity and religious identity coincided and the old English law of 1861 was made more stringent and elevated into a constitutional principle by means of a referendum. To be Irish was to be Catholic, was to reject abortion. In Britain, the crusade against abortion was fought by a well-organized and cohesive minority whose ancestral Irish identity was turning into or had turned into a British Roman Catholic identity. By the 1930s, the old, fiercely Protestant "no Popery" form of British nationalism had faded and the main cultural conflicts in which Britain's Roman Catholics were involved were with more secular forces in British society, notably over abortion.

The reason for the ferocity with which the British and Irish Catholics have fought against abortion lies in the Roman Catholic Church's adoption in the nineteenth century of the view that a human person exists from the very moment of conception, a statement of certainty about an issue on which most non-Catholics are markedly uncertain. The latter feel that at some time between conception and birth (or even some time after birth) a bundle of cells becomes a person. They aren't sure when, and when non-Catholic legislators and judges in Britain have been called to make decisions about the legality of abortion they have proceeded to fix and alter the conditions under which and the stages in pregnancy at which abortion is permitted or forbidden by a mixture of hunch, intuition, feelings, discussions with scientists and doctors and legal precedent. Obedient Roman Catholics, by contrast, have since the mid-nineteenth century been obliged by the Pope to believe that abortion is totally prohibited at all stages and for whatever reason. Prior to the Holy Father's ruling, Roman Catholics had not been particularly prominent in the movement to ban abortion, but from that time onward abortion became a distinctively Catholic issue.

It is debatable whether, prior to the nineteenth century, abortion before the stage in pregnancy known as quickening was seen as a sin let alone a crime (Brookes 1988: 24-26; Keown 1988: 3-10). As the distinguished theologian and historian Paul Badham (1992: 58) has noted: "for the first 1,900 years of the Christian tradition a distinction was made between early and late abortion...it is not possible to claim that the Fathers of the Church thought that the embryo was a human being from the moment of conception. They did not." However, in the nineteenth century two major changes occurred. First, the physiologists had concluded that pregnancy is a continuous process and that the time of quickening, the point when traditionally ensoulment was thought to have taken place, was of no significance (Brookes 1988: 25; Keown 1988: 12). Second, and for our present purposes more importantly, there was:

The decisive change in the Roman Catholic attitude to the status of the early foetus (which) stems from the proclamation of the dogma of the Immaculate Conception in 1854. In his statement Pope Pius IX affirmed that "the Virgin Mary was in the first instant of her conception, preserved untouched by any taint of original sin" but this is intelligible only if it can be supposed that Mary's personhood and moral sense could be thought of as already present "in the first instant of her conception." Consequently Pius IX found it necessary to break with past teaching and insist that from the moment of conception a human being, with full status as a person, already exists. And so, in 1869 Pius IX dropped reference to an "ensouled fetus" in the grounds for excommunication for abortion, thus making, for the first time, early as well as late abortion a ground of excommunication. This teaching was further explicated in the papal decrees of 1884, 1889 and 1902, which forbade direct termination of a pregnancy even in circumstances where, as in ectopic pregnancies, the result of non-intervention was the certain death of both mother and child. (Badham 1992: 58-59)

The British Attitude toward Mothers Who Kill Their Own Children

The Roman Catholic position in regard to the relative standing of mother and child is in marked contrast to, say, the long-standing British attitude to infanticide where a mother kills her own child shortly after its birth. In their textbook on criminal law, Smith and Hogan (1978) wrote in reference to the 1922 Infanticide Act:

The 1922 Act was itself the result of an agitation over many years during which it was practically impossible to get convictions of murder by mothers of their young children because of the disapproval by public and professional opinion of a law which regarded such killings as ordinary murder. Where a conviction was obtained the judge had to pronounce a sentence of death which everyone except perhaps the prisoner knew would not be carried out. A number of reasons were advanced why infanticide should be considered less reprehensible than other killings: (i) The injury done to the child was less, for it was *incapable of the kind of suffering* which might be undergone by the adult victim of a murder; (ii) the loss of its family was less great; (iii) the crime did not create the *sense of insecurity* in society which other murders caused; (iv) generally the heinousness of the crime was less, the motive very frequently being the concealment of the shame of the birth of an illegitimate child; and (v) where the killing is done by the mother, her responsibility may be reduced by the disturbance of her mind caused by the stress of the birth. (Smith and Hogan 1978: 338, emphasis added)

In 1922, the law was changed so that such a killing need no longer be treated as murder but as the lesser crime of infanticide if the child were newly born, and, in 1938, this was extended to the case of a child under the age of twelve months. The reason that was given was diminished responsibility as a result of birth or lactation, yet as Smith and Hogan (1978: 338) pointed out this may no longer be relevant and in most cases "the relationship of incomplete recovery from the effects of childbirth or lactation to the child-killing is remote." What we may infer from this is that murder was seen as an abhorrent crime in Britain not because of the sanctity of life but because of the suffering it caused. The killing of a newly born child is less serious because its capacity for suffering is less; even *after* its birth it is in some senses only a potential person and not a full and particular person. If someone other than the mother were to kill the child, it would be seen as a particularly vile murder and would provoke public outrage, but it would be seen as a crime against the mother since it would involve the infliction of great suffering on her. The very closeness of the tie between mother and child both diminishes her guilt in killing the child and enhances the culpability of someone else who does so. In theory, a woman convicted of infanticide rather than murder was still guilty of a felony punishable like manslaughter with a possible sentence of life imprisonment. Yet in practice she was usually treated with great leniency. Thirteen women were convicted of statutory infanticide in England in 1955, but most of them were discharged without punishment or given probation and only two went to prison, one for three years and one for twelve months (Williams 1958: 37). Even this causalist, harm-minimizing solution did not go far enough for the radical reformer Glanville Williams (1958: 42), who felt that the authorities should use their discretion and refrain from prosecuting the killing mother altogether in order to save the woman concerned the distress that would result from her being tried in public and convicted with all the attendant publicity. For Williams, the trial itself caused suffering which served no social purpose and he saw it as an unjustified concession to the prejudices of religious minorities obsessed with the sanctity of life.

It is also worth noting in passing that the British treated mothers who killed their older children more leniently than other murderers. Between 1900 and 1949, 45.7 percent of all death sentences for murder in England and Wales were commuted or respited, but in the case of women it was 90.8 percent and only eleven women were executed all told, not because of sex discrimination against men by the Home Secretary but because 102 of the 130 women sentenced to death had killed their own child (*Report of the Royal Commission on Capital Punishment 1949-53* [1953]: 13, 326).

In many other cases, the mother would plead insanity as a defense and if this were accepted she would have been sent to Broadmoor, Britain's criminal lunatic asylum whose female inmates were nearly all there because they had killed one of their own children. It was more or less established practice to keep such women in Broadmoor for three years and then release them (Williams 1958: 42), presumably on the grounds that they neither needed treatment nor constituted a danger to society. Glanville Williams, characteristically, wanted to go even further and to use the law of diminished responsibility in cases of homicide brought into effect in England and Wales by the Homicide Act of 1957 to allow such women to be released on probation immediately (Williams 1958:42).

Roman Catholic Resistance to Abortion in Britain

The opposition to abortion in Britain throughout the twentieth century among the leaders of Roman Catholic opinion has been so much stronger than among the Protestant and agnostic majority that it calls for special consideration. Roman Catholic views on abortion lay outside the mainstream thinking of moral Britain, but the Catholics were Britain's most important minority and no account of the death of "moral Britain" would be complete without a discussion of the decline of the influence and confidence of Roman Catholic Britain.

The Roman Catholics were already prominent in the debate on abortion in Britain in the 1930s. It is notable, for example, that *only* two religious groups were keen to give evidence before the Inter-Departmental Committee on Abortion between 1937 and 1939 or sent written statements to the Committee. One was the Modern

Churchmen's Union, and in particular its most prominent supporter though not member, Ernest William Barnes, the Anglican Bishop of Birmingham, which was concerned to advance the cause of abortion on eugenic grounds, and the other was the Roman Catholics, including the Union of Catholic Mothers, the Westminster Catholic Federation, the Midland Catholic Medical Society, the Catholic Nurses Guild of Great Britain, and the Catholic Women's League. No representatives of the Protestant Nonconformist churches took part or made statements (*Report of the Inter-Departmental Committee 1939*). The Nonconformists who were the leading force in campaigns for temperance and Sunday observance and against gambling and prominent in the causes of pacifism and of opposition to capital punishment had nothing to say about abortion. Opposition to abortion, birth control, and divorce, by contrast, lay at the core of Roman Catholic moral Britain, and of these three things, abortion was the most important. The Protestant Nonconformists were preoccupied with the sins of men (see Martin 1990: 38, 92) and Catholicism with the sins of women and particularly abortion, women's sin against life itself. By definition, men cannot have abortions and a majority of the unskilled back-street abortionists were women. In the 1930s, more than twice as many women as men were convicted of offenses relating to abortion and this represented the real relative involvement of the two sexes as illegal abortionists (*Report of the Inter-Departmental Committee* 1939: 45, 143; Simms and Hindell 1970: 36). No doubt this reflected the nature of the Roman Catholic Church as a celibate all-male hierarchy. By contrast a Nonconformist minister had to take into account the views and feelings of the congregation that employed him, a majority of whom would have been female, and of his wife. By the 1930s, the more democratic denominations, such as the Congregationalists and the Unitarians, permitted the ordination of women, something that is anathema to Roman Catholics. Roman Catholicism represented the oppression of women by men. Protestant Nonconformity had leanings in the opposite direction.[1]

The famous judgment delivered by Mr. Justice McNaughton in *R v Bourne* (1938), which explicitly stated the medical grounds under which an abortion was legal in England, provoked considerable condemnation by leading Roman Catholics. They were particularly alarmed at the judge's comment that it was a doctor's duty to perform an abortion if the mother's life was in danger and that if he or she neglected this duty and the woman died, the doctor could be prosecuted for manslaughter; even worse was his comment that if doctors were conscientiously opposed to this, they shouldn't be practicing in that area of medicine. This was directly contrary to the central beliefs of the Roman Catholics and carried with it the threat of the use of the power of the state against those Roman Catholic doctors who ranked their duty to their church's teachings higher than their legally defined medical responsibilities. The Theologian Father Alphonsus Bonnar lamented that "the Bourne case is merely a symptom of the downward trend of our civilization away from Christian standards. The dechristianization of Europe, which began with the jettisoning of authority at the Reformation has proceeded apace and seems to be approaching its climax. Only God knows whether Europe can be saved" (cited in Simms and Hindel 1971: 79). Father Bonnar's linking of abortion and the Reformation is an indication of how far apart, indeed how opposed to one another were moral Britain and Roman Catholic moral Britain.

The point was emphasized by the response in Britain to Pope Pius XI's reiteration in 1951 of his church's traditional and absolute view that abortion was never permissible even to save the life of the mother, which produced an outraged response from the non-Catholic press in Britain. The Church of England newspapers called the Pope's pronouncement "inhuman, callous and cruel" (Simms and Hindell 1970: 80; Williams 1958: 177). There was no agreement between Roman Catholics and Protestants on a common set of Christian values to be applied to such a situation. Roman Catholic casuists when faced with these objections by the Protestants or agnostics to the sacrifice of the life of a full particular person in this way retreated into the slippery doctrine of double effect, whereby the death of the fetus in life-saving surgery on the mother is defined as an unintended byproduct of a worthy act. This kind of verbal trickery to preserve the integrity of an absolute principle or even of a particular law while permitting exceptions for pragmatic reasons is, however, very common in all legal and constitutional systems and it was unfair of Glanville Williams (1958: 182) to single out the Roman Catholics for special criticism on this point. The doctrine of double effect is not that distant from such British legal fictions as the distinction between infanticide and murder on the basis of an assumed rather than demonstrated diminished responsibility on the part of the mother, or the decision to prosecute the abortionist but not the mother, when the former is really a mere hit-person for the guilty woman being treated as innocent.

In 1952 and 1961, bills to put into statutory form what had become accepted practice in the English courts in regard to abortion were put forward in the House of Commons. The only opposition to them within Parliament came from Roman Catholic MPs of all parties who defeated both Bills by strong organized filibustering; they also talked out two further abortion reform bills in 1965 and 1966. The only strident criticism of these moderate measures for reform that came from outside Parliament was from the Roman Catholic hierarchy and the Roman Catholic press (Simms and Hindell 1971: 81-86; see also Brookes 1988: 154).

The Roman Catholic voters were only about a tenth of the electorate and to a substantial extent concentrated in working-class areas settled by Irish immigrants in the nineteenth century, such as Lancashire, notably Merseyside, and in and around Glasgow where they controlled the local Labour parties. Nonetheless, the ferocity of Roman Catholic letter writers was such as to make politicians fighting to retain or to win marginal seats nervous of provoking Roman Catholic opposition by visibly taking a lead in the politics of reforming the law on abortion. Gerald Gardiner Q.C., later to become a Labour Lord Chancellor, wrote in a letter to a leading proponent of reform:

> I should not feel able to take any personal part with regard to a bill.... I am a Labour candidate in a marginal constituency and as you will appreciate, any marked public support for abortion law reform immediately antagonises the whole of the Catholic vote. (quoted by Simms and Hindell 1971: 81)

When, in 1966, the Liberal MP David Steel proposed to put forward a bill in Parliament to liberalize the law on abortion, he came under strong and hostile pressure from Roman Catholic organizations to get him to withdraw it; there was no such pressure from any of the other major churches. Roman Catholic MPs from all political parties were extremely active and vocal in both debates and committees and once again tried to talk the bill out of existence by the length of their speeches. This brought retaliation and mockery from those MPs who were supporters of reform, "lolling back horizontally in their seats they held loud private conversations, occasionally interjecting remarks such as 'filibuster' and 'Pope'" (Simms and

Hindell 1971: 182). The voting figures show decisively that the opposition to the reform of the law on abortion was strongly Roman Catholic in character. The Roman Catholic MPs voted 9 to 1 against the liberalization of the law on abortion whereas those MPs known to be affiliated to the Free Churches, the most strongly Protestant churches, voted 9 to 1 in favor of reform[2] (Richards 1970: 183).

The supporters of reform tended to be in the Labour and Liberal parties, as did the Free Church MPs, but it is particularly noticeable that the Roman Catholic Labour MPs not only voted against reform but often led the opposition to it. In many cases we do not have reliable information about an MP's religious affiliations, but the MP's whose religion was unknown tended to vote in favor of reform. However, they were less in favor of reform than the MPs listed as affiliated to the Protestant Free Churches. The Anglican MPs were almost equally divided in their voting on abortion, but there were far more of them in the Conservative Party than in the other parties. It is also striking how very assiduous the Roman Catholic MPs were in turning up to vote on abortion, far more so than MPs with Protestant affiliations of any kind. Abortion was a Roman Catholic issue and indeed continued to be, for many of the unsuccessful attempts to curtail the liberal 1967 Act between 1971 and 1992 were sponsored by Roman Catholic MPs (often also with a strong Roman Catholic presence in their constitutencies) from all three of the main parties, notably James White (Labour), John Corrie (Conservative), and David Alton (Liberal, Liverpool, Morsley Hill)—the three MPs who came closest to modifying the law in a restrictive direction. Indeed, Alton did succeed in reducing the time limit for abortions from 28 weeks to 26 weeks in line with medical advances that had made the survival of those born prematurely more probable and thus changed the point of viability which was the generally agreed limit. Alton was not able though to stop late abortions being carried out on eugenic grounds or where there was a serious threat to the mother's life or health.

The Strange Death of Roman Catholic Labourism

In the Roman Catholic countries in Europe, those who wanted to remove the restrictions on abortion tended to be found in the parties of the left, many of which had an anti-clerical ideology and defined themselves in opposition to a Roman Catholic establishment or tradition (Berlinguer 1978, Institut 1981). In Britain, by contrast, a large proportion of Britain's Roman Catholics, until recently, have been found among Labour voters and activists for reasons of ethnicity and social class. In 1966-67, Roman Catholic MPs of Irish ancestry, representing old centers of Irish immigrant settlement in Lancashire in England and Glasgow and Clydeside in Scotland, were at the forefront of the fight against abortion. At that time, the Irish were Britain's largest ethnic minority, with a million people who had been born in the Republic of Ireland living in Britain. Also at least 10 percent of the British population are of Irish descent, most of them being Roman Catholics. Some Polish and Italian Catholics have also emigrated to Britain and there have been a few prominent converts, but in the main to be Roman Catholic was to be Irish, by ancestry (Hornsby-Smith, 1987: 116-20, 131), though most of those of Irish descent had come to regard themselves as English, Scots, or Welsh, depending on where their ancestors had settled. The original Irish emigrants had tended to take up unskilled employment on arrival in Britain, constructing in turn Britain's canals, railroads, and freeways, and working on building sites, as longshoremen and in factories, particularly on automobile assembly lines. When the Irish took part in politics, not surprisingly, they joined Britain's largest working-class party, the Labour party, much as in the United States they were to be found in the Democratic party and in Australia in the Australian Labour party and later in their very own breakaway Roman Catholic party, the Democratic Labour party (Bayor 1978; Herberg 1960; Hornsby-Smith 1987: 44; Pringle 1958: 73-95; Sowell 1981).

In the 1960s, when Labour and Liberal members of the British Parliament turned their attention to social issues such as the reform of the law relating to divorce and abortion, those Roman Catholic MPs of Irish ancestry who were on the left on economic and class issues but socially conservative found themselves trapped. On issues such as the abolition of capital punishment, they had consistently voted the same way as their fellow Labour MPs, but on abortion and divorce they split away from them and voted against reform and were in consequence exposed to strong and. indeed, hostile criticism and pressure from other Labour MPs and political activists, which left them feeling greatly embittered.

The Roman Catholic Labour MPs who voted against abortion were not only heavily defeated by the votes of their fellow Labour MPs on issues about which they felt very strongly, but were also made the subject of unpleasant personal attacks. Simon Mahon, the Roman Catholic Labour MP for Bootle, was particularly angered when the British left-wing journal *Tribune* referred to him and a like-minded group of Roman Catholic Labour MPs as "reactionaries"; the Members of Parliament under attack all represented working-class Lancashire constituencies whose voters were the Roman Catholic descendants of Irish immigrants. Mahon declared in Parliament that it was grossly unfair that such a term should be applied to "Liverpool Labour Members who have spent a lifetime working among slum conditions and trying to get rid of the environment in which we were born...we have spent our adult lives in the Labour movement as did our fathers and grandfathers before us.... I am not a reactionary in any way." (*Hansard,* House of Commons 1966, vol. 738, col.1083).[3] His brother Peter Mahon, one of nine siblings, who was the Roman Catholic Labour MP for Preston South, another Irish Catholic constituency in Lancashire from 1964-1970, was even more upset when it came to the final stages of the Third Reading of the Medical Termination of Pregnancy (Abortion) Bill and it was clear that the abortion reformers had won:

> I have been in politics, a member of the Labour Party, for 44 years and I have never had the word "unworthy" used to me. I hope that I will go to my grave without that word ever having been said to me. I have never been an unworthy member of the Labour movement.... I must calm down. I am rather over-emotional about this.... It has puzzled me that there should be so much support in Parliament for the Measure. I never anticipated that after three years in office the Labour Party would allow such a Bill to come forward. Not in my wildest imagination could I have imagined such a thing.... In the whole of my public life I have never felt so badly about anything as I do about the Bill. (*Hansard,* Commons 1967, vol. 750, col. 1354)

In 1971, Peter Mahon became Britain's first anti-abortion candidate when he stood against his own party in a by-election for the Liverpool Scotland constituency, one of Britain's most fervently Irish Catholic constituencies, indeed, a seat formerly held by the Irish Nationalists. Even so, he won only just over 10 percent of the vote in a mere by-election, but as a result of his candidacy he was expelled from the Labour party. The anger and anguish expressed by the Mahons was not just an expression of their personal feelings but was the last moral outcry of an important ethnic, religious, and political movement in British society: Irish Catholic Labourism. Time had caught up with them. To be of Irish descent was to be Roman Catholic was to be against abortion, a strongly held tribal ethic. Then, quite suddenly, the members of the Labour Party, which represented the social class to which most of the Irish belonged, chose to support the radical reform of the laws relating to divorce and abortion in a way that they could never have envisaged and they were crushed between their church and their party.

Though the Labour Catholic MPs probably did not know it, the late 1960s was also a turning point in other ways for Roman Catholics in Britain. After World War II, British Catholics enjoyed considerable upward social mobility. They became more educated and more flexible and they left the old areas of Irish Catholic immigration of their ancestors to live in middle-class suburbs, where their ancestry and religion were not an issue (Hornsby-Smith 1987: 72-78, 206). Many voted Conservative, both out of conscious self-interest and as an expression of what they had become socially, that is, ordinary middle-class British people. Even more radically, they began to depart from the traditional teachings of their church, especially over questions such as birth control and divorce (Hornsby-Smith 1987: 111-14). Secularization and the fall in church membership and attendance hit the Roman Catholics in Britain later than the Protestants (Brierly 2000; Bruce 1996: 55-58; 2002: 65-66), possibly because many of them had originally lived in immigrant enclaves, which insulated them from change. However, once they had left the old Catholic areas and mingled with mainland Britain's increasingly indifferent Protestant majority, who no longer defined their own identity in opposition to Catholicism in general and Irish Catholicism in particular, they ceased to be a distinctive religious and ethnic sub-culture (Hornsby-Smith 1992: 123-130); Catholicism lost its tribal significance. British Catholicism had a brief moment of triumph when it seemed that the Roman Catholic church alone was maintaining its numbers (albeit with a good deal of help from continued and substantial migration from Ireland to Britain) while its Protestant rivals were dwindling, but then Catholicism itself entered a steep curve of decline (Bruce 1996; 2002: 66). Not merely have the numbers attending mass fallen drastically (Bruce 1996: 29) but those who remain no longer accept what were once seen as eternal certainties.

By the 1990s most of the Catholics of Irish descent in mainland

Britain had become completely assimilated (Hornsby-Smith 1992: 128). In Northern Ireland, the tension between Protestant Unionists and Roman Catholic Republicans continued and national-religious affiliations were, and remain, very strong. In the rest of England, the weakening of collective identities, whether national or religious, has come to the point where no one much cares who is Protestant and who is Catholic or whether your ancestors came from Cork or Coleraine, let alone Cardiff, Corstorphine, or Colchester. The strange death of Catholic Labourism is just one instance of the strange death of many old national-religious identities in Britain and of the moralities that were once strongly linked to them. The absence in Britain of an American-style polarization on abortion between supporters of the right to choose and supporters of the right to life is proof of this.

The Death of Roman Catholic Britain

During the 1997 British general election, right to life groups put up single-issue pro-life candidates in fifty-six constituencies. In some cases, they targeted sitting MPs or new candidates known to be in favor of abortion, but in each case the pro-life candidate polled only a derisory number of votes, even though the Roman Catholic hierarchy had told the faithful to take account of a candidate's views on abortion before casting their votes. The total number of votes for these candidates was 17,335, an average of 345 per seat. Even those who stood in traditionally Roman Catholic areas such as Liverpool and Glasgow did badly with the highest vote for one of their candidates being 1,170 in strongly Roman Catholic East Kilbride. In Liverpool Wavertree the pro-life candidate obtained 346 votes, 0.75 percent of the total votes cast, and in Glasgow Maryhill 344 votes, or 1.16 percent of the total votes cast. They had failed even in the heartlands of Irish Roman Catholic settlement. The pro-lifers fared even worse in the 2001 general election when they were only able to put up thirty-seven candidates. Twenty-six of them came in at the bottom of the poll, well below other independent candidates, some of whom were not merely eccentric but self-consciously foolish. In Cheltenham, the Pro-Life Alliance gained fewer votes than the Raving Loony Party and one of their main leaders gained only 179 votes, slightly more than the Jam Wrestling Party. The *total* number of votes for the Pro-Life Alliance in 2001 was only 9,453 in thirty-seven seats, giving an average vote for the Alliance of 255, with the highest vote only 475.[4] When voters have felt strongly about a non-party issue, then they have been willing to vote for an independent in a particular constituency, even in a general election as we saw in the case of capital punishment. The preservation of the life of the fetus was not such an issue. At the end of the twentieth and beginning of the twenty-first century, opposition to abortion had ceased to be a major political force in Britain, even among members of Britain's oldest, largest, and most important ethnic and religious minority, the Irish Roman Catholics. This manifest coolness about the abortion issue was an unmistakable demonstration of the strange death of Roman Catholic moral Britain, for when the leaders of the British Roman Catholic hierarchy called upon their troops to march in defense of traditional morality, they declined to do so.

Towards the Strange Death of Moral Ireland: The Erosion of the Roman Catholic Church's Moral Monopoly in Ireland

The situation was and is quite different in Ireland. In Ireland Sections 58 and 59 of the English 1861 Offenses Against the Person Act, which only permitted abortion if the mother's life was in danger, remained in force both in the British province of Northern Ireland and in the Republic of Ireland (Institut 1981, Rynne 1982). The British Abortion Act of 1967 did not apply to Northern Ireland and the situation there was ambiguous. There was no such ambiguity in the Republic of Ireland where the existing prohibition of abortion was written into the very constitution of the Republic following the Constitutional Referendum on Abortion of 1983 (Inglis 1998: 82-84).

No other country in Western Europe has had such a monolithic Roman Catholic identity as the Republic of Ireland and until recently the Roman Catholic Church enjoyed a moral monopoly in that country (Inglis 1998). To be Irish was to be Catholic, was to be totally opposed to abortion. In both Germany and the Netherlands, by contrast, there are large Protestant populations who would not permit the Roman Catholics to impose a total ban on abortion in their country, though such an attempt has been made in Bavaria. In France, Italy, and Spain there are strong anti-clerical as well as Catholic national traditions (Martin 1978: 120-26) that date respectively from the French Revolution, the unification of Italy at the expense of the

Papal states in the nineteenth century, and the events in Spain that culminated in the Spanish Civil Wars. A French or Italian or Spanish patriot does not have to be a supporter of the majority church and, indeed, can be openly hostile to it without any loss of national fervor. In the referenda on abortion in Italy, all the secular parties, the Liberals, Republicans, Social Democrats, Socialists and Communists, supported the liberalization of the law in Italy. Only the fascist Italian Social Movement and the Roman Catholic Christian Democrat Party were opposed to the change (Berlinguer 1978). Perhaps the nearest case to that of Ireland was Belgium, the last country in Western Europe to accept reform, where in 1990 the strongly Roman Catholic King Baudoin chose to resign for just one day, so that an act of Parliament permitting abortion could become law without his signature. Nonetheless, and despite the ease with which Belgian women could get abortions in the Netherlands, the liberalization of the Belgian law on abortion was supported by a sizeable parliamentary majority.

Until the mid-1970s the Republic of Ireland was a mighty fortress of traditional Roman Catholicism and church and state were strongly, almost totally, locked together (Blanshard 1954; Inglis 1998). Contraception, divorce, and abortion were completely prohibited and there was a greater degree of censorship of publications than in the other countries of Western Europe; indeed newspapers and magazines from abroad would regularly have substantial sections snipped out by the censor before they were delivered to their purchasers (Blanshard 1954: 89, 97, 107). Homosexual acts between males, even in private, were prohibited by law, and a strong hostility towards homosexuals was prevalent.

It was possible to maintain such a position because Ireland was a homogeneous and isolated island. The vast majority of the population of the Republic of Ireland were Roman Catholic and fervently so (Inglis 1998; Bruce 1986: 152). There was extensive emigration out of but no movement into this distant island on the Atlantic edge of Europe and no significant foreign minorities. The Roman Catholic Church controlled all aspects of life (Inglis 1998), and moral Ireland had a rock-like stability. However, within the last thirty years of the twentieth century, rapid social changes shattered this stability. Some of the most striking of these came from outside and disrupted and broke through Ireland's moral borders in ways that the Irish political elite did not and could not have predicted but to which they were forced to adjust.

Abortion and the Moral Boundaries of Ireland

Abortion, though totally prohibited in Ireland, became in the 1980s a crucial and controversial source of conflict. Anti-abortion groups in the Republic of Ireland were concerned lest a decision by an *external* body such as the European Court of Human Rights or one of the institutions of the European Community might force the Irish to permit abortion on lines similar to the rest of Europe (Hesketh 1990: 351, 354, 387; Holden 1994; 48-49). In order to prevent this, Irish Roman Catholic anti-abortionists obtained and won by a two-thirds majority the referendum of 1983 (Hesketh 1990: 52; Holden 1994; Inglis 1998: 83-84), which made the total prohibition of abortion a part of the Irish *constitution*. Abortion was already strongly forbidden by law and any significant liberalization of this law by the Irish Parliament or by the Irish Supreme Court was very unlikely indeed, so it seems probable that this was an attempt to safeguard Ireland's moral borders against external penetration.

Confronted with a ban on abortion at home, thousands of Irish women sought abortions abroad, especially in Britain (Rynne 1982: 19, 22-5). The Irish authorities tried to prevent this by stopping them from obtaining the information necessary if they were to locate and contact British abortion clinics (Holden 1994: 165, 180-81) and by restricting their right to travel to other countries for this purpose. However, these prohibitions could have been overruled by the European Community (the E.C. now the E.U.), as they violated the principle of the freedom of movement of persons, services, and information throughout Europe. In 1991, to forestall any such move, the Taoiseach (Irish prime minister) Charles Haughey talked the European foreign ministers into accepting an Irish-sponsored amendment to the Maastricht treaty saying, "Nothing in the Treaty on the European Union or in the treaties establishing the European Communities or in the treaties or acts modifying or supplementing those treaties, shall affect the application in Ireland of Article 40.3.3 (i.e., prohibiting abortion) of the Constitution of Ireland" (Holden 1994: 185). Haughey's aims were to strengthen the Irish ban on abortion and to stop any attempt to give Irish women the right to travel to other countries to obtain abortions; in this way, he could buy off

Roman Catholic anti-abortion opposition to the overall Maastricht treaty in the subsequent Irish referendum on the treaty. The rapidly growing Irish economy was heavily dependent on European grants, subsidies, and markets (Holden 1994: 183) and Haughey knew that the other European countries were keen to avoid the embarrassment of an anti-Europe vote in the forthcoming Maastricht referendum in Ireland and were thus highly susceptible to blackmail. In this way he sought to reinforce Ireland's moral borders against the influence of Europe; the other European countries were far more concerned with economic, financial, and monetary issues and in order to get an agreement on these they were prepared to allow Ireland a degree of local moral autonomy. The forces of economic continentalization were thus shown to be capable of being manipulated by the political elite of a small and socially threatened country trying to secure its moral borders. The most staunchly pro-life Roman Catholics, however, remained fearful of the impact of the European Union on Ireland's independence in relation to abortion. In April 1992, Mr. Justice O'Hanlon was sacked as president of the Irish Law Reform Commission, only one month after he had been appointed to the post. The new Taoiseach, Albert Reynolds, said it was inappropriate for a president of the Law Commission "to express publicly views which tend to suggest to the Government how the policy of the state should be formulated." Mr. Justice O'Hanlon had argued that Ireland should abandon its membership of the European Union rather than permit abortion in Ireland (http://www.cin.org/archives/cintuus/199806/0022.html).

A further crisis arose in 1992 when a pregnant girl aged 14, well under the Irish age of consent and the victim of unlawful carnal knowledge, who had traveled to England with her parents to seek an abortion was compelled to return to Ireland by the Irish attorney general. The family was told that if the abortion went ahead in England they would be severely punished when they returned to Ireland. The Irish Supreme Court later ruled that the girl, 'X', should be allowed to seek an abortion abroad because a psychologist testified that she was suicidal and that her life was in danger (*Attorney-General v X and others* (1992), I.R.1 at 66-70, 90; Holden 1994: 140-3;). The Irish judges refused to refer the question of her right to travel under European Community law to the European Court of Justice in Luxembourg; they declared that this was a matter for Irish law alone.

In 1992, the European Court of Human Rights awarded damages and costs of £IR200,000 (Irish pounds), about $300,000, against the Irish government, which was held to have violated its citizens' human rights in 1988 when the Irish authorities had ordered the Dublin Well Woman Centre and Open Line Counselling to stop issuing information about abortion (Holden 1994: 180-81; *Open Door Counselling and Well Woman v Ireland* (1993) 15, E.H.H.R., 244). The European Court of Human Rights noted that Ireland had breached the Convention for the Protection of Human Rights and Fundamental Freedoms. As had happened previously in the case of male homosexuality, the moral boundaries of Ireland were shattered and the values of Europe prevailed over the local and particular morality of Ireland. The Irish government tried to avoid the negative implications of these rulings for its image in Europe by sponsoring new and complicated referendum questions on abortion and, in November 1992, Irish voters decided (by a two-thirds majority in each case) in favor of both the right to travel for this purpose and the right to obtain information about abortion facilities abroad. It was one more indication that Ireland's moral boundaries and moral identity had foundered, in part at least because of critical decisions made by two external European institutions to which Ireland was now irreversibly committed.

Ireland's moral boundaries and particular moral identity were thus eroded by the institutional imperialism of the European center which forced this small country on the periphery of Europe to accept the norms of the hedonistic, individualistic, and rights-obsessed core of Europe. Individuals in Ireland are freer in consequence, but Ireland is now less Irish. That country is now less morally distinctive than it was and is becoming a mere suburb of Europe. However, Irish moral identity with regard to abortion continued to be defined in a nationalistic way, but against Britain where Irish abortions took place rather than abortion-permissive Europe as a whole. This was vividly revealed in a letter to the *Irish Times* of 28 February 1995, written by Father Tom Ingoldsby of Salesian House, Portlaoise, Ireland, in which he strongly criticized the Irish Labour Party's attitude to abortion referrals and to the provision of information about facilities for abortion outside Ireland, which he called "complicity in murder." Father Ingoldsby wrote:

> Yet it is intolerable that overseas magazines be allowed to carry adverts for so-called "clinics"—in reality baby extermination centres. This too must be outlawed.... We have

been sickened by the killings in the North over 25 years. We are still more sickened by
the daily killings of Irish pre-born babies in British abortuaries.

The *dichotomy* between Irish good and British evil, between home
and overseas, between innocent Irish pre-born babies and murderous British abortuaries was further emphasized by Father Ingoldsby
in his deliberate use of the Irish Gaelic phrases, *A chara* and *Le
meas*, to begin and end his letter in place of the standard English
language forms such as "Sir" and "Yours" more usually found in
letters to the *Irish Times*. It is unlikely that he was merely brushing
up his Erse. Father Ingoldsby was very definitely defending a *national* morality and a *national* identity. There was nothing peculiar
about his doing so for he was writing from the rural heart of Ireland
where moral issues were still perceived in national terms.

Further External Threats to Moral Ireland

At the beginning of the twenty-first century, the future of the Irish
ban on abortion, which embodies the unchallengeable central values of a distinctive Irish and Catholic moral identity appears uncertain. In the 1992 abortion referendum, despite the concessions on
travel and information, Irish voters had rejected the section that would
have permitted abortion when due to illness or disorder that was a
real and substantial risk to the mother's health (Inglis 1998: 220).
Abortion was still only possible if there was a direct threat to life.
But what if, as in the 'X' case in 1992, the pregnant woman or girl
threatened to take her own life? The 14-year-old 'X' had been specifically allowed to seek an abortion in England because she was
suicidal, but by implication this was also a valid ground for abortion
in Ireland, since there was a direct threat to her life. In 2002, a further referendum on abortion sponsored by the Irish government took
place in order to block off this possible loophole, and to prevent
women from threatening suicide in order to get an abortion. The
Taoiseach Bertie Ahern warned that a "No" vote would pave the
way for the same liberal abortion regime as in Britain and at masses
across the country priests read out letters from their bishops pressing parishioners to vote "Yes" and calling the referendum "An opportunity not to be missed." The electorate rejected the government's
proposal, albeit by a very small margin indeed, on an ambiguously
worded question with more than one clause. What is most relevant
to any discussion of social change in Ireland is that afterwards the

Irish bishops expressed disappointment at the defeat of the referendum proposal and the Family Planning Association thanked those who had voted "No."[5]

The next undermining of resistance to abortion in the Republic of Ireland may well come from an external threat to moral Ulster, much as the victory of Ulster homosexual Mr. Dudgeon led inexorably to that of homosexual Senator Norris in the Republic in the European Court of Human Rights. Mr. Dudgeon's victory was assisted by the political tie between England and Wales, where homosexual acts were permitted, and Northern Ireland where they were not. It was difficult to justify such a difference within a single legal and political system, particularly at a time when devolution had been suspended.

In 1994, the Standing Advisory Commission on Human Rights in Northern Ireland declared that the law on abortion in Northern Ireland (the old law of 1861 as modified by case law in the English courts) was so unclear that it would not stand if a case were taken to the European Court of Human Rights. Between 1997 and 1998 there were only seventy-seven medically induced abortions carried out therapeutically in Northern Ireland's hospitals, but 1,572 women from Northern Ireland were recorded as having therapeutic abortions in England in 1997, making a total of 40,000 since 1967, and this greatly underestimates the total since many more will have given an address in England to the provider. This was an anomaly since it meant that women from Northern Ireland incurred greater costs and had later abortions than their English counterparts, even though they enjoy common citizenship. Furthermore, five women have died from back-street abortions in Northern Ireland.

In 2001, the Family Planning Association was granted leave for a judicial review of the providing of abortion rights in the province. The FPA had claimed that the Department of Health was acting unlawfully in failing to issue guidance on what abortion services were available in Northern Ireland, and in what circumstances, and in failing to provide proper public health care to women with unwanted pregnancies. The situation in Northern Ireland in 2002 was uncertain in the same way as it had been in England and Wales prior to 1967 when abortion seemed to be legal if there was a serious threat to the health of the mother, but no one was entirely sure. One of the reasons for the 1967 legislation was to make the law clear by statute, but in the process it was also considerably liberalized. The opponents of abortion in Northern Ireland are fearful that this was the family planners' aim in calling for judicial review and that in the long run they will succeed. The human rights lawyer Lord Lester, Q.C., representing the Family Planning Association, spoke of the unnecessary burden faced by women in Northern Ireland and said that the Department of Health must ensure that under European Human Rights legislation women had proper access to termination.[6]

In the past, the European Court of Human Rights has refused to hear cases about abortion whether brought by those in favor of abortion or by those against. It is quite clear that a ruling could be made on the basis of a variety of clauses in the European Convention on Human Rights. However, in the past whereas a decision could be made against Ireland over homosexuality because a majority of Council of Europe countries did not have such legislation, in the case of abortion there were strong differences of views between the more strongly Roman Catholic countries and the Protestant or secular members. Hence, there was no *agreed* criterion on which a decision could be based and the Court is once again revealed as not so much a court of human rights as a court committed to *Gleichschaltung,* a court seeking to bring into line those countries that diverged from the European norm and make things uniform.

In the case of abortion, there was no such norm and if a case had come before the Court seeking to restrict or expand the grounds on which an abortion could be granted then the Court would have taken refuge in the doctrine of "margin of appreciation," that is, leaving the individual countries to balance the claims of rights and morality for themselves. Depending on the degree of divergence between the laws of the members of the Council of Europe the degree of margin of appreciation allowed by the court can be broad (as would have been the case with abortion) or narrow (as was the case with homosexuality). Unlike the U.S. Supreme Court in *Roe v Wade* (1973), the E.C.H.R. is not going to strike down the abortion legislation of several European states at once. The European Convention on Human Rights does not represent a system of checks and balances designed by those suspicious of the power of government, but rather seeks to make countries conform to a modal point representing the position taken by a majority of its member states. Where, as in the case of abortion, there was no clear mode, the European Court of Human Rights was stymied, and in the case of Ireland could only rule on peripheral matters such as the right of Irish women to information about abortion facilities in other countries.

However, the peculiar circumstances of Northern Ireland may (if a reconvened Northern Irish Assembly, the British Parliament, and English judges now able to apply the European Convention as part of domestic law all prove unsympathetic) in the future lead the European Court of Human Rights to rule that the women of the province are entitled to the same local access to abortion as other British subjects. Should this happen, pro-abortion activists in the Republic of Ireland will also bring a case to the E.C.H.R. and there are now, apart from Ireland, very few members of countries of the Council of Europe in which abortion is totally prohibited. Moral Ireland could well be slain by foreign judges. Defeat over homosexuality was damaging; defeat on abortion would be devastating for an independent Irish moral identity.

The continued rapid pace of social change in Ireland in the early years of the twenty-first century, however, may well lead to the Irish choosing by themselves to topple this last pillar of moral Ireland, much as they have chosen to legalize and extensively use artificial forms of contraception (Inglis 1998: 226-67) including ones, such as I.U.D.s, that permit conception but prevent implantation and which involve the destruction of a genetically unique zygote, which, from a Roman Catholic point of view, is a human being. Indeed, one of the ambiguities of the complicated Irish referendum question on abortion in 2002 was whether it confirmed or undercut the legality of contraceptives that prevent implantation. In a letter dated 8 January 2002 to Cardinal Re, Prefect of the Congregation of Bishops in Rome, the former Irish Supreme Court Justice, Roderick J. O'Hanlon, deplored among other things the fact that in 2001 the Irish government had in proposed legislation spoken of "unborn life after implantation in the womb of a woman"[7] (www.theflanagan.com/abortionreferendum2002/frames/roryohanlan2.htm; December 2002).

The Waning of Moral Ireland

By the end of the twentieth century, the Roman Catholic Church's influence and power in Ireland was waning. Although it had been successful in preventing sterilization, artificial sterilization, and amniocentesis from being available even in public (as distinct from Catholic voluntary) hospitals in 1997, it failed to prevent the provision of a vasectomy clinic in Letterkenny, in the heart of rural Ireland. The clinic's operation was briefly suspended due to picketing by Pro-Life groups and opposition from the local Roman Catholic bishop, Bishop Boyce of Raphoe, who called it a rejection of God's gift of life, but soon reopened with the explicit support of the Irish government (Inglis 1998: 226).

It may now simply be a question of time before pressure from Irish voters themselves leads the guardians of Irish morality and identity into losing a more vital referendum on abortion that will force the Irish Parliament, the Dáil, to enact a rather more liberal law on abortion. Vox populi will have defeated vox Dei, and a distinctively Irish moral identity will have been dismantled by the will of an anonymous aggregate of Irish citizens. Oddly, it will have been made possible by the greater degree of democracy built into the Irish constitution in 1922 at British insistence than was or is the case in Britain. Already in 2001 an opinion poll revealed that 60 percent of Irish women aged 18-34 wanted easier access to abortion facilities (*Ireland on Sunday*, 28 October 2001), and every year 7,000 women travel to Britain for abortions. When abortion does become available in Ireland it will mean the strange death of moral Ireland. Moral Britain and moral Ireland will be united in death. The islanders will both live in a similar demoralized world of rootless individualism in which there is neither British nor Irish, neither Catholic nor Protestant. The process would have been even faster but for the conflict in Ulster.

Religion in Ireland declined much later than in Britain but also faster, with a turning point around 1990, after which Mass attendance and attendance at monthly confession fell and belief in a personal God became transmuted into belief in a mere impersonal lifeforce. Most remarkable was the decline in the numbers of those wanting to enter the priesthood and even more so, the religious orders. In 1966, there were nearly 600 vocations to orders of religious sisters in Ireland, but in 1996 only nineteen, and there was only one vocation to the various orders of religious brothers. In the past, Ireland exported priests to Britain, but between 1966 and 1996 the number of vocations to become diocesan clergy fell by nearly 80 percent and to clerical religious orders by 90 percent (Inglis 1998: 212-13). The decline in the numbers of those willing to bind themselves completely to a hierarchical, "greedy," and, in some cases, total institution (Coser 1974; Goffman 1961), and a life of service, sacrifice, and subordination is an index of a total transformation of an Irish society that had been based formerly on the ideal of self-denial and the surrender of individual interests to those of family and community. Not surprisingly, the death of religious Ireland was accompanied by the death of respectable Ireland. There was a marked rise in crime and drug abuse in late twentieth-century Ireland and the proportion of births outside marriage rose from 2 percent in 1961 to 20 percent in the 1990s, with one in three of first births being illegitimate (Inglis 1998: 240). It was the death of that respectable Ireland that had been created in the late nineteenth and early twentieth centuries partly in emulation of moral Britain and partly in opposition to it. Moral Britain was emulated because it was moral and repudiated because it was British and Protestant. This national dialectic was replaced from the 1960s onward by the same creeping disease of rootless individualism that had already afflicted Britain. Indeed, Ireland may well have caught the disease from Britain, for the early undermining of moral Ireland came through the enticing plural and permissive images available from British television transmitters in Wales, often aided by boosters and later supplemented by cable. It could not be subjected to the same kind of censorship as books and newspapers and it undermined the Roman Catholic Church's moral monopoly, much as West German and Austrian television had undermined the political monopoly of the East German government. It may well be that the strange death of moral Britain led to the decay of moral Ireland. Ireland was seduced by the beguiling and betraying quality of British television with its affluent glitter, its flaunted sexuality and, above all, its lack of deference towards, and its sidelining and even mockery of figures of authority such as priests and bishops (Inglis 1998: 246). Once this pattern was familiar and accepted in Ireland the local media produced its own version and in particular revelled in clerical scandals that in a previous generation would have been successfully hushed up. Those acquainted with the activities of the Irish teaching order known as the Christian Brothers have always known, and said in private, that it contained a substantial minority of sadists and predatory homosexual pedophiles who tormented and exploited their charges, but the power of the Roman Catholic Church and universal deference to it ensured that such matters were never discussed in public. Once the mold of deference had been broken in the 1990s every single act of cruelty or illicit sexuality perpetrated by a priest or a member of an order, sometimes long ago (Inglis 1998: 216-19, 291-303), sometimes merely alleged, sometimes probably fictitious, was dragged out into the open as part of a hysterical denunciation of an entire institution, much as had happened in the far more plural societies of Australia, Britain, Canada, and the United States. Anti-clericalism had come to Ireland not as a foreign import but as a local product, not as a form of resentment of a church that was strong but as an attack on one that had been weakened by indigenous social changes, as the bitterness of those whose loyalty and affection had been betrayed.

However, moral Ireland still had far more life in it than moral Britain at the beginning of the twenty-first century; even though its rate of decay had been faster than that of Britain, it began later. Ireland will only have caught up with Britain if and when abortion becomes legal and widely available. The prohibition of abortion is the central defining element both of Irish morality and of Irish identity. Should it crumble it will mark the death of moral Ireland.

Notes

1. In Latin America, the Roman Church opposes birth control and crusades against abortion (Rahaim 1969). The now expanding and flourishing Protestant churches in Latin America may well also be against abortion but their most distinctive characteristic is their willingness to curb machismo. From the women's point of view abortion is *not* a family issue, but restraining the man of the household from squandering its resources on drink and gambling is (Martin 1990: 181-82). Protestant pastors and their wives tend to see the point and act on it. An ounce of Protestant ethic is worth more to women than a ton of liberationist theology. Or, as the Europeans would say, 28.35 grams of Protestant ethic is worth more to a woman than 1016 kgs. of liberationist theology.

2. The relationship holds up even when other factors such as party affiliation are allowed for.

3. He was speaking not in a debate on abortion but on the Sexual Offences Bill concerning the decriminalization of homosexual acts.

4. These voting figures were found on www.prochoiceforum.org.uk/comm18.asp, December 2002, but their source is the official electoral returns published after each election. The compilers were probably being malicious, but the facts are accurate and representative

5. www.cathtelecom.com/news/202/46.php; www.ifpa.ie/campaigns/abortion/ref.html; www.rnw.nl/hotspots/html/irelando20305.html; www.katolsk.no/nyheter/2002/03/

04-0002.htm; www.cnn.com/2002/world/europe/03/04/irish.abortion/; December 2002.

6.   www.cnn.com/2002/world/europe/06/13/nireland/abortion/ab-northireland.html; news.bbc.co.uk/1/org.uk/northire.html; www.spuc.org.uk/releases/20010508.htm; www.johnstonarchive.net/policy/abortion/ab-uknorthireland.html; December 2002

7.   Rory O'Hanlon gave a carefully considered legal opinion that the proposed Twenty-Fifth Amendment to the constitution of Ireland was an attack on the very integrity of the constitution and amounted to the repeal of sections 58 and 59 of the Offences Against the Person Act of 1861. He described the Taoiseach's original proposal as intrinsically evil. The amendment does seem to have been ambiguous given the odd patterns of support and opposition it produced. Justice O'Hanlon, a member of Opus Dei, was strongly pro-life. See also www.iol.ie/~hlii/commentary-factsheet.html; February 2004.

6

Conclusion

Each of the preceding chapters outlining a different facet of the strange death of moral Britain has been reasonably self-contained and so this final section seeks to build upon the conclusions arrived at in each of the chapter and also to provide a tentative overall assessment of the losses and, indeed, gains incurred due to the strange death of moral Britain. In the twenty-first century, this can only be done from within the causalist mode of thinking that has now become dominant in Britain. We began by looking forward and we now end by looking backwards. Before doing this, however, it is worth reminding ourselves that many aspects of moral Britain, notably the era of respectable Britain, were only a phase, perhaps just an interlude, in the history of a rough people. Curiously, the death of moral Britain has been accompanied by the equally strange rebirth of the Liberal England (or rather the Liberal Britain) that George Dangerfield (1936) thought was gone forever. The coincidence reveals how little direct relationship there was between moral evolution and the mainstream British politics of electoral competition of the twentieth century, a politics of material things that never resulted in serious internal conflict or violence, in part because moral absolutes were never at stake. The peculiar nature of the one exception, the violent conflicts over the secession and sovereignty of Ireland strengthens the argument about the stability of Great Britain itself. In all other respects, violence in Britain has rarely had anything to do with social conflict; it has been merely the sum of the crimes of egoistic individuals seeking excitement, gain, or the fulfillment of spite.

Finally. brief comparisons will be made between Britain and other closely related societies, notably the United States, but also Ireland and Sweden, whose experience of moral change has been in many respects similar to that of Britain, but in other more interesting ways, very different. Such a comparison naturally brings us to the problem of the "dog that did not bark in the night" (Davies 1998), the unimportance of any talk about entrenched rights in Britain until towards the end of the twentieth century. Britain's national identity, for hundreds of years, has been closely tied to the idea of British liberty and opposition to foreign absolutism and to pride in the fact that its people have been far more free than they were in other more restrictive and authoritarian European countries. The new European "rights and fundamental freedoms," by contrast, are a major threat to a post-moral Britain that has lost its moral confidence. The growing power and intrusiveness of the European Court of Human Rights is going to prove a serious threat to Britain's constitutional and democratic traditions. When the British dismantled moralist Britain they did so in their own way, in their own time, and for their own reasons, even in those cases where essentially similar changes occurred in many other countries. Moralist Britain jumped off the tower of tradition when it was ready to do so, in contrast to moral Ireland, which was pushed. So far as Great Britain was concerned, for most of the last half of the twentieth century, the European Convention on Human Rights, which the British had not only signed but helped draft and its subsequent alien enforcer, the E.C.H.R., were merely a cloud no bigger than a lawyer's hand. By the beginning of the twenty-first century that cloud showed signs of becoming a fog through which the British people will stumble, blinded, confused and angry. The response of the British government to losing numerous cases in the E.C.H.R. of incorporating the Convention into domestic law is a reckless and dangerous constitutional innovation. If we shift the emphasis within the phrase "moral Britain" from "moral" to "Britain" it should be clear that what will be at stake in the twenty-first century is not the moral Britain of 1900 or 1925 or 1955, all of which have long vanished, but the existence of Britain as a nation that makes its own decisions about law and morality.

What follows is, in some respects, a set of reflections rather than conclusions. Indeed it is also of necessity a set of speculations and I do not propose to document them in the kind of detail that was vital to the construction of the substantive chapters. However, the reflections and speculations do rest on top of the conclusions of those earlier chapters and the reader may find a brief recapitulation of these helpful:

1. The last half of the nineteenth century and the twentieth century saw the rise and fall of respectable Britain, a process directly linked to the rise and fall of the influence on popular morality of institutions, notably the Sunday Schools, rooted in religion. It was thus indirectly linked to the rise and fall of the confidence, commitment, and strength in numbers and resources of that section of the population that was sufficiently imbued with religion to invest time, resources and, most important of all, commitment in the running of these institutions. The changes are reflected in and best measured by what I have termed the U-curve of deviance, the fall and subsequent rise of crime, illegitimacy, and drug and alcohol abuse, a U-curve whose turning points were World War I and the latter half of the1950s.

2. There has been a decline in moralism with its emphasis on autonomous individuals who were free to choose either virtuous innocence or deliberate guilt and to whose choices society responded with appropriate forms of reward, protection, and penalties. It was replaced by causalism, especially in regard to policymaking, namely the minimizing of harm regardless of moral status. Both this change and the decline of religion and respectability are related to the rise of large, bland, impersonal, and contractual institutions for the administration of production or welfare that are far more concerned with the smooth working of their everyday rules and activities than with matters of individual character or morality. They can neither demand nor expect strong loyalties nor a sense of duty beyond the call of contract.

3. There has been a loss of commitment to and identification with religion and country, and in consequence a loss of the idea of service and sacrifice and the moral imperative of duty. One welcome byproduct of the worrying weakening of Britain's identity and boundaries has been a movement towards the toleration and acceptance of homosexuals and their sexual behavior.

4. The political defeat and inner decay of both Conservative hierarchical moral Britain and Roman Catholic moral Britain has resulted in a curious triumph for an utterly secularized version of non-conformist Protestant individualism. It is curious because it was accompanied by the almost total eclipse of the nonconformists, now a lost culture (Munson 1991), and the collapse of the respectability that they had so strongly fostered. Roman Catholic Ireland followed a different trajectory but we may predict the strange death of moral Ireland within the early decades of the twenty-first century.

Before and After Respectable Britain

The rise and fall of respectable Britain is an account of changes that took place between the mid-nineteenth century and the end of the twentieth century. It makes no claims about what went before, nor strong predictions about the future. Respectable Britain is dead but the British social order has survived and there is no reason to suppose that it is going to collapse for purely internal reasons. Societies with low levels of respectability and high levels of deviant behavior do persist and adapt, albeit uncomfortably and with a certain loss of pride and confidence.

Moral Britain has died, but there still exists a British society that continues to function more or less adequately, even though religion and its associated morality have withered away. People do not have to be good for their societies to be viable. By the end of the twentieth century, individuals in Britain had adapted to high levels of crime by installing burglar alarms and more sophisticated locks on their homes and cars, and this frustrated the criminals, such that car theft and burglary actually fell in the late 1990s. Staff in casualty reception in hospitals have been issued stab-proof vests and local police forces have instructed the public on how to avoid being mugged, the advice being based on interviews with experienced muggers who have been happy to share their expertise with potential victims. Likewise, sending more people to prison may have had an effect, in that those in jail, who, on average, claim to have committed 140 crimes a year (250 in the case of regular drug users)[1] are prevented from committing further crimes for the duration of their sentences. These material substitutes for respectability may be unsatisfactory but they do help to preserve order and security; when morality fails, other more expensive and coercive remedies are always available. Crime affects two-thirds of Britain's larger companies every year (*The Times, Business,* 21 April 2003: 19), but the cost is passed on to customers, and the loss to shareholders and thence to pension-holders; it gets lost among other larger economic shocks.[2]

More generally, it would be foolish to project the changes of the last half of the twentieth century forward into an imagined future Britain in which crime cripples all honest endeavor, family life is nonexistent, and drunkenness and addiction ubiquitous. Projecting trends, whether linear or exponential, into the future is dangerous as many demographers, economists, psephologists, and investors in the stock market have discovered to their cost; observers of shifts in morality should learn from this to be cautious. Readers who have hoped, expected, or feared that I would conclude with predictions of total disaster will be disappointed; skeptical pessimism is the best I have to offer.

I make this mild comment partly in response to the criticisms of my original account of the U-curve of deviance put forward in 1983 (Davies 1983) by Gertrude Himmelfarb (1994: 234). She wrote of my U-curve that: "It might be more accurately described as a 'J-curve' for the height of deviancy in the nineteenth century was considerably lower than it is today." However, the use of the term "J-curve" has quite unjustified implications, both for what may have happened in the more distant past and for what the future may bring. The use of a J rather than a U shape suggests inevitable, accelerating, and apocalyptic future increases in levels of crime in Britain, rather than the once and for all shift from a low crime to a high crime society that I have called the strange death of respectable Britain. No simple prediction about twenty-first-century crime rates can be made; they may rise, they may fall. In post-respectable Britain, there will be marked short-term fluctuations driven by demographic and economic factors (Davies 1986) and by the hardening of targets and of penalties. Crime rates will, though, remain at a high level and will never return to the very low levels that characterized the last years of the nineteenth century and the first half of the twentieth. The same point can be made in relation to fatherlessness, or drug and alcohol abuse. Severe problems have come to stay. The forces that created moral Britain had dwindled by the 1990s to the point where they were largely unimportant. Little further decline in a religion-driven respectability is possible because the fortunes of the religious institutions are already at such a low level. Why should the right hand side of the U-curve continue to rise?

Himmelfarb's preference for a J-curve likewise implies that there cannot have been a period prior to the mid-nineteenth century when levels of crime were comparably high with those of the last decades of the twentieth century. Yet such limited and speculative evidence as we have suggests that levels of violent crime were far higher in the *distant* past than they have ever been in the twentieth century (Hanowalt 1979: 45, 98-101, 270-73). Indeed, Gurr (1989: 304-15) has suggested that homicide rates, that is, murder *and* manslaughter taken together and by implication the incidence of other serious violent assaults, were several times higher in the thirteenth century than at the present day. Lane (1992: 37) has called Gurr's description of the long decline in the incidence of homicide and violence in England down to the mid-twentieth century, followed by a rise in the last half of that century, a "huge reverse J-shaped curve." Given the much longer time span (more than six hundred years) during which homicide rates fell relative to the last fifty years of the twentieth century during which they rose, it makes as little sense to speak of a reverse J-curve as of a J-curve. My only purpose in citing this long-run study is to indicate the arbitrariness of Himmelfarb's decision to begin her study with the 1840s, when crime, as measured by the numbers of people committed for trial, peaked prior to the birth of respectable Britain (Himmelfarb 1994: 225; see also Alison 1840, vol. 2: 97-8, 317, 325; Gatrell 1980: 239; Phillips 1977: 141-47; Jones 1992: 30-43, 241).

It is quite possible that this peak in malefactors being brought to trial was merely a result of the introduction of the first modern and reasonably efficient police forces by the Metropolitan Police Act of 1829, the Municipal Corporations Act of 1835, and the County Police Acts of 1839 and 1840 (Phillips 1977: 189; Gatrell 1980: 280-81). It was now possible for the first time effectively to detain and prosecute substantial numbers of criminals, rather than haphazardly to seize and in some cases to execute a small proportion of a large number of violent and dishonest individuals. It is, of course, far beyond the scope of this book to speculate as to levels of crime in the very early years of the nineteenth century and before. The point being made here is merely the skeptical one that whereas we can be reasonably certain at the beginning of the twenty-first century that persons and property are far more at risk from crime than was the case in 1955 or 1925 or 1905, we cannot say whether they are more at risk than they would have been in 1750 or 1800. Indeed, the opposite might well be the case and the same point can be made in relation to the proliferation of foundlings and gin-swiggers in the eighteenth century. We have no reason to suppose that the high levels of deviance in contemporary Britain are unprecedented and we should settle for the more modest claim that they were far higher at the end of the twentieth century than in the late nineteenth century and the first half of the twentieth. The British do not live in a uniquely amoral and dissolute age. They have "merely" destroyed the respectable Britain that they had previously created and then sustained;

respectable Britain was a phase in British history, not a natural state that an unnatural generation has abandoned.

Looking Backwards

The account given here of the strange death of Moral Britain began by asking how the changes that have taken place would have been perceived by an imaginary person traveling forward in time, one who was firmly embedded in the assumptions of moral Britain, and assessing how he or she would have been surprised and shocked by its death. It is now time to look backwards at that same transformation and given the prominence achieved by the moral perspective I have called causalism, it is appropriate to look back at moral Britain and assess it in those terms. It is, of course, impossible even to attempt to estimate the overall increase or diminution in harm resulting from the strange death of the former moral order. To do so would only demonstrate how difficult it is to use causalism in other than a very narrow context. Besides, everything else has changed. How could one isolate the impact of the death of moral Britain from that of other equally important changes in the course of the twentieth century? All that is really feasible is to take the particular changes that have already been analyzed in detail and to assess the losses and gains. It is possible that on this basis a causalist would be able to argue that the strange death of moral Britain has actually benefited the individuals who make up that country (Davies 1988a).

As a result of the liberalization of the laws on abortion, many women have been freed from the suffering associated not only with back-street abortions but with years of stress that could result from the bearing of and caring for numerous unwanted children. Whether or not a fetus can feel pain, it cannot suffer in the same way, for it cannot contemplate its own situation or its own demise. The abolition of capital punishment has taken away from the state the power to inflict a major form of suffering on a particular known individual and to curtail completely that individual's existence. Unlike the fetus, the person executed has hopes, plans, expectations, and relationships and thus a capacity for suffering. It is perhaps significant in this context that those Europeans who claim that capital punishment as exercised in the United States is cruel and unusual and who oppose the extradition of murderers to America to face trial are as much concerned about the sufferings of those on death row as they are about the executions. Dostoyevski (1955 [1869]) would have seen the point. From a causalist point of view, the American concern for equal justice and due process that leads to such delays is thus in itself a cause of suffering and all suffering is to be deplored. Whether the abolition of the death penalty in Britain has caused even more suffering elsewhere, as a lower level of deterrence has led to more killings, is a matter unresolved by the statisticians, but these victims are mere statistical persons who can less easily be fitted into causalist calculations.

There has been a significant whittling away of the harm done to Britain's male homosexuals, not just by arbitrary criminal prosecutions but by social stigma and the associated need for secrecy, by enforced sexual deprivation, by blackmail, and the deliberate aggressions of others which could not be reported or prevented. All of these forms of harm have been reduced, though by no means eliminated. Male homosexuals experience far less suffering imposed by others in post-moral Britain than they did in moral Britain. It would not be unreasonable for them to look back at the past and say with feeling in the British and Australian idiom, "Bugger moral Britain!" Why should they regret the passing of a moral order that persecuted them first as a byproduct of the maintenance of British identity and boundaries and then as a scapegoat for the decay of family life?

By contrast, the massive growth of both acquisitive and violent crime, the breakdown in family life creating fatherless families of many kinds, and the resurgence in drug and alcohol abuse, particularly since 1955, have inflicted great harm on a very large number of individuals. The time-traveler from 1900 would condemn these changes as the growth of wickedness and an index of the collapse of that self-control that is a necessary, if not sufficient, condition for virtue. The twenty-first century causalist would point to the harm inflicted on the victims of crime and to the increased number of children growing up without fathers. Families without fathers are, even when judged by narrowly causalist standards, not alternative families but inferior families. The fact that the best examples of these families are better for their children than the poorest examples of the traditional English nuclear family is an irrelevance. Those who use it as an argument are not merely insulting the numeracy of their audiences but are guilty of a dishonest attempt to distract our attention from the very clear evidence that, on average, even when all other social variables are held constant, children are badly harmed by being deprived of the kind of stable, if often flawed, family life that most of them enjoyed for, say, the first two-thirds of the twentieth century (Booth and Crouter 1998; Cockett and Tripp 1994; Flood-Page et al. 2000; Sweeting et al. 2000; Whelan 1994). Children are harmed by being deprived of a full family life, which includes a father, ideally a biological father, and it is a harm that stays with them for the rest of their lives, a harm that they, in turn, transmit to their own children. It is not necessary to postulate that families in the past were idyllic when pointing out that children without fathers are not only worse off themselves but also, as a consequence of their lack of a father, are more likely to harm others and indeed to harm other children. Likewise, the return of drug abuse and public drunkenness leading to disorder and aggression (a problem that had all but disappeared by 1925) in the latter years of the twentieth century creates harm both for the abusers, whether aggressive drunks or obsessional and desperate addicts, and for those unfortunate enough to be in contact with them. A society that permits its members extensively to damage one another in any of these ways causes far more harm than a respectable and judgmental society that represses these forms of deviance through forms of informal social disapproval that include, where appropriate, stigma and social exclusion.

Politics Before and After:
The Irrelevance of Conventional Politics

One notably striking aspect of the strange death of moral Britain is the extent to which it took place outside conventional British politics, the politics of electoral competition between parties. In the case of the birth and death of respectable Britain, the important changes took place in the realm of spontaneous order outside the plans and policies of the state, and with the exception of temperance they were not subjects of electoral competition between the parties. In the case of the changes in the laws relating to moral issues enacted by Parliament, these were kept out of electoral politics; they were a matter for individual MPs. The fundamental cleavage in outlook between Conservatives and non-Conservatives was very much present, notably in relation to capital punishment, but in a way quite different from the politics of the material world that for most of the electorate most of the time in twentieth century Britain was British politics. If the moral issues had been placed before the people either as contested electoral issues or in a referendum, they might well have been re-solved quite differently. We can see, for example, from the nervous way in which politicians handled proposals for the abolition of the death penalty that the people would have upheld it for murder but not for desertion from the army. For what they are worth, the opinion polls always showed consistent support for the execu-tion of at least some categories of murderer (Cameron 2002: 139; Christoph 1962: 44; Erskine 1970; Tuttle 1961: 71). It is difficult to say what would have happened in the case of the decriminal-ization of homosexuality, given the widespread combination of strong prejudice against male homosexuals, particularly among working-class males, the group most likely to vote Labour, with a gen-eral reluctance to see the law used to deprive people of their liberty. The liberalization of the law regarding abortion would probably have hap-pened much earlier and the old restrictive law would have been at-tacked and eliminated as a "law for the rich," for they alone were able to get round it.

However, all this is speculation. There has been no open politics of abortion or capital punishment in Britain of the kind that has been so prominent in the United States, which is now a far more moralist and far less secular society than Britain and one where the checks on direct democracy are legal and constitutional, rather than, as in Britain, a matter of custom. Likewise the politics of law and order and of respectability in Britain has been largely a matter of mere rhetoric and small adjustments. Respectable Britain was neither cre-ated nor dismantled by the state. It is difficult to see, for example, how official crime or penal policy in Britain was ever of anything other than marginal significance in the massive fall and rise in crime that has been discussed. The changing policies implemented and to a large extent manipulated by the Home Office might just as well never have happened for all the impact they had.

In Britain, even the politics of temperance was temperate. Before World War I the anti-Conservatives pursued a political agenda of restricting the availability and consumption of alcohol and the Con-servatives opposed them. It was a particularly popular policy with the Nonconformists who supported the Liberal Party. There was never any possibility of such a politics culminating in the imposition of a national policy of prohibition. Drinkers were inconvenienced but never threatened. The anti-Conservatives' only substantial gain in the enforcement of respectability occurred during World War I when the conservative forces in society whose main concern was with wartime efficiency and orderliness were willing to support their efforts. There was never a victory for drys over wets. Britain remained respectable in the 1920s at a time when there was a marked upsurge of crime in the United States precisely because in Britain there was no attempt to enforce respectability by law. There was in Britain a willingness to deal with deviant markets in other ways and a realization that suppressing them by law in the name of morality does not work. The same point may be made in relation to prostitution, which has never been made illegal in Britain, merely subjected to a variety of restrictions in how and where it can operate.

Where problems have arisen, as in the case of abortion and off-course betting in the past, the black markets of the 1940s driven by price control and rationing, and more recently in relation to recreational drugs, it has been because the British state has departed from the path of moderation. Trying to discourage demand by suppressing supply in the name of morality creates and produces the same kind of unintended if entirely foreseeable consequences as attempts to suppress markets for more purely economic reasons (Block 1976; Neal and Davies 1998). At this point, powerful and valid causalist objections to moralist policies of suppression are raised, but it is often difficult to reach an agreement as to where the point of minimum harm lies. Estimates of the net harm caused by imposing, retaining, or abolishing a particular restriction are skewed by the differing moral outlook of the protagonists, and the ghost of moralism lurks behind all decisions about harm reduction (Davies 1997); we can see this in the British controversies about needle-exchange schemes, about the imposition of a level of taxation of tobacco, which has led to smuggling or about the sale without prescription of drugs that induce early abortion.

The strange death of the moral Britain that flourished before World War I may be contrasted with George Dangerfield's *The Strange Death of Liberal England* (1936), a death that never really happened. The respectable Britain and Nonconformist Britain that were so much a part of "Liberal England" have disappeared, and viewed from the twenty-first century they seem strange and remote. Yet in many ways Liberal England survived and was born again in the 1990s as "New

Labour." We can now see that it is "Liberal England's" rivals that have died. The remnants of a Conservative England based on dominance and hierarchy and the tight unity of the United Kingdom were defeated by the rise of New Labour and the revival of the Liberals as the Liberal Democrats in the general elections of 1997 and 2002. "Old Labour" England, which was rising in power before World War I, died with the Trade Union movement in the 1980s. Britain has also seen the strange death of Socialist Britain, for it was only the ruthless jettisoning of the fantasy of collective ownership and central planning within the Labour Party that enabled New Labour to come to power in 1997. The strange, or perhaps not so strange (Shtromas 1981), death of the Union of Soviet Socialist Republics in 1991 also helped socialist Britain into its grave. The "Liberal England" of global free trade, home rule, promises of welfare, high-minded talk of internationalism and a resolute opposition to hierarchy and dominance had returned. Ninety years on, the suffragettes had been embraced, the Ulster Unionists squashed, and the labor unions tamed. "Liberal England" had triumphed against its enemies after all. All that had really died was moral Britain, not "Liberal England," and it did not die as a result of political conflict. Moral evolution and political conflict have been largely unrelated in Britain. Those who argue otherwise have confused crime and conflict even though the former is an individual and the latter a collective phenomenon. Political violence has been rare in Britain, except when it has spilled over from the conflicts in Ireland over the sovereignty of that island, and labor disputes in Britain, though common, have been remarkably peaceful and law-abiding by the standards of other countries. There never has been any significant link between industrial conflict and crime in Britain. In South Wales in the late nineteenth (South Wales Colliers 1875: 52-58) and early twentieth centuries, the low crime rates of a Nonconformist Protestant people existed alongside the frequent and protracted labor disputes that often characterize coal mining regions. There was no U-curve of conflict in Britain, nor have political conflicts distracted the police from recording crime in Britain; conflict has been neither an incentive to nor a substitute for crime. It makes no sense to study the U-curve of crime in connection with political conflict; it belongs with the U-curves in illegitimacy and drug and alcohol abuse for crime is a form of individual moral failure, not of protest.

How is Britain Different?

Many of the changes that make up the strange death of moral Britain have no doubt also taken place in other Western societies, notably in the rise and fall of respectability. A U-curve of crime is to be found in the history of Sydney and in that of Stockholm (Grabosky 1977; Grabosky, Perrson, and Spurlings 1977; Gurr 1977). Sweden is one of the few European countries besides Britain whose continuity has not been interrupted in the twentieth century by invasion or civil war and it seems to be characterized by a U-curve of deviant behavior that is essentially similar to that found in Britain ; presumably this signifies the rise and fall of respectable Sweden. Jerzy Sarnecki (1985) has independently linked the Swedish U-curve in crime to the evolution of the Swedish welfare state in a very similar way to the account given of Britain in chapter 1. Subsequent Swedish commentators have, rather predictably for Sweden, suggested that the key factor might be the U-curve in alcohol consumption. National trends in alcohol consumption in Sweden in litres per capita for the years 1851-1988 show a U-curve trend that matches the Swedish U-curve for homicide and assault quite well both in its general pattern and in its short-term fluctuations, the details of which are strikingly similar to what happened in Britain. The U-curve for repeated theft also matches the long-term trend in alcohol consumption, but, as in Britain, the *short-term fluctuations* in theft and alcohol consumption moved in opposite directions in the nineteenth century and indeed this remained true until after World War II. In hard times in the nineteenth and early twentieth centuries, the Swedes stole but could not afford to get drunk (particularly since the state restricted the supply and controlled the price of alcohol in Sweden) and in good times alcoholic excess led to a rise in assault and murder. Swedes are inclined to see shifts in recourse to alcohol in Sweden as the crucial forces driving their entire U-curve in crime. Rather it makes sense to ask why all these U-curves in homicide, assault, theft, and overall alcohol consumption in a society with a tendency toward binge drinking and an unfortunate mode of drunken deportment fell and rose together. What lay behind this pattern? It is possible, and I would hope a Swedish scholar could investigate this, that the fortunes of religious institutions rose and fell in Sweden over this time period in a way similar to the British experience; certainly by the late twentieth century Sweden had become one of the most secular countries in the world.

Studies of particular cities in the United States suggest that the U-curve model also characterizes the United States (Lane 1992: 35), though in such a diverse country where for much of the period there were no national statistics it is difficult to be sure. Nonetheless, the work of Wilson and Herrnstein (1985: 430-37) does seem to confirm that there was a U-curve in deviance in the United States and they relate it to a "changing investment in impulse control," which would, of course, have been tied to the fortunes of America's religious institutions.

However, the very strength of religious institutions in the United States has led to a fiercer politics of respectability than was the case in Britain. In both countries, adherence to the standards of respectability grew in the nineteenth century through the activities of voluntary institutions, but in the United States this came to be supplemented both then and in the early twentieth century by attempts to enforce respectability by law, which tended to destroy what they were trying to preserve, notably at the time of Prohibition. The British Conservative elite who were opposed to this kind of populist imposition of morality ensured that there could be no prohibition experiment in Britain. In consequence, Britain was able to avoid the upsurge of crime that disrupted the low point of the U-curve in deviance in the United States in the first half of the twentieth century. The British Conservatives did not like experiments in the name of moral uplift. Politicians in Britain never seriously tried to eliminate altogether the markets for alcohol, gambling, and prostitution that catered to male pleasure; they merely sought to restrict and regulate them. The female and popular Protestant forces, such as the W.C.T.U. (Women's Christian Temperance Union) that sought to enforce virtue by political means in America, were never as strong in Britain. Their militant attitude was abhorrent to British Conservatives who had strong ties to the all-male hierarchical institutions (see W. Churchill 1930: 64-71; R. Churchill 1966: 232-34) in which men constrained men and where male vices were tolerated, provided that they did not threaten order and discipline. Such Conservatives were strongly hostile to male homosexuality, which they saw as a threat to the stability of the male hierarchies, but drink, gambling, and prostitution could be tolerated. The opposition to male weaknesses was female and the Conservatives were the masculine party. For the Conservatives male aggressiveness was to be channelled and placed at the service of society, not suppressed as something fearful.

The weakness of religious and moral fervor in Britain relative to the United States or Ireland in the latter part of the twentieth century accounts for the absence in Britain of culture wars over abortion, homosexuality, or capital punishment. There was still skirmishing over these issues in Britain at the beginning of the twenty-first century, but they were not a source of major division within the society. Britain's Roman Catholic minority is smaller and less powerful than that of the United States where it controls certain states, and this has reduced the level of conflict over abortion. Also Britain lacks the kind of moral majority Protestantism that in the United States gave added strength to the crusade against abortion and provided support for capital punishment and opposition to homosexuals and their sexual practices. In the United States, prospective judges of the Supreme Court are nominated, cross-examined, and approved or rejected on the basis of their attitudes toward abortion. In Britain, abortion is no longer a political issue that could excite that kind of interest and concern.

In Britain, the Nonconformist Protestant denominations have always constituted a counterculture opposed to an established church; in the twentieth century they came to oppose capital punishment, which was taken as a symbol of the power of the ruling hierarchies. emigrated to America, they became the dominant culture in that country (Martin 2002: 103); they knew this and their confidence in their own position affected their perception of capital punishment. In America capital punishment was not seen as the symbol of a traditional hierarchy to which they were opposed but as the will of the people and as God's universal and eternal instruction to Noah. In time, many leaders of the main Protestant denominations in America, as in Britain, became liberal in their theology and in their interpretation of the Bible, and in line with this, their attitudes towards capital punishment and homosexuality changed. However, in the United States, in marked contrast to Britain, there remained a substantial population of unchanging fundamentalists and a strong growth of new and flourishing hard-line denominations also appeared; both of these groups were strong upholders of traditional morality. The same elements existed in late twentieth-century Britain and indeed showed greater powers of survival than the more liberal denominations, but with the exception of Northern Ireland, they were small and unimportant. They had neither cultural influence nor political clout. Because these denominations were weak—but were not perceived as "minorities" to be cosseted—they did not have to be appeased and indeed were often treated with an unpleasant degree of disregard that amounted to discrimination. They were not allowed, for example, to own radio or television stations and those who control these media have an informal policy of excluding them from broadcasting altogether. The "religion" section in British bookshops does not contain paperbacks full of moral exhortation in favor of retaining capital punishment or denouncing homosexuals, except, of course, in Northern Ireland. U.S. paperbacks such as William H. Baker's *On Capital Punishment* (1985) (formerly *Worthy of Death* [1973]) or E. Lagard Smith's *Sodom's Second Coming* (1993), which integrate social and political data and analysis with biblical quotations seen as unchallengeable revealed truth, do not have popular British equivalents. It is not that there was any lack in Britain of individuals who support capital punishment or were hostile to homosexuals, merely that there were no sizeable institutions with a Bible-based morality that could legitimate their views by reference to the word of God. The U.S. or Irish politics of morality were and are simply baffling to most people in Britain, as indeed they are to the citizens of most of the highly secularized countries of north-west Europe.

In chapter 3, the abolition of capital punishment in Britain was related to the decline in the significance of the British hierarchies that exercised force on behalf of the state. It is a point that is reinforced by comparisons with its abolition in other Western democratic societies. There is a curious relationship between the power and external assertiveness of individual European countries and their willingness to execute those found guilty of murder. The first of these countries to abolish capital punishment for murder were Portugal (1867), the Netherlands (*de facto* 1860, formal abolition 1870), Belgium (*de facto* 1863), Denmark (*de facto* 1892s), formal abolition 1930), Sweden (*de facto* 1910, formal abolition 1921), Iceland (1928), all of them small, neutral *pays fainéants,* who hoped that by remaining passive and quiet and avoiding provoking others they could hide away from the wars of their more powerful and assertive neighbors, protected by their very inability and unwillingness to fight.

The second group of countries to abolish capital punishment were those such as Germany and Italy, which had engaged in a politics of deliberate external aggression and the wanton use of capital punishment that had led them to total defeat, disaster, and ignominy. In Italy, Mussolini's death penalty was abolished by decree in 1944, and the outlawing of capital punishment altogether was part of the basic law of the new Federal Republic of Germany when it was set up in 1949. The third group of countries to give up capital punishment were the former major imperial powers, Britain (1965) and France (1981), who did so after they had lost their empires (Amnesty International 1979; Amnesty International 1989).

The United States, now the world's lone superpower, is the only Western democratic country to retain capital punishment. It is powerful and well armed, and even willing to act to pre-empt an attack from outside, in contrast to the feeble and demographically declining countries of Europe, most of which are unable to defend themselves. The United States has a confident sense of its own special destiny and is willing to ignore and defy external and international pressure, notably in relation to capital punishment. There is a principled willingness in the United States to employ force to achieve good ends; whether it is always employed wisely, or even sensibly, is another matter. Britain, too, once had this kind of imperial power and a sense of destiny that was central to its people's sense of what Britain was. Even now there is a very un-European resilience about Britain, shown by its willingness to fight and win the Falklands War at the other end of the world and its partnership with the United States against Iraq (see also Ashford and Timms 1992: 90; Harding et al. 1986: 94). In contrast to other European countries, support for capital punishment continued to be strong in Britain long after its abolition in 1965; an opinion poll as late as 1989 suggested that 89 percent of its people were in support (Cameron 2002: 139). This in marked contrast to the widespread indignation found elsewhere in Europe at the continued employment of capital punishment in the United States and expressed through popular campaigns against the extradition of U.S. murderers who have fled to Europe to avoid arrest and trial; these campaigns also draw indirectly upon a widespread resentment in Western Europe of the United States's overwhelming military strength. Britain does not fit easily into the supposed dichotomy between the United States, the warrior country, and a timid, feeble, over-civilized Europe.

Britain avoided the U.S. culture wars over abortion, capital punishment, and homosexuality not only because Britain is far more secular than the United States but also because of the absence in Britain of the kind of entrenched fundamental legal rights seen as central to U.S. national identity. The free availability of abortion in America is based on the woman's right to privacy in her dealings with her doctor, a right that has been constructed by the U.S. Supreme Court from various elements in the United States constitution in *Roe v Wade* (1973) and building on the precedent of *Griswold v Connecticut* (1965). In Britain, abortion is not a right but merely something permitted by Parliament under specified circumstances. The British medical profession's liberal interpretation of the permitted circumstances is such that in effect there is abortion on demand. Women have less difficulty in practice in obtaining abortions in Britain than they do in most U.S. states, partly because many of them do not have to pay for it; abortions are provided under the National Health Service, which is paid for by the taxpayer. The provision of abortion is not a right but something provided by the British welfare state within the limits of what it can afford, in exactly the same way that it might pay for the treatment of arthritis or pneumonia, for vaccinations against flu, for in-vitro fertilization, or sex change operations or for contraceptives, some of which work by inducing early abortions. These benefits are in no sense rights, since it *can* not be specified as a matter of right how much and what kinds of medical or quasi-medical services shall be made available to an individual; that depends on the decisions of politicians who levy taxes and fund the N.H.S. and on the bureaucrats and doctors who allocate resources within it. Welfare is a substitute for rights; it provides protection for individuals against the insecurities of life. There is a parallel here with the far greater volume of private litigation in the United States concerned with personal injury, malpractice, and accidents than is the case in Britain. In Britain, people tend first to look to the state to provide the medical treatment, compensation for loss of earnings, and even *"counselling,"* which are seen as appropriate responses to such misfortunes. In the United States where such assistance is often not available, personal insurance cover patchy, and the cost of medical treatment very high, an individual's first and only resort may well be to phone one of the many and aggressively advertised "no win, no fee" lawyers who will process his or her claim for damages against a real or imagined perpetrator. In Britain, the government provides ambulances, in the United States lawyers chase them. In Britain, state administrators and regulators with their tribunals and committees lie at the heart of society, not, as in the United States, lawyers and the courts. They are alternative means of both redress and frustration.

Likewise, during the campaign to abolish capital punishment in Britain, little use was made of the argument that it was a "cruel and unusual punishment" forbidden by the British Bill of Rights of 1688.[3] (At that time the death penalty was not seen as cruel and unusual and was widely if erratically employed.) It was not open to British judges in the twentieth century to rule that changing notions of what is "cruel and unusual" eliminated the use of the death penalty. Senior judges did not like the way in which the royal power to pardon, that is, to commute a sentence of death to one of life imprisonment, was exercised on behalf of the monarch by the Home Secretary (a government minister advised by civil servants) because it was not subject to due process or external scrutiny, but there was nothing they could do about it. Between 1957 and 1964 British judges were outraged by the workings of the Homicide Act because it did not provide equal justice for those convicted of murder; however, they had no choice but to carry out the will of Parliament. Individuals were executed or not executed according to categories based on deterrence and if an individual was convicted of a capital murder the death sentence was mandatory. Neither the judge nor the appeal court could take into account the aggravating or mitigating circumstances involved[4] in a particular individual case. When deciding sentence they had to carry out the law as enacted by a Parliament that was sovereign. The senior judges, the Law Lords did play a part in the eventual abolition of capital punishment in 1965 since they saw abolition as the only way to eliminate what they saw as offensive anomalies, but they did so as legislators, as individual members of the House of Lords, not as judges sitting in court. The British have government not by lawyers but by men.

The lack of formal constitutional individual rights enforced by judges in Britain did not mean that Britain was a less free society than the United States, merely that British liberty was maintained in other ways, namely by tradition, by popular sentiment, by the vigilance of MPs and peers, and by the way in which individual judges extended the common law and interpreted the statutes. Britain was a free society created by the spontaneous interaction of individuals with a shared culture of individual freedom and independence. The Bill of Rights of 1688 guaranteed fair trials free from arbitrary interference and ensured that the executive would not have the means to govern by physical force alone but it also enshrined Parliamentary sovereignty. Parliament could legislate as it saw fit and no Parliament could bind its successors to retain a particular law, even one that upheld an essential liberty. The Britain that emerged in the eighteenth century was not a notably equitable society, but it was a free society especially when compared with its absolutist European neighbors. It was also the ancestor of another free society, the United States, much of whose original Constitution and Bill of Rights was a codification of British ideas and traditions as seen by colonists who in the main were the descendants of British emigrants.

The basis of British liberty was not rights but good government, government that did not override the liberties of the people partly because those who had political power and influence themselves believed in liberty and partly because they did not have at their command any sizeable standing army or even national police force. They would have been unable to crush the resentment and disorder that would have followed any attempt to circumscribe seriously what were seen as the traditions of liberty of a society of free individuals; even more important the British elite would have been badly divided by such an attempt. When police forces were established in Britain in the early part of the nineteenth century they were unarmed; since then the use of soldiers to maintain order has been both rare and unpopular with public opinion.[5] English individualism was a social reality; there was never any occasion for an assertion of the rights of man.

Looking back over the twentieth century, it would be difficult to argue that a Britain without rights was a less free society than the United States; in some respects it was more free and in some ways less, but overall the difference between the extent and degree of freedom enjoyed by right-full America and rightless Britain was small. The American tradition of enforcing freedom of speech by a legal decision of the courts is a thoroughly admirable one, but in many cases it has had to be employed to resolve infringements of free speech that would not have arisen in Britain in the first place. Likewise in Britain there was no need for a *Griswold v Connecticut* (1965) to protect the rights of those wishing to obtain and use contraceptives. There was no restrictive law in existence to be struck down. The United States has had more need of rights because of its relative lack of informal and traditional checks to the exercise of moral and political indignation.

The libertarian reader will no doubt point out that the laws operative in Britain criminalizing homosexuals and prohibiting abortion were an infringement of liberty and a contradiction of my claim that Britain was a free society. It is a strong point and I have no wish to contest it. I would merely point out that Britain liberalized its abortion law by act of Parliament earlier than the great majority of U.S. states and more radically than most of those that did, and six years before *Roe v Wade* (1973) was decided by the Supreme Court. At the very end of the twentieth century, the U.S. Supreme Court still had not extended the right to privacy laid down in regard to contraception and abortion to the practitioners of sodomy.

Rights are neither a necessary nor a sufficient guarantee of liberty. In unfree countries such as the former Soviet Union, declarations that their citizens have constitutional rights are meaningless, a hypocritical attempt to legitimize vicious societies in which individuals have little freedom and lack even the security of their own lives (Lamont 1952: 68-89; Rummel 1990). Likewise, the Tasmanians had a point when they were able to show that some of the members of the U.N. Committee on Human Rights deciding the case against them, discussed in chapter 4, came from societies with despotic governments. In a society such as Britain, where freedom was assured, there never has been a need for formal rights and their introduction would have proved a nuisance for it would have impeded and distorted the evolution of that country's established tradition of freedom. In a free society, rights are not about liberty, they are about power, about the question of who the guardians of freedom shall be, about whether they shall reside in a Parliament or in the judiciary. The values of individualism and freedom are distinctively Anglo-American and are shared by few countries outside the English-speaking world, even those with democratic institutions (Harding et al. 1986: 78). The United States sought to express and preserve these ideals through a written constitution to which was added a set of strongly entrenched rights and Britain did not. The values are shared but the traditions are different. In Britain, law is a means to an end, whereas in the United States it takes on a quasi-sacred quality. The idea of rights enshrined in law is central to the definition of what the United States is; take it away and there would be no America. However, the opposite is also true, for to impose a cage of rights on Britain, a cage alien to its entire history and tradition, would be to destroy Britain itself. Yet this is precisely the threat that faces post-moral Britain in the twenty-first century, as we have already seen from the experience of Britain's closest neighbor Ireland.

The Threat of the European Court of Human Rights

The European Court of Human Rights is a powerful institution with an alien way of thinking to which Britain's politicians have stage by stage subordinated ever larger portions of Britain's moral autonomy. When Britain became the first country to ratify the European Convention on Human Rights and Fundamental Freedoms in March 1951 no changes were made in domestic law or in the workings of the legal system. It was assumed, perfectly reasonably, that the law and the legal system as they stood were sufficient to provide any remedies necessary for the upholding of the rights and freedoms outlined in the Convention on any reasonable interpretation of the text. It was never envisaged that the interpretation of the Convention would evolve in ways that would undermine Britain's constitutional traditions and indeed British sovereignty. Major problems only really arose after it was decided by Britain in 1966 to allow individual British citizens to bring cases to what had become the Convention's watchdog, the European Court of Human Rights. The problems that have arisen are two-fold. First, there are the problems that have arisen in many democratic countries since World War II from the ambition of judges to usurp the power of the elected politicians (Berger 1994); in Britain this was held in check by a strong tradition of parliamentary sovereignty that was respected by the judges. This was now undermined by the E.C.H.R. and in a way that led to the second problem, namely that judges from countries with completely different legal and political traditions were able to erode Britain's independence. What is now at stake in the twenty-first century is not the preservation of moral Britain, for that has vanished, but the power of the British people, expressed through their own institutions to make their own decisions rather than to have them imposed from outside.

When male homosexual behavior was decriminalized in England and Wales in 1967 the armed forces were by general agreement specifically exempt from the new dispensation (*Report of the Committee on Homosexual Offences* 1957: 122, para. 144; *Hansard,* House of Commons 1966, vol. 738, cols. 1073-4, 1109; House of Lords 1966, vol. 266, cols. 709-10). However, there was a shift away from the use of courts-martial to try those detected in homosexual acts and then impose severe punishments on them. Instead, the armed forces tried to prevent anyone with a homosexual orientation from joining and automatically administratively discharged those of its members against whom evidence of homosexuality could be found or who had been informed on, even if their conduct while on duty had been entirely satisfactory (Hall 1995: 5-6). Homosexuality gradually ceased to be regarded as morally disgraceful, but it led to automatic expulsion. The rationale was that the presence of such individuals would tend to disturb the comradeship of tightly knit groups of males in combat and also that homosexual relationships might cut across the boundaries of rank; either way it was bad for discipline. The new perception of homosexuality as an orientation rather than mere wanton activity led to increased numbers of expulsions and of women as well as men. What had once been a largely invisible phenomenon, though when detected severely punished, now became the subject of intrusive investigation.

In the late twentieth century, it became difficult to justify excluding in this way patriotic gay men and lesbians who merely wanted to serve quietly and unobtrusively in Britain's armed forces; far too many individuals with an exemplary service record were suddenly having their careers cut short and their lives disrupted by a sudden investigation based on rumor or a malicious informant. A man who was seen in a gay pub, a servicewoman sharing a flat with a female civilian, the possession of the wrong kind of magazines, an indiscreet letter that fell into the wrong hands might be enough to end a promising career. The leaders of Britain's armed forces pointed out justifiably enough that their institution did not and could not operate according to the liberal rules that prevailed in civilian life and that those entering one of Britain's all-volunteer services knew this when they enlisted. They even carried out a survey of a random sample of those serving in the armed forces that indicated how strongly its members were opposed to any relaxation of the rules against homo-sexuality (*Report of the Homosexuality Policy Assessment Team* 1996).

In time, however, Parliament would probably have overridden the views of the army leadership, much as it had done in relation to the abolition of capital punishment for desertion in 1930. By the 1980s the influence of the traditional hierarchies was weak in an essentially commercial Conservative party that sought to civilianize the army. In the 1980s and 1990s, civil law was increasingly used in the military sphere and the standard civilian regulations derived from legislation such as the Health and Safety at Work Act 1974 and the Employment Protection Act 1978 applied to the armed services at all times except during actual conflict. From 1987 onward, it be-came possible for the first time for members of the armed services to bring civil actions against the Crown if injured on duty and there was a seven-fold increase in negligence claims against the Ministry of Defence between 1991 and 1996. Those injured in these peace-time accidents were better treated than servicemen wounded in battle (Brazier 1998: 65-67; Frost 1998: 15). The taking of risks by the individual in the interest of comrades, regiment, and country, which was the distinctive feature of the armed forces, was, in peacetime at least, subordinated to other considerations.

It was thus likely at the end of the twentieth century that the ban on homosexuals and lesbians serving in the military would soon be discarded. It would have been discarded for the causalist reason that the harm suffered by particular individuals due to the ban was greater than any harm it precluded; the military leadership's fear of loss of control was, as in 1930, unjustified. In particular, it could have been argued that in the period before 1967 when homosexual acts were seen as morally disgraceful, the armed services had done little to investigate and detect them and indeed had consciously ignored the flagrant involvement of some of their members in homosexual pros-titution. In both Britain and the United States so long as the soldiers and sailors concerned did not take on a passive role their behavior was not even defined as homosexual (Ackerly 1971: 90, 118-19, 176-77; Chauncey 1991: 229-317; Harvey 1971: 104-12; Melly 1978: 14, 26, 36, 67-77, 93-104, 170-73). The armed forces had not screened out homosexual conscripts during and after World War II with any degree of thoroughness and had on the whole chosen not to notice the existence of homosexual behavior among men for whom it was not a preference but a response to being isolated from women for long periods of time (Smith 2002). The homosexual orientation of those who were administratively discharged from the armed forces had often been known for a long time before to those working with them; indeed in many cases they continued working together and sharing the same sleeping quarters while the case against the person to be discharged was being processed (Lustig-Prean 1999; *Lustig-Prean and Beckett v United Kingdom* 2000 E.H.R.R. 548 at 557 para. 21). None of these phenomena seemed to have ever reduced the fighting capacity of the armed forces, so why was there a need for a ban?

However, this British way of resolving the question was never tried because of the intervention of the European Court of Human Rights. In 1995, former Royal Navy Lieutenant-Commander Duncan Lustig-Prean, former RAF Sergeant Graeme Grady, former RAF nurse Jeanette Smith, and former Royal Navy weapons engineer John Beckett, all of whom had been dismissed from the armed services because of their sexual orientation (rather than for any specific acts or conduct), despite in each case an exemplary service record and good relations with their colleagues and senior officers, sought judicial review in the English High Court. They sought to have quashed the decisions that had been made to discharge them from the armed forces and to have these decisions and the policy underlying them declared unlawful. None of them had committed homosexual acts on duty, on armed services premises, or with other service personnel.

Their lawyers argued that the Ministry of Defence policy to discharge individuals automatically on the basis of their homosexuality was "irrational" and in breach of the European Convention on Human Rights. The High Court judges and later the judges in the Court of Appeal refused their application, on essentially constitutional grounds. The judges in the appeal court noted that "the constitutional balance in this country between the courts and the executive is a delicate one," and declined to intervene in a matter involving the defense of the realm, an area on which they, by reason of their limited experience, were not well equipped to form a view and which had long been recognized as unsuitable for judicial review (*R v Ministry of Defence ex parte Smith* (1996), Q.B. 517 at 535). They ruled that the European Convention on Human Rights was not part of domestic law and so was inapplicable. The petitioners had also hoped that the judges would apply the Wednesbury principles developed under the common law to decide that the Ministry of Defence's general and absolute policy of excluding homosexuals regardless of circumstances and without exception was "irrational," that is, that it could not be related by a process of logical reasoning to a central and legitimate purpose of the institution. The Ministry of Defence opposed this, saying that the ban was there to safeguard the morale and unit cohesiveness necessary to operationally efficient and effective fighting units and that the presence of homosexuals would endanger the trust and respect necessary for cohesion and performance between all ranks.

There was little chance that the applicants would succeed. In order to prove the "irrationality" of the ministry's policy they would have had to show that it was "plain beyond sensible argument that no conceivable damage could be done to the armed services as a fighting unit" (*R v Ministry of Defence ex parte Smith* (1996) Q.B.517 at 541). There was nothing peculiar about the various courts' decisions. The judges were merely applying the correct if very high threshold for ruling that a policy or decision was irrational that had been applied in previous cases of a more mundane kind. It was indeed the appropriate test to apply. The judges followed precedent and in keeping with British constitutional tradition were not prepared to depart from it merely because the lawyers for the complainants argued that this was a question of human rights. The complainants sought leave to appeal to the highest court in England, the House of Lords, but leave to appeal was refused by the Appeal Committee of the House of Lords on 19 March 1996.

In 1999, Lustig-Prean and Beckett and Smith and Grady took their cases to the European Court of Human Rights and won. The European court ruled that the Ministry of Defence's policy of excluding personnel on the basis of mere orientation and not just conduct when on duty, and also the exceptionally intrusive investigations to which it inevitably gave rise, constituted a grave interference in the private lives of the applicants (*Lustig-Prean and Beckett v United Kingdom* [2000] 29 E.H.R.R. 548; *Smith and Grady v United Kingdom* [2000] E.H.H.R. 493). The European Court conceded that such interference could be said to pursue the legitimate aim of safeguarding national security and preventing disorder but added that it was not "necessary in a democratic society" to override the complainants' rights in the pursuit of these aims (*Lustig-Prean and Beckett v United Kingdom* [2000] 29 E.H.R.R. 548 at 549). The most important criterion for judging this was that the great majority of the countries making up the Council of Europe had no such regulations excluding homosexuals from their armed forces. It was, therefore, concluded that the British government's policy was disproportionate to the aim pursued (*Lustig-Prean and Beckett v United Kingdom* [2000] 29 E.H.R.R. 548 at 552).

In saying this, the court used its power to impose on Britain and its armed services decisions made by politicians in other European countries with quite different constitutional traditions and often without a particularly lengthy experience of stable democracy. Whereas the U.S. Constitution was a codification of an existing democratic tradition, some of the Council of Europe countries had adopted written constitutions to compensate for and guard against a repetition of their past record of dictatorship, persecution, and genocide or even as a way of pretending that these things had never happened. Such constitutions are often a substitute for a careful regard for the freedom of their individual citizens that is taken for granted in the Anglo-Saxon countries.

It is clear from the written judgments that the members of the court showed a complete lack of understanding of British constitutional conventions (*Lustig-Prean and Beckett v United Kingdom* [2000] 29 E.H.R.R. 548 at 579 para. 79). The Cypriot judge, Loukis Loucaides, who would have had an acquaintance with British traditions and English law, dissented from his fellow judges on the grounds that the court had not allowed a "sufficient margin of appreciation" to the British government in deciding what was and what was not disproportionate (*Lustig-Prean and Beckett v United Kingdom* [2000] 29 E.H.R.R. 548 at 588-590). The Albanian, Austrian, and Lithuanian judges, by contrast, no doubt drew upon their own countries' long and unbroken histories of freedom, toleration, and respect for the individual and concurred in the E.C.H.R.'s condemnation of Britain's lack of a written constitution and, in consequence, respect for human rights (*Lustig-Prean and Beckett v United Kingdom* [2000] 548 at 579 para. 79). The European Court had usurped the sovereignty of the British Parliament and an unelected and unaccountable group of foreign lawyers had made a political decision about a question of British defense policy.

The E.C.H.R.'s arrogance is particularly questionable given that shortly before, in 1997, it had refused to uphold the rights of a group of homosexuals, Colin Laskey, Roland Jaggard, and Anthony Brown who in 1990 had been sentenced by an English judge, Judge Rant, to four and a half years, three years, and two years and nine months imprisonment, respectively, for what were essentially private consensual sexual acts (Grey 1993: 40; Law Commission, *Consent in the Criminal Law* 1995: 133-36; Madeson 1998). They had cunningly enough not been prosecuted for group sex, which was at that time forbidden to homosexuals, but for offenses of violence based on the sado-masochistic nature of some of their activities. The damage inflicted had been considerably less than in a legal boxing match and required no medical treatment and the level of bodily risk involved was less than in the case of sodomy. There was no threat to public order from these private activities, which only became known to the authorities when an amateur video made by one of the participants fell into the hands of the police. They were the victims of the same kind of moral indignation that had led to the criminalization of all kinds of male homosexual acts prior to 1967. Their convictions were upheld by the Court of Appeal in 1992 (though the sentences were reduced) (*Brown [Anthony], Lucas, Jaggard, Laskey, Carter, and Cadman v R* [1992] 1Q.B.491) and also by a majority (two of the five judges dissented) of the judges in the House of Lords (*Brown [Anthony], Lucas, Jaggard, Laskey, Carter v R* [1994] 1 A.C. 212).

When their case went to the European Court of Human Rights it might have been expected that in such a clear instance of the rights of the individual being overridden as a matter of public policy the E.C.H.R. would be sympathetic to the appellants. Yet the E.C.H.R. judges declared by 11 votes to 7 that there had been no violation of the applicants' rights under Article 8 and that each country had considerable latitude to decide its own policy in such matters (*Laskey, Jaggard and Brown v United Kingdom* [1997], 24, E.H.R.R. 39 at paras. 45, 61, and pp. 53-4). Whereas the United Kingdom had been allowed only a very narrow margin of appreciation in the cases involving Lustig-Prean and Beckett and Smith and Grady, in this case the margin of appreciation was of equatorial latitude, as indeed the dissenting judges pointed out. The contrast between the two judgments reveals that the outcome of cases of this kind in the E.C.H.R. is arbitrary and largely a matter of the prejudices of individuals, as is clear from the hysterical comments made by one of the judges (*Laskey, Jaggard, and Brown v United Kingdom* [1997]: 24, E.H.R.R. 39 at 60-61).

Why then were the two sets of cases decided so differently? When all the high-minded language and the rationalizations that justify underlying bundles of sentiments are stripped away it is clear that what drives the international men and women of words and ink is a distaste for even the *appearance* of force or aggression or dominance and submission. Laskey, Jaggard, and Brown had made the mistake of playing sex games that made use of the fears and dislikes of this class of people and scared as well as offended them. What chance then did the armed services, those specialists in the use of collective force on behalf of the state, have when judged by those with this kind of mind-set, one derived from years devoted to the delusion that the world is but a reflection of its documents? Judges of this type are hardly likely to listen sympathetically to the argument (whether correct or not) that a category of individuals defined by orientation should be dismissed from their jobs in the interests of the more efficient and disciplined use of violence by the military.

The distress suffered by Lustig-Prean and Beckett should have been remedied by the British Parliament for the causalist reasons indicated earlier and along the lines of the decriminalization of homosexuality by the British Parliament in 1967; it was extremely unfortunate that the delay in doing this led to the imposition of an alien decree on their country. The crucial reason for repudiating the meddling of the E.C.H.R. is that the British Parliament has final responsibility for defending Britain against outside aggression or terrorism. If the British government had of its own accord lifted the ban on homosexuals serving in the armed forces, it would also have taken responsibility for any possible adverse consequences. Ultimately, it is the politicians who are answerable for the shortcomings of the military. Should Britain be defeated in a war or its people slain by militant terrorists, it is not only Britain's military leaders but Britain's politicians who will be held responsible. International tribunals alone can afford to live in a theoretical world of abstract rights where these vulgar material considerations do not intrude.

Furthermore, the British Parliament (mainly through the executive composed of ministers drawn from the party in power but also through specialist committees) has considerable experience in making decisions, not just about military matters in general but about the British armed forces with their particular needs and traditions and is advised by both civil servants and military specialists on this. The British judges conceded in the case of *R v Ministry of Defence ex parte Smith* (1995 [1996] Q.B. 517 at 532-4) that their expertise was limited to legal questions and that this rendered them an unsuitable tribunal for passing judgments on defense policy. The European Court of Human Rights was even less suited to such a task and was in no position to assess the Ministry of Defence's case.

It is irrelevant that most of the member states of the Council of Europe do not ban homosexuals from their armed services. The armed services of many of these countries are unable to cope with even an unexpectedly robust bout of peacekeeping let alone defend their countries. Surveys of differences in values across Europe regularly show that citizens of the various European countries are far more reluctant to contribute to their own national defense than is the case in Britain (Ashford and Timms 1992: 90). The British armed forces acquitted themselves well in several wars and also against terrorism in the last twenty years of the twentieth century and into the twenty-first. It hardly makes sense to reduce them even in theory to the Council of Europe countries' average level of morale and preparedness to fight.

The removal of the ban on homosexuals has, by the British military's own admission (*Daily Telegraph*, 1 September 2000; *Observer*, 19 November 2000), had no adverse effects, any more than the abolition of capital punishment for desertion did in 1930, but that is beside the point. What is important is that an irresponsible international body, the E.C.H.R, arrogated to itself the power to intervene in the organization of that most vital and national of institutions, Britain's armed forces. It is not the outcome of the case (which has had little practical effect on the capacity of Britain to defend itself) but the manner in which, and the grounds on which, it was taken that is thoroughly objectionable and indeed threatening. It should also be viewed against the background of other E.C.H.R. decisions impeding Britain's as well as other Council of Europe countries' capacities to defend themselves against terrorism. The E.C.H.R.

can in effect force nations into a kind of unilateral disarmament by constraining them with rules that do not and cannot constrain the terrorists.

In 1998, the British added the entire European Convention on Human Rights to their domestic law by the Human Rights Act. It was in part at least an attempt to avoid further defeats in the E.C.H.R. where Britain, together with Sweden, was the country that lost most often. The numerous British defeats in the E.C.H.R. in the past about the liberties to which individuals are entitled are not indications of an absence of liberty in Britain; they merely reveal a difference in priorities between Britain and the other countries of the Council of Europe. Where the British enjoy freedoms that most of these other countries lack, for example, in the market place, or rights peculiar to Britain such as the right to trial by jury, these rights and freedoms will never be imposed by the E.C.H.R. on one of the other Council of Europe countries at the request of one of its citizens. They cannot be fitted into the E.C.H.R.'s method of proceeding by *Gleichschaltung,* by making Europe uniform and will be dismissed as mere Anglo-Saxon oddities. On the contrary, these British liberties may well be destroyed in the future as a byproduct of E.C.H.R. judgments about other matters.

The transfer of the initial stages of decision-making involving the European Convention on Human Rights to British judges will not improve the situation. The British judges will be making decisions based not only on the text of the Convention but shaped by the strongly persuasive precedents set by previous decades of cases heard by the E.C.H.R and decided by judges drawn from countries with considerably different legal systems and political traditions and priorities, which have warped the interpretation of the Convention in exceedingly un-British directions. Furthermore, an individual dissatisfied with a judgment based on the Convention reached in Britain can still appeal to the European Court of Human Rights in Strasbourg and have it overturned. Now that the Convention has been incorporated into domestic law in both England and Scotland it is difficult to see why this avenue of further appeal is either necessary or desirable. The sole function of this final avenue of appeal is to subordinate British traditions and preferences in regard to liberty to those of lawyers drawn from countries with a different and often deficient record of upholding freedom. The British Human Rights

Act of 1998 solves none of the problems connected with the loss of British sovereignty.

Different free societies have different preferences and make different choices when there is a clash of liberties or objectives; the United States alone, for instance, is the true upholder of a legal right to the unfettered freedom of political speech, one untrammeled by the restrictions to be found in most European countries. It is thanks to U.S. decisions not the E.C.H.R. that British subjects and European citizens can enjoy a relatively uncensored Internet. This happy situation is an expression of indigenous American values about freedom of speech (which the people of Britain share, but most Europeans do not, or at least with so many reservations as effectively to deny them) that have been exported by the operation of global economic and technical forces, not one created by a clutch of international lawyers and bureaucrats. Yet precisely for this reason U.S.-sponsored Internet freedom is likely to come under attack from one European institution or another; in particular, the Europeans will seek to restrict the freedom of those who are prevented by law from presenting their views in their own countries but who can have a website in America that their fellow citizens can read. European notions of rights, unlike those of America, are not rooted in British individualism and British traditions of liberty.

From the Strange Death of Moral Britain to the Strange Death of Britain

Britain as a society survived the strange death of moral Britain, survived the radical secularization of the last half of the twentieth century, survived the ending of the phase in its history I have termed respectable Britain, and survived the replacement of moralist by causalist policies. Its very continuity is a denial of the assertion that a society needs a strong common morality to survive (Devlin 1965: 18, 22). The assertion is a piece of bad functionalism that cannot specify how much or what common morality is needed. At the same time, it is easy to see that post-moral Britain is only sustained by residual and now weakening moral habits from the past, habits of orderliness, honesty, duty, and loyalty. How long can they survive when they are no longer being praised and promoted? The British top still spins but it is slowing down and will soon begin to wobble, even though it is a long way from falling over.

Post-moral Britain is a viable if defective social order. If and when the society falls it will be for other purely political reasons that may be discerned from this study of the crumbling of moral Britain and indeed may have common origins but are not in themselves part of the death of moral Britain. The willingness of successive British governments to relinquish British sovereignty over moral issues to the European Court of Human Rights has been matched by their far more dangerous willingness to hand over political and economic decision-making to the European Union. The E.U. is an alien and essentially bureaucratic monster that has far more extensive powers and a broader reach than the European Court of Human Rights. The adoption by many European countries of a single European currency has meant for them a loss of control over monetary policy and is a prelude to their loss of power over taxation. The historic British principle of no taxation without representation has no place in Europe. Likewise, the adoption of an ever-tightening European constitution will mean the end of Britain as a nation. Britain will fall and it will have fallen because of the prior death of moral Britain, which reduced the national will to resist. A loss of national boundaries and identity today makes easier the loss of national independence tomorrow.

If Britain is swallowed up politically by Europe there will be no moral Britain to provide an alternative mode of continuity and distinctiveness. Yet, politically, Britain does not share a common history, values, and tradition with Europe (Ashford and Timms 1992: 112). A United Europe would not be a happy or stable union such as that of the United States. The United States was by origin a new nation, but it was created out of self-governing colonies with a common language and a common, preexisting set of traditions and perceptions; even then it nearly foundered in civil war. A United Europe would have nothing to sustain it but fear, the fear of a return to the conflicts between its nations that tore it apart in the past. Britain, an island separated from Europe by a protecting sea was, it is true, dragged into these conflicts, but then so was the United States. The peoples of the European nations who choose to sink into the bog of Europe will lose their old identities without gaining new ones, a recipe for total alienation. Who is going to be loyal to a United Europe? Who would sacrifice or subordinate their own interests for the sake of Europe? Who is going to feel pride at seeing its flag, that thin circlet of yellow stars flying in the wind? It is perhaps significant that it is among the people of countries such as Belgium or Italy, which have failed as political and military units, that there is most enthusiasm for this leviathan (Harding et al. 1986: 94; Ashford and Timms 1990: 90-92). Should Britain as a political entity slide into subordination to a European state, then the British will come to re-gret that there is no moral Britain to sustain and distinguish their nation when all other sources of pride and independence have been lost.

Notes

1.   This is the figure being leaked from the Home Office. It is due to be published but will probably be tucked away somewhere obscure as its implications are contrary to their preferred policy.
2.   These crimes get left out of victim surveys as do crimes whose victims are under 16, that is, the surveys underestimate the volume of crime and should not be treated as a better measure than the police figures. They are two different measures, each with strengths and weaknesses.
3.   It reads: "That excessive Baile ought not to be required nor excessive Fines imposed nor cruell and unusuall punishments inflicted." Executing someone for murder was not unusual in 1688 and the Bill of rights was not a "living" document that could be manipulated at will to suit the whim of later generations. It was a guard against absolutism, which is all a Bill of Rights can or should be.
4.   The Homicide Act of 1957 did, however, import into England from Scotland much broader notions of diminished responsibility.
5.   It is the contrast between Britain and Ireland that again emphasizes the point. The Royal Irish Constabulary were armed and soldiers were stationed there in case of trouble. In Britain, neither was needed and indeed would have been opposed.

References

Ackerley, J. R. (1992) (1968). *My Father and Myself*. London: Pimlico.

Alison, Archibald. (1840). *The Principles of Population and Their Connection with Human Happiness* (2 vols.). Edinburgh: Blackwood.

Amnesty International. (1979). *The Death Penalty*. London: Amnesty International.

_____. (1989). *When the State Kills*. London: Amnesty International.

_____. (1990). *Amnesty International Report*. London: Amnesty International.

Anderson, Stuart, and Virginia Berridge. (2000). "Opium in 20th Century Britain: Pharmacists, Regulation and the People." *Addiction* 95 (1): 23-36.

Armitage, Air Chief Marshal Sir Michael. (1998). *Gay Warriors, Implications for Military Cohesion*. In Gerald Frost (ed.), *Not Fit to Fight*, 39-46. London: Social Affairs Unit.

Armytage, W.H.G., R. Chester, and John Peel (eds.). (1980). *Changing Patterns of Sexual Behaviour*. London: Academic Press.

Ashford, Sheena, Noel Timms. (1992). *What Europe Thinks*. Aldershot: Dartmouth.

Babington, Anthony. (1983). *For the Sake of Example, Capital Courts Martial 1914-20*. London: Leo Cooper.

Badham, Paul. (1992). "Christian Belief and the Ethics of In-vitro Fertilization Research." In Paul Badham (ed.), *Ethics on the Frontiers of Human Existence*. New York: Paragon.

Baechler, Jean. (1979). *Suicides*. Oxford: Basil Blackwell.

Bailey, Derrick Sherwin. (1975) (1955). *Homosexuality and the Western Christian Tradition,* Hamden, CT: Archon.

_____. (ed.). (1956). *Sexual Offenders and Social Punishment*. London: The Church Information Board.

Baker, William H. (1985). *On Capital Punishment* (previously *Worthy of Death*). Chicago: Moody.

Barber, Malcolm. (1981). "Lepers, Jews and Moslems—The Plot to Overthrow Christendom in 1321." *History* 66 (216): 1-17.

Barry, Norman. (1982). "The Tradition of Spontaneous Order." *Literature of Liberty* 5: 7-58.

Bayer, Ronald H. (1978). *Neighbors in Conflict, The Irish, Germans, Jews and Italians of New York City 1929-41*. Baltimore: John Hopkins Press.

Bean, Philip. (1974). *The Social Control of Drugs*. London: Martin Robertson.

Bedau, Hugo Adam (ed.). (1983). *The Death Penalty in America* (3rd ed.). New York: Oxford University Press.

Beloff, John. (1989). "Do We Have a Right to Die?" In Berger et al. (eds.), *Perspectives on Death and Dying: Cross-cultural and Multi-Disciplinary Views*, 163-171. Philadelphia: Charles.

Benson, Bruce L., and David W. Rasmussen. (1996). *Illicit Drugs and Crime*. Oakland: The Independent Institute.

Bentham, Jeremy. (1978). "Offences Against One's Self: Paederasty, Part One. *Journal of Homosexuality* 3 (4) (Summer): 389-405; Part Two, *Journal of Homosexuality* 4 (1): 91-110 (Written but not published, 1785).

Berger, Arthur, Paul Badham, Austin, H. Katscher, Joyce Berger, Michael Perry, and John Beloff. (1989). *Perspectives on Death and Dying: Cross-cultural and Multi-Disciplinary Views*. Philadelphia: Charles.

Berger, Raoul. (1994). *Government by Judiciary*. Indianapolis, IN: Liberty Fund.

Berlinguer, Giovanni. (1978). *La Legge Sull' Aborto*. Rome: Riunite.

Berridge, Virginia. (1999). *Opium and the People*. London: Free Association.

Betts, G. Gordon. (2002). *The Twilight of Britain*. New Brunswick, NJ: Transaction Publishers.

Bewley, Thomas H., Oved Ben-Arie, Pierce James, Vincent Marks. (1968). "Morbidity and Mortality from Heroin Dependence." *British Medical Journal* 23 (March): 725-40.

Bible, King James Version. (1611).

Bible, New English. (1970). Oxford and Cambridge: Oxford University Press and Cambridge University Press.

Bienot Sarah, Barry Anderson, Stephanie Lee, David Utting. (2002). *Youth and Risk. London*: Communities that Care.

Bird, Steve. (2002). "Half Gay 'Fleet Fuelled Admirals Fear' of Blackmail and Treachery." *The Times*, 31 October, 1-2.

Blanshard, Paul. (1954). *The Irish and Catholic Power, an American Interpretation*. London: Derek Verschoyle.

Block, Walter. (1976). *Defending the Undefendable*. New York: Fleet Press.

Booth, Charles. (1903). *Life and Labour of the People of London*. London: Macmillan.

Booth A., and A. Crouter (eds.). 1998. *Men in Families: When Do They Get Involved? What Difference Does It Make?* Mahwah NJ: Lawrence Erlbaum.

Boswell, John. (1980). *Christianity, Social Tolerance and Homosexuality*. Chicago: University of Chicago Press.

_____. (1994). *Same-Sex Unions in Pre-modern Europe*. New York: Villard.

Brazier, Julian. (1998). "Who Will Defend the Defenders?" In Gerald Frost (ed.), *Not Fit to Fight,* 63-75. London: Social Affairs Unit.

Brierley, Peter. (2000). "Religion." In A. H. Halsey and Josephine Webb (eds.), *Twentieth Century British Social Trends*, 650-674. Basingstoke: Macmillan.

British Medical Association. (1987). *Living with Risk*. Chichester: John Wiley.

Brooke, C.N.L. (1964). "Gregorian Reform in Action: Clerical Marriage in England 1050-1200." In Sylvia L. Thrupp (ed.), *Change in Medieval Society: Europe North of the Alps 1050-1500.* New York: Appleton-Century-Crofts.

Brookes, Barbara. (1988). *Abortion in England: 1900-1967*. London: Croom Helm.

Brown Callum, G. (1992). *A Revisionist approach to Religious Change*. In Steve Bruce (ed.): 31-58.

_____. (2001). *The Death of Christian Britain, Understanding Secularisation 1800-2000*. London: Routledge.

Browne, Douglas G., and E. V. Tullett. (1952). *Bernard Spilsbury: His Life and Cases*. London: Conpanicon.

Bruce, Steve. (1986). *God Save Ulster: The Religion and Politics of Paisleyism*. Oxford: Clarendon.

_____ (ed.). (1992). *Religion and Modernisation: Sociologists and Historians Debate the Secularization Thesis*. Oxford: Clarendon,

_____. (1996). *Religion in the Modern World, From Cathedrals to Cults*. Oxford: Oxford University Press.

_____. (2002). *God is Dead: Secularization in the West*. Oxford: Blackwell.

Bullough, Vern L. (1976). *Sexual Variance in Society and History*. Chicago: University of Chicago Press.

Calvert, E. Roy. (1936). *Capital Punishment in the 20th Century*. London: Putnam.

Cameron, Samuel. (2002). *The Economics of Sin*. Cheltenham: Edward Elgar.

Carlson, Allan. (1993). "Liberty, Order and the Family." In Jon Davies (ed.), *The Family: Is It Just Another Lifestyle Choice?* London: IEA Health and Welfare.

Carroll, Lewis. (1965)(1895). "Eternal Punishment." *The Works of Lewis Carroll*. Feltham, Spring, 1110-17.

Charlton, John, Sue Kelly, Karen Dunnell, Barry Evans, Rachel Jenkins. (1994). "Suicide Deaths in England and Wales: Trends and Factors Associated with Suicide Deaths." In Jenkins et al. (eds.), *The Prevention of Suicide*, 13-21, London: H.M.S.O.

Charlton, John, Sue Kelly, Karen Dunnell, Barry Evans, Rachel Jenkins, and Ruth Walls. (1994). Trends in Suicide Deaths in England and Wales in Jenkins et al. (eds.), 6-12.

Chauncey, Jr., George. (1991). "Christian Brotherhood or Sexual Perversion? Homosexual Identities and the Construction of Sexual Boundaries in the World War I Era." In Duberman et al. (eds.), *Hidden from History: Reclaiming the Gay and Lesbian Past*, 129-140, Harmondsworth: Penguin.

Christoph, James B. (1962). *Capital Punishment and British Politics*, London: Allen and Unwin.

Church Assembly Board for Social Responsibility. (1965). *Abortion, an Ethical Discussion*. London: Church Information Office.

Church of England Moral Welfare Council. (1954). *The Problem of Homosexuality*. London: Church Information Board.

Churchill, Randolph. (1966). *Winston S. Churchill, Vol. 1, Youth, 1874-1900*. London: Heinemann.

Churchill, Winston S. (1930). *My Early Life: A Roving Commission*. London: Thornton Butterworth.

The Cleansing of a City. (1908). London: The National Social Purity Crusade and Greening and Co.

Clinard, Marchall B. (1978). *Cities with Little Crime: The Case of Switzerland*. Cambridge: Cambridge University Press.

Clutterbuck, Richard. (1995). *Drugs, Crime and Corruption*. Basingstoke: Macmillan.

Cobbe, Frances Power. (1902). "A False Philosophy—The Cause of the Evil in Public Morals." In James Marchant (ed.), *Public Morals*, 251. London: Morgan and Scott.

Cockett M., and J. Tripp. (1994). *The Exeter Family Study: Family Breakdown and Its Impact on Children*. Exeter: University of Exeter Press.

Cohen, P. (1990). "Desires for Cocaine." In Warburton (ed.), *Addiction Ccontroversies*, 212-222. Chur, Switzerland: Harwood Academic Publishers.

Coker, Charles. (1998). "Selling the Regimental Silver." In Gerald Frost (ed.), *Not Fit to Fight*, 19-30. London: Social Affairs Unit.

Coleman, David. (2000). "Population and Family." In A. H. Halsey and Josephine Webb (eds.), *Twentieth Century Social Trends*, 27-93. Basingstoke: Macmillan:

Coleman, Peter. (1980). *Christian Attitudes to Homosexuality*, London: SPCK.

Collins, Sylvia. (2001). "Faith, Ethics and Young People in Late Modernity." In Kieran Flanagan and Peter C. Jupp (eds.), *Virtue Ethics and Sociology*. Basingstoke: Palgrave.

Conley, Carolyn A. (1991). *The Unwritten Law, Criminal Justice in Victorian Kent*. Oxford: Oxford University Press.

Coser, Lewis. (1974). *Greedy Institutions, Patterns of Undivided Commitment*. New York: Free Press.

Crozier, Frank Percy. (1937). *The Men I Killed*. London: Michael Joseph.

Dalrymple, Theodore. (1998). "Straight and Narrow." *Sunday Times*, (London), 23 August.
Dangerfield, George. (1936). *The Strange Death of Liberal England*. London: Constable.
Davenport-Hines, Richard P. T. (1990). *Sex Death and Punishment,: Attitudes to Sex and Sexuality in Britain since the Renaissance*. London: Fontana.
Davies, Christie. (1976). "The Relative Fertility of Hindus and Muslims. *Quest* 99, 18-27.
_____. (1978). "How Our Rulers Argue about Censorship." In R. Dhavan and C. Davies (eds.), *Censorship and Obscenity*, 9-36. London: Martin Robertson.
_____. (1980). "Moralists, Causalists Sex, Law and Morality." In W.H.G. Armytage, R. Chester, and J. Peel (eds.), *Changing Patterns of Sexual Behaviour*, 13-43. London: Academic Press.
_____. (1982). "Sexual Taboos and Social Boundaries." *American Journal of Sociology* 87, 5 (March): 1032-1063.
_____. (1982a). "Itali sunt imbelles." *Journal of Strategic Studies* 5, 266-69.
_____. (1983). "Crime, Bureaucracy and Equality." *Policy Review* 23 (Winter): 89-105.
_____. (1983a). "Handling the Abortion Issue: An Intercontinental Divide". *Wall Street Journal*, 19 December.
_____. (1983b). "Abortion Needn't be a Matter of Rights." *Wall Street Journal*, 28 December.
_____. (1983c). "Religious Boundaries and Sexual Morality." *Annual Review of the Social Sciences of Religion* 6 (Fall): 45-77.
_____. (1986). "A Breathing Space to Bring Down Crime." *The Times*, 8 October.
_____. (1987). "Witches at the Church Door." *The Times*, 21 February.
_____. (1988). "British Abortion Debate Obscures Issues." *Wall Street Journal*, 17 February.
_____. (1988a) "What Prevents Life from Being Worthwhile?" *The World and I* 3, 5 (May): 665-85.
_____. (1993). "The Criminals' Charter." *The Lawyer*, 11 April.
_____. (1997). "Prohibiting and Taxing Everyday Pleasures." In D Warburton and Neil Sherwood (eds.), *Pleasure and Quality of Life,* 199-207. Chichester: Wiley.
_____. (1997a). "Coffee, Tea and the Ultra-Protestant and Jewish Nature of the Boundaries of Mormonism." In Douglas J. Davies (ed.), *Mormon Identities in Transition*, 35-45. London: Cassell.
_____. (1998). The dog that didn't bark in the night in Willibald Ruch (ed.) *The Sense of Humor*, Berlin and New York, Mouton de Gruyter, 1998 pp 293-306.
_____. (1999). "The Creation, Morality, the After-life and the Fission of Religious Tradition: Modernity Not Post-modernity. *Journal of Contemporary Religion* 14, 3: 339-360.
_____. (2002). *The Mirth of Nations*. New Brunswick NJ: Transaction Publishers.
Davies, Christie, and Mark Neal . (2000). "Durkheim's Altruistic and Fatalistic Suicide." In W.S.F. Pickering and Geoffrey Walford (eds.), *Durkheim's Suicide: A Century of Research and Debate*, 36-52. London: Routledge.
Davies , Christie, and Eugene Trivizas. (1986). "Tactics of Legal Reform: Learning from the Recent Past. *The Howard Journal* 25, 1: 25-32.
_____. (1994). "A Neo-Paretian Model of Discourse about Penal Policy: Basic Sentiments and Public Argument." *Revue Europeenne des Sciences Sociales* 32, 99: 147-67.
_____. (2000). "Sadomazochismos ke Sinenese sto Piniko Thiekeo" (Sado-Masochism and Consent in the Criminal Law). In Nestor Kourakis (ed.), *Pinika Anteglimatiki Politiki, Meletes gia ta Oria tus Orus ke tis Katefthensis*, 475-494. Athens: Ant. N. Sakulas.
Davies, Ebenezer Thomas. (1981). *Religion and Society in the Nineteenth Century.* Llandybie: Christopher Davies.
Dennis, Norman. (1993). *Rising Crime and the Dismembered Family*. London: I.E.A. Health and Welfare.

_____. (1997). *The Invention of Permanent Poverty*. London: I.E.A. Health and Welfare Unit.

Dennis, Norman, and George Erdos. (1993). *Families without Fatherhood*. London: I.E.A. Health and Welfare.

Dernley, Syd, with David Newman. (1990). *The Hangman's Tale, Memoirs of a Public Executioner*. London: Pan.

Devlin, Patrick Lord. (1965) *The Enforcement of Morals*, London: Oxford University Press.

Dhavan, Rajeev, and Davies, Christie (eds.). (1978). *Censorship and Obscenity*. London: Martin Robertson.

Dostoyevski, Fyodor. (1955, orig. 1869). *The Idiot* (trans. David Magarshack). Harmondsworth: Penguin.

Douglas, Mary. (1966). *Purity and Danger*. London: Routledge and Kegan, Paul.

Dover, Kenneth James. (1978). *Greek Homosexuality*. London: Duckworth.

"Drugs Uncovered." (2002). *The Observer*, 21 April.

Du Cane. E. F. (1893). "The Decrease of Crime." *The Nineteenth Century*. xxxiii, (March): 480-492.

Duberman, Martin Bauml, Martha Vicinus, and George Chauncey, Jr. (eds.). (1991). *Hidden from History: Reclaiming the Gay and Lesbian Past*. Harmondsworth: Penguin.

Dulles, Avery Cardinal. (2001). "Catholicism and Capital Punishment." *First Things*, 112 (April): 30-35.

Durkheim, Emile. (1933) (1st French ed. 1893). *The Division of Labor in Society*. New York: Free Press.

_____. (1952) (1st French ed. 1897). *Suicide*. London: Routledge and Kegan Paul.

Ehrlich, Isaac. (1975). "The Deterrent Effect of Capital Punishment: A Question of Life and Death. *American Economic Review* 68 (June): 397-417.

Enloe, Cynthia. (1983). *Does Khaki Become You?* London: Pluto.

Erskine, Hazel. (1970). "The Polls—Capital Punishment." *Public Opinion Quarterly* 34 (Summer): 290-307.

Escott, Thomas Hay Sweet. (1885). *England, Its People Polity and Pursuits*. London: Chapman and Hall.

Evans, Eifion. (1969). *The Welsh Revival of 1904*. London: Evangelical Press.

Fitzpatrick, Ray, and Tarani Chandola. (2000). "Health." In A. H. Halsey and Josephine Webb (eds.), *Twentieth Century British Social Trends*, 94-127. Basingstoke: Macmillan.

Flood-Page, Claire, S. Campbell, V. Harrington, and J. Miller. (2000). *Youth Crime: Findings from the 1998/99 Youth Lifestyles Survey*. London: Home Office Research, Development and Statistics Directorate.

Frean, Alexandra. (2002). "Adoption Ban 'Breaches Basic Human Rights'." *The Times*, 31 October, 4.

Frost, Gerald. (1998). *Not Fit to Fight*. London: Social Affairs Unit.

_____. (1998). "How to Destroy an Army." In Gerald Frost (ed.), *Not Fit to Fight*, 1-18. London: Social Affairs Unit.

Fry, Geoffrey Kingdon. (2001). *The Politics of Crisis*. Basingstoke: Palgrave.

Furedi, Frank. (1998). *Culture of Fear.* London: Cassell.

Gatrell, V.A.C. (1980). "The Decline of Theft and Violence in Victorian and Edwardian England." In V.A.C. Gatrell (ed.), *Crime and the Law: the Social History of Crime in Western Europe since 1500*, 238-370. London: Europa.

Gatrell, V.A.C., and T. B. Hadden. (1972). "Criminal Statistics and their Interpretation." In E. A. Wrigley (ed.), *Nineteenth Century: Essays in the Use of Quantitative Methods for the Study of Social Data*, 336-95. Cambridge: Cambridge University Press.

Gilbert Alan D. (1980). *The Making of Post-Christian Britain*. London: Longman.

Gilbert, Arthur N. (1976). "Buggery and the British Navy 1700-1861." *Journal of Social History* 10 (1): 72-98.

Gill, Robin, (1992). "Secularization and Census Data." In Steve Bruce (ed.), *Religion and Modernisation: Sociologists and Historians Debate the Secularization Thesis*, 90-117. Oxford: Clarendon.

Glatt, M. M. (1958). "The English Drink Problem: Its Rise and Decline through the Ages." *British Journal of Addiction* 55, 51-65.

Gosden, P.H.J.H. (1960). *The Friendly Societies in England 1815-1875*. Manchester: Manchester University Press.

_____. (1973). *Self-Help, Voluntary Association in the Nineteenth Century*.London: Batsford.

Goffman, Erving. (1961). *Asylums*. Garden City NY: Anchor.

Goldsmith, Netta, Murray. (1998). *The Worst of Crimes, Homosexuality and the Law in Eighteenth Century London*. Aldershot: Ashgate.

Goodich, Michael. (1979). *The Unmentionable Vice: Homosexuality in the later Medieval Period*. Santa Barbara: ABC-Clio.

Gorer, Geoffrey. (1955). *Exploring English Character*. London: Cresset.

Gourevitch, Peter Alexis. (1977). "International Trade, Domestic Coalitions and Liberty: Comparative Responses to the Crisis of 1873-1896." *Journal of Interdisciplinary History* viii-2 (Autumn): 281-313.

Gowers, Sir Ernest. (1956). *A Life for a Life? The Problem of Capital Punishment*. London: Chatto and Windus.

Grabosky, Peter, N. (1977). "Sydney: The Politics of Crime and Conflict, 1788 to the 1970s." In Gurr et al. (eds.), *The Politics of Crime and Conflict*, 323-466.Beverly Hills: Sage.

Grabosky, Peter, N., Leif Persson, and Sven Spurlings. (1977). "Stockholm: The Politics of Crime and Conflict 1750 to the 1970s." In Gurr et al. (eds.), *The Politics of Crime and Conflict*, 256-319. Beverly Hills: Sage.

Green, David G. (1993). *Reinventing Civil Society, the Rediscovery of Welfare without Politics*. London: I.E.A. Health and Welfare Unit.

Green, Simon J. D. (1996). *Religion in the Age of Decline: Organization and Experience in Industrial Yorkshire*. Cambridge: Cambridge University Press.

Greenaway, John R. (1990). The Drink Problem Back on the Political Agenda? *Political Quarterly* 61, 80-92.

Grey, Antony. (1992). *Quest for Justice*. London: Sinclair-Stevenson.

_____. (1993). *Speaking of Sex*. London: Cassell.

Griffith-Edwards J. (1978). "Some Years On. Evolution in the British System." In D. J. West (ed.), *Problems of Drug Abuse in Britain*, 1-51. Cambridge: University of Cambridge Institute of Criminology.

Gurr, Ted Robert. (1977). "The Best of Times The Worst of Times." In Gurr et al. (eds.), *The Politics of Crime and Conflict*, 619-650. Beverly Hills, Sage.

Gurr, Ted Robert. (1989). "Historical Trends in Violent Crime: Europe and the United States." In Ted Robert Gurr (ed.), *Violence in America, Vol. 1, The History of Crime*. Newbury Park: Sage.

Gurr, Ted Robert, Peter N. Grabosky, Richard C. Hula (eds.). (1977). *The Politics of Crime and Conflict*. Beverly Hills, Sage.

Hall, Edmund. (1995). *We Can't Even March Straight: Homosexuality in the British Armed Forces*. London: Vintage.

Halsey, A. H. (1993). Foreword to Norman Dennis and George Erdos, *Families without Fatherhood*, ix-iii. London: I.E.A. Health and Welfare.

Halsey, A. H., and Josephine Webb. (2000). *Twentieth Century British Social Trends*. Basingstoke: Macmillan.

Hanafin, Patrick. (2000). Rewriting Desire in Carl Stychin and Didi Herman (eds.), *Sexuality in the Legal Arena*, 51-66. London: Athlone.

Hanawalt, Barbara A. (1979). *Crime and Conflict in English Communities 1300-1348.* Cambridge, MA: Harvard University Press.

Harding, Stephen, David Phillips, and Michael Fogarty. (1986). *Contrasting Values in Western Europe.* Basingstoke: Macmillan.

Harrison, Brian. (1994). *Drink and the Victorians, The Temperance Question in England 1815-1872.* Keele University, Staffordshire: Keele University Press.

Hartley, Shirley Foster. (1975). *Illegitimacy.* Berkeley: University of California Press.

Harvey, Arnold, D. (2001). *Sex in Georgian England.* London: Phoenix.

Harvey, Ian. (1971). *To Fall Like Lucifer.* London: Sidgwick and Jackson.

Heer, Friedrich. (1962). *The Medieval World, Europe 1100-1300.* London: Weidenfeld and Nicholson.

Henderson, Emma M. (2000). "I'd Rather be an Outlaw, Identity, Activism and Decriminalization in Tasmania." In Carl Stychin and Didi Herman (eds.), *Sexuality in the Legal Arena*, 35-56, 232-37. London: Athlone.

Herberg, Will. (1960). *Protestant, Catholic, Jew.* Garden City, NY: Doubleday.

Hesketh, Tom. (1990). *The Second Partitioning of Ireland, the Abortion Referendum of 1983.* Dun Laoghaire: Brandsma.

Himmelfarb, Gertrude. (1995). *The De-Moralization of Society.* New York: Alfred A. Knopf.

Hindmarch Ian, Neil Sherwood, and John S. Kerr. (1994). "The Psychoative Effects of Nicotine, Caffeine and Alcohol." In David M. Warburton (ed.), *Pleasure: The Politics and the Reality*, 50-57. Chichester: John Wiley.

Hilton, Matthew. (2000). *Smoking in British Popular Culture 1800-2000.* Manchester: Manchester University Press.

Holden, Wendy. (1994). *Unlawful Carnal Knowledge, the True Story of the Irish X Case.* London: Harper Collins.

Hood, Roger, and Andrew Roddam. (2000). "Crime, Sentencing and Punishment." In A. H. Halsey and Josephine Webb, *Twentieth Century Social Trends*, 675-709. Basingstoke: Macmillan.

Hornsby-Smith, Michael P. (1987). *Roman Catholics in England, Studies in Social Structure since the Second World War.* Cambridge: Cambridge University Press.

———. (1992). "Recent Transformation in English Catholicism: Evidence of Secularization?" In Steve Bruce (ed.), *Religion and Modernisation: Sociologists and Historians Debate the Secularization Thesis*, 118-144. Oxford: Clarendon.

Horton, R. F. (1910). "Methods to be Employed by the Church to Retain Young People When They Reach the Ages of 14 to 17." In *The Nation's Morals*, 57-64. London: Cassell.

Hough, Mike, Pat Mayhew. (1983). *The British Crime Survey: First Report* (Home Office Research Study No. 76). London: H.M.S.O.

Howe, Adrian. (2000). "Homosexual Advances in Law, Murderous Excise, Pluralized Ignorance and the Privilege of Unknowing." In Carl Stychin and Didi Herman (eds.), *Sexuality in the Legal Arena*, 84-99. London: Athlone.

Huie, William Bradford. (1954). *The Execution of Private Slovik.* New York: New American Library.

Hull, Stephen. (2002). "Robbers Help Cops in Crime Campaign. Officers Issue Tips to Beat Muggers." *The Midweek* 12 June, www.icBerkshire.co.uk

Inglis, Tom. (1987). *Moral Monopoly. The Catholic Church in Modern Irish Society.* Dublin: Gill and Macmillan.

———. (1998). *Moral Monopoly: The Rise and Fall of the Catholic Church in Modern Ireland.* Dublin: University College Dublin Press.

Ingoldsby, Tom. (1995). Letter to *The Irish Times*, 28 February.
Institut National d'Etudes Demographiques (INED). (1981). *L'interruption volontaire de grosseuse dans l'Europe des neuf* (Cahier No. 91). Paris: Presses Universitaires de France.
Jeffery-Poulter, Stephen. (1991). *Peers, Queers and Commoners*. London: Routledge.
Jenkins, Rachel, Sian Griffiths, Ian Wylie, Keith Hawton, Gethin Morgan, André Tylor (eds.). (1994). *The Prevention of Suicide*. London: H.M.S.O.
Jones, David J. V. (1992). *Crime in Nineteenth Century Wales*. Cardiff: University of Wales Press.
Jones, David J. V., (1996). *Crime and Policing in the Twentieth Century, The South Wales Experience*. Cardiff: University of Wales Press.
Keown, John. (1988). *Abortion, Doctors and the Law*. Cambridge: Cambridge University Press.
Kesteven, J. N. van, P. Mayhew, and P. Nieuwbeerta. (2000). *Criminal Victimisation in Seventeen Industrialised Countries: Key Findings from the 2000 International Crime Victims Survey*. The Hague: Ministry of Justice, WODC, Onderzoek en beleid nr 187.
Keynes, John Maynard. (1936). *The General Theory of Employment, Interest and Money*. London: Macmillan.
Kipling, Rudyard. (1990). *War Stories and Poems*. Oxford: Oxford University Press.
Kitson, Clark G. (1962). *The Making of Victorian England*. London: Methuen.
Klein, Lawrence R., Brian Forst, and Victor Filato. (1983). "The Deterrent Effect of Capital Punishment: An Assessment of the Evidence." In Hugo Adam Bedau (ed.), *The Death Penalty in America* (3rd ed.), 138-58. New York: Oxford University Press.
Lahr, John. (1980). *Prick up your Ears: The Biography of Joe Orton*. Harmondsworth: Penguin.
Lambert, M. D. (1977). *Medieval Heresy: Popular Movements from Bogomil to Hus*. London: Arnold.
Lamont, Corliss. (1952). *Soviet Civilization*. New York: Philosophical Library.
Lane, Roger. (1992). "Urban Police and Crime in Nineteenth Century America." In Michael Tonry and Norval Morris (eds.), *Modern Policing, Vol. 15*, 1-50. Chicago: University of Chicago Press.
Laqueur, Thomas Walter. (1976). *Religion and Respectability, Sunday Schools and Working Class Culture 1780-1850*. New Haven: Yale University Press.
Lea, Henry Charles. (1932). *History of Sacerdotal Celibacy in the Christian Church*. London: Watts.
Lee, W.L. Melville. (1901). *A History of Police in England*. London: Methuen.
Lee, Ellie. (2001). "Reinventing Abortion as a Social Problem." In Joel Best (ed.), *How Claims Spread, Cross-National Diffusion of Social Problems*, 39-67. New York: Aldine de Gruyter.
Lefebure, Molly. (1977). *Samuel Taylor Coleridge: A Bondage of Opium*. London: Quartet.
Leighton, Albert C. (1967). "The Male as a Cultural Invention." *Technology and Culture*, 8, 1: 45-52.
Lloyd, Roger. (1966). *The Church of England: 1900-1965*. London: S.C.M.
Longmate, Norman. (1972). *If Britain Had Fallen*. London: B.B.C. and Hutchinson.
Lowe, Geoff. (1994). "Pleasures of Social Relaxants and Stimulants—the Ordinary Persons' Attitudes and Involvement." In David M. Warburton (ed.), *Pleasure: The Politics and the Reality*, 95-108. Chichester, John Wiley.
Lustig-Prean, Duncan. (1999)." Last Night I Dreamt of the Sea Again." *Gay Times* (November) [also ww.davidclemens.com/gaymilitary/duncan].
Lynn, Richard, and S. L. Hampson. (1977). "Fluctuations in National Levels of Neuroticism and Extroversion 1935-1970." *British Journal of Social and Clinical Psychology* 16: 131-38.

MacKenzie, Compton. (1957). *Sublime Tobacco*. London: Chatto and Windus.

MacNamara, J. J. (1910). "Home, School and Nation." An introduction in *The Nation's Morals*, 13-29. London: Cassell.

Madeson, JJ (1998). "SM, Politics and the Law." In Charles Moser and JJ Madeson, *Bound to be Free*. New York: Continuum.

Malcolm, Joyce Lee. (2002). "Targeting a Myth." *Boston Globe*, 26 May, D1.

Mann, Henry. (1904). "Facts and Forces not Enumerated." In Richard Mudie-Smith (ed.), *The Religious Life of London*, 273-280. London: Hodder and Stoughton.

Mannheim, Hermann. (1940). *Social Aspects of Crime in England Between the Wars*. London: George Allen and Unwin.

Marchant, James. (1902). *Public Morals*. London: Morgan and Scott.

_____. (1909). *Aids to Purity*. London: Health and Strength.

Maritain, Jacques. (1948). *St. Thomas Aquinas*. London: Sheed and Ward.

Marrin, Albert. (1974). *The Last Crusade: The Church of England in the First World War*. Durham, NC: Duke University Press.

Martin, David. (1967). *A Sociology of English Religion*. London: Heinemann.

_____. (1978). *A General Theory of Secularisation*. Oxford: Basil Blackwell.

_____. (1990). *Tongues of Fire, The Explosion of Protestantism in Latin America*. Oxford: Blackwell.

_____. (1997) *Does Christianity Cause War?* Oxford: Clarendon.

_____. (2002) *Christian Language and its Mutations*. Aldershot: Ashgate.

Marwick, Arthur. (1965). *The Deluge, British Society and the First World War*. London: Bodley Head.

Masters, R.E.L. (1962). *Forbidden Sexual Behavior and Morality*. New York: Julian.

Mayhew, Pat, David Elliott, and Lizanne Dowd. (1989). *The 1988 British Crime Survey* (Home Office Research Study No. 111). London: H.M.S.O.

Mayhew, Pat, Natalie Aye Maving, and Catriona Mirrlees Black. (1993). *The 1992 British Crime Survey* (Home Office Research Study No. 132). London: H.M.S.O.

McCabe, Joseph. (1925). *1825-1925: A Century of Stupendous Progress*. London: Watts.

McClintock, F. H., N. Howard Avison. (1968). *Crime in England and Wales*. London: Heinemann.

McDonald, Lynn. (1982). Theory and Evidence of Rising Crime in the Nineteenth Century. *British Journal of Sociology* 33, 3 (September): 404-20.

McLeod, Hugh. (2000). *Secularization in Western Europe, 1848-1914*. Basingstoke: Macmillan.

Melly, George. (1978) (1977). *Rum, Bum and Concertina*. London: Futura.

Merry Jules. (1994). "A Short History of Narcotic Addition and the Case for Regulation and Legalisation." Commentary in Richard Stevenson, *Winning the War on Drugs: To Legalise or Not?* 71-82. London: Institute of Economic Affairs.

Miller, Neil. (1995). *Out of the Past, Gay and Lesbian History from 1869 to the Present*. London: Vintage.

Montgomery, John. (1963). *Toll for the Brave, The Tragedy of Hector Macdonald*. London: Max Parish.

Moore, William. (1974). *The Thin Yellow Line*. London: Leo Cooper.

Morris, Miranda. (1995). *The Pink Triangle. The Gay Law Reform Debate in Tasmania*. Sydney: University of New South Wales Press.

Morris, Terence. (1989). *Crime and Criminal Justice since 1945*. Oxford: Basil Blackwell.

Morton, Desmond. (1972). "The Supreme Penalty: Canadian Deaths by Firing Squad in the First World War." *Queen's Quarterly* [Kingston, Ontario] 29: 345-52.

Mott, Joy. (1978). "A Long Term Follow-Up of Male Non-Therapeutic Opiate Users and Their Criminal Histories." In D. J. West (ed.), *Problems of Drug Abuse in Britain*, 80-94. Cambridge: University of Cambridge Institute of Criminology.

Mudie-Smith, Richard (ed.). (1904). *The Religious Life of London*, London: Hodder and Stoughton.
Munson, J. (1991). *The Nonconformists: In search of a Lost Culture*. London: SPCK.
Murray, David W. (1994). "Poor Suffering Bastards." *Policy Review* 68 (Spring): 9-15.
Nakell, Barry. (1983). "The Cost of the Death Penalty." In Hugo Adam Bedau (ed.), *The Death Penalty in America* (3rd ed.), 241-46. New York: Oxford University Press.
The Nation's Morals: Being the Proceedings of The Public Morals Conference held in London on 14-15 July. (1910). London: Cassell.
Neal, Mark, and Christie Davies. (1998). *The Corporation under Siege*. London: Social Affairs Unit.
Orwell, George. (1968) (1944). "The English People." In Sonia Orwell and Ian Angus (eds.), *The Collected Essays, Journalism and Letters of George Orwell vol iii As I Please-1943-45*, 1-38. London: Secker and Warburg.
Parker, Howard, Judith Aldridge, Fiona Measham. (1998). *Illegal Leisure*. London: Routledge.
Passingham, Bernard. (1970). *The Divorce Reform Act, 1969*. London: Butterworths.
Paton, J. B. (1908). "The Moral Training of Our Youth." In *The Cleansing of a City*, 1-26. London: The National Social Purity Crusade and Greening and Co.
Patrick, Ray, and Tarani Chandola. (2000). "Health." In A. H. Halsey and Josephine Webb (eds.),*Twentieth Century British Social Trends*, 94-127. Basingstoke: Macmillan.
Pearson, Hesketh. (1936). *Labby, the Life and Character of Henry Labouchere*. New York: Harper.
Phadraig, Maire NicGhiolla. (1981). "Alternative Models to Secularisation in Relation to Moral Reasoning." In *Actes 16 ième Conference International de Sociologie des Religions, Lausanne 1981*. Paris: CISR.
Phillips, David. (1977). *Crime and Authority in Victorian England, The Black Country 1835-60*. London: Croom Helm.
Phillips, David P. (1980). "The Deterrent Effect of Capital Punishment, New Evidence on an Old Controversy. *American Journal of Sociology* 86: 139-48.
Phillips, Roderick. (1988). *Putting Asunder, a History of Divorce in Western Society*. Cambridge: Cambridge University Press.
The Phoenix of Sodom or the Vere Street Coterie. (1813). In Trumbach (ed.) 1986 (facsimile).
Pierce, David, Peter N. Grabosky, and Ted Robert Gurr. (1977). "The Dimensions of London Life: 1800 to the 1870s and Crime Conflict and Public Order from the 1870s to the Great Depression." In Ted Robert Gurr, Peter N. Grabosky, and Richard C. Hula (eds.) *The Politics of Crime and Conflict*, 35-213. Beverly Hills: Sage.
Pierce, David, Peter N. Grabosky, and Ted Robert Gurr. (1977). "London the Politics of Crime and Conflict: 1800 to the 1870s" In Ted Robert Gurr, Peter N. Grabosky, and Richard C. Hula (eds.) *The Politics of Crime and Conflict*, Beverly Hills: Sage.
Pike, Luke Owen. (1876). *A History of Crime in England, vol. 2, From the Accession of Henry VII to the Present Time*. London: Smith Elder.
Potter, Harry. (1993). *Hanging in Judgement: Religion and the Death Penalty in England*. London: SCM.
Pratt, Michael. (1980). *Mugging as a Social Problem*. London: Routledge and Kegan Paul.
Pringle, John Douglas. (1958). *Australian Accent*. London: Chatto and Windus.
Pugsley, Christopher. (1990). *On the Fringe of Hell, New Zealanders and Military Discipline in the First World War*. London: Hodder and Stoughton.
Putkowski, Julian, and Julian Sykes. (1992). *Shot at Dawn*, London: Leo Cooper.
Putting Asunder, A Divorce Law for Contemporary Society: A Report of a Group Appointed by the Archbishop of Canterbury in January, 1964. (1966). London: SPCK.

Quinton, Richard Frith. (1910). *Crime and Criminals, 1876-1910.* London: Longmans Green.

Quirke, Thomas. (1990). "Coming Out and Catching Up." *Sunday Correspondent*, 25 March, 1.

Radzinowicz, Sir Leon, and Joan King. (1979). *The Growth of Crime.* Harmondsworth: Penguin.

Rahaim., Salomon. (1969). *Que hay por fin sobre el Control Natal?* Oaxaca, Mexico: Sociedad E.V.C.

Ramsay, Dean Edward Bannerman. (1874). *Reminiscences of Scottish Life and Character.* Edinburgh: Gall and Inglis.

Richards, Jeffrey. (1991). *Sex Dissidence and Damnation, Minority Groups in the Middle Ages.* London: Routledge.

Richards, Peter G. (1970). *Parliament and Conscience.* London: Allen and Unwin.

Robertson, Alex, and Raymond Cochrane. (1976). "Deviance and Cultural Change." *International Journal of Social Psychiatry* 22: 1-6.

Rock, Paul. (1998). *After Homicide.* Oxford: Clarendon.

Rose, Lionel. (1986). *The Massacre of the Innocents, Infanticide in Britain 1800-1939.* London: Routledge and Kegan Paul.

Rowell. G. (1974). *Hell and the Victorians.* Oxford: Clarendon.

Rummel, R. J. (1990). *Lethal Politics, Soviet Genocide and Mass Murder since 1917.* New Brunswick, NJ: Transaction Publishers.

Rynne, Andrew. (1982). *Abortion, the Irish Question.* Dublin: Ward River.

Sarnecki, Jerzy. (1985). "Some Mechanisms in the Growth of Crime in Sweden." *Archiwum Kryminolgii* TXXII: 199-210.

Schur, Edwin M. (1963). *Narcotic Addiction in Britain and America.* London: Tavistock.

Segalman, Ralph. (1986). *The Swiss Way of Welfare Lessons for the Western World:* New York: Praeger.

Segalman, Ralph, and David Marsland. (1989). *Cradle to Grave.* Basingstoke: Macmillan.

Sheridan, Alan. (1998), *André Gide: A Life in the Present.* London: Hamish Hamilton.

Shtromas, Alexander. (1981). *Political Change and Social Development: The Case of the Soviet Union.* Frankfurt-am-Main: Peter Lang.

Simms, Madelaine, and Hindell, Keith. (1971). *Abortion Law Reformed.* London: Peter Owen.

Simpson, H. B. (1898). Introduction to the "Criminal Statistics for the Year 1896." In *Statistics Relating to Criminal Proceedings, Police, Coroners, Prisons, Reformatory and Industrial Schools and Criminal Lunatics for the Year 1896, Part I—Criminal Statistics.* London: H.M.S.O.

Sindall, Rob. (1990). *Street Violence in the Nineteenth Century: Media Panic or Real Danger.* Leicester: Leicester University Press.

Skidelsky, Robert. (1983). *John Maynard Keynes: A Biography, vol. 1: Hopes Betrayed 1883-1920.* London: Macmillan.

Smith, Arthur. (1959). *Lord Goddard, My Years with the Chief Justice.* London: Weidenfeld and Nicolson.

Smith, E. LaGard. (1993). *Sodom's Second Coming.* Eugene, OR: Harvest House.

Smith, J. C. and Brian Hogan. (1978). *Criminal Law* (4th ed.). London: Butterworths.

_____. (1986). *Criminal Law: Cases and Materials* (3rd ed.). London: Butterworths.

Smith, Michael. (2002). "Sacking All Gay Sailors Would Have Scuppered the Fleet.' *The Daily Telegraph*, 31 October.

Smith, Peter. (1983). "Inflation Before and After Keynes." *The Journal of Economic Affairs* 3, 3: 219.

Smithies, Edward. (1982). *Crime in Wartime, A Social History of Crime in World War II.* London: George Allen and Unwin.

"South Wales Colliers." (1875). *All the Year Round*, xiv (New Series) (17 April): 52-58.
Sowell, Thomas. (1981). *Ethnic America, a History*. New York: Basic.
Spear H. B. (1969). "The Growth of Heroin Addiction in the United Kingdom." *British Journal of Addiction* 64: 246-258.
Spencer, Herbert. (1884). *The Man versus the State*. London: Williams Norgate.
Springhall, John, with Brian Fraser and Michael E. Hoare. (1983). *Sure and Steadfast, a History of the Boy's Brigade 1883-1983*. London: Harper Collins.
Stephen, James Fitzjames. (1885). "Variations in the Punishment of Crime." *The Nineteenth Century* xvii: 755-776.
Stevenson, Richard. (1994). *Winning the War on Drugs: To Legalise or Not?* London: Institute of Economic Affairs.
Stimson G. V., and A. C. Ogborne. (1970). "A Survey of Addicts Prescribed Heroin at London Clinics. *The Lancet* (30 May): 13-22.
Stone, Lawrence. (1990). *Road to Divorce, England 1530-1887*. Oxford: Oxford University Press.
"Street Terrors." (1863). *All the Year Round*, viii (14 February): 533-38.
Stychin, Carl, and Didi Herman (eds.). (2000). *Sexuality in the Legal Arena*. London: Athlone.
Sweeting H., P. West, and M. Richards. (2000). "Teenage Family Life, Lifestyles and Lifechances: Associations with Family Structure, Conflict with Parents, and Joint Family Activity." *International Journal of Law, Policy and the Family* 14: 15-46.
Television and Religion Report by Social Surveys Ltd. (1964). London: University of London Press.
Thurtle, Ernest. (n.d.). *Shootings at Dawn, The Army Death Penalty at Work*. London: Victoria House Printing.
_____. (1920). *Military Discipline and Democracy*. London: C. W. Daniel.
_____. (1945). *Time's Winged Chariot*. London: Chaterson.
The Times' House of Commons. (1929). London: *The Times*.
Toscano, Roberto. (1999). "The United Nations and the Abolition of the Death Penalty." In *The Death Penalty Abolition in Europe*. Strasbourg, Alsace: Council of Europe.
Treasure, Catherine. (1992). "The Enemies in the Closet." *The Guardian*, 10 November.
Troup, C. E. (1900). Introduction to the *Criminal Statistics, Judicial Statistics for England and Wales 1898, Part One Criminal Statistics*, London: H.M.S.O.
Trumbach, Randolph. (1991). "The Birth of the Queen, Sodomy and the Emergency of Gender Equality in Modern Culture 1660-1750." In Martin Bauml Duberman, Martha Vicinus, and George Chauncey, Jr. (eds.), *Hidden from History: Reclaiming the Gay and Lesbian Past*. Harmondsworth: Penguin.
_____ (ed.). (1986). *Sodomy Trials Seven Documents* (facsimilies). New York: Garland.
Tuttle, Elizabeth Orman. (1961). *The Crusade against Capital Punishment in Great Britain*. London: Stevens.
Van der Elst, Violet. (1937). *On the Gallows*. London: Doge.
Vanggaard, Thorkil. (1972). *Phallos*. New York: International Universities Press.
Vere Street Coterie, or The Phoenix of Sodom, London, 1813. (Facsimile in Trumbach [ed.], 1986).
Wadsworth, J., I. Burnell, B. Taylor, and N. Butler. (1985). The Influence of Family Type on Children's Behaviour and Development at Five Years." *Journal of Child Psychology, and Psychiatry* 26:245-54.
Warburton David M. (ed.). (1990). *Addiction Controversies*. Chur Switzerland: Harwood Academic Publishers.
_____. (1990). "Heroin, Cocaine and Now Nicotine." In David M. Warburton (ed.), *Addiction Controversies*, 21-35. Chur Switzerland: Harwood Academic Publishers.
_____. (ed.). (1994). *Pleasure: The Politics and the Reality*. Chichester: John Wiley.

_____. (ed.). (1996). *Pleasure and Quality of Life*. Chichester: John Wiley.

Weeks, Jeffrey. (2000). *Making Sexual History*. Cambridge: Polity.

Wellings Kaye, Julia Field, Anne M. Johnson, and Jane Wadsworth, with Sally Bradshaw. (1994). *Sexual Behaviour in Britain, the National Survey of Sexual Attitudes and Lifestyles*. Harmondsworth: Penguin.

Werner, Barry. (1982). "Recent Trends in Illegitimate Births and Extra-Marital Conceptions." *Population Trends* 30 (Winter): 9-12.

West, D. J. (1960). *Homosexuality*. Harmondsworth: Penguin.

West, D. J. (1977). *Homosexuality Re-examined*. London: Duckworth.

West D. J. (ed.). (1978). *Problems of Drug Abuse in Britain*. Cambridge: University of Cambridge Institute of Criminology.

Whelan, R. (1994). *Broken Homes and Battered Children*. Oxford: Family Education Trust.

Wiener, Martin J. (1990). *Reconstructing the Criminal, Culture, Law and Policy in England 1830-1914*. Cambridge: Cambridge University Press.

Wilkinson, A. (1978). *The Church of England and the First World War*. London: SPCK.

Williams, Glanville Llewelyn. (1958). *The Sanctity of Life and the Criminal Law*. London: Faber and Faber.

Williams, Kenneth (ed. Russell Davies). (1993). *The Kenneth Williams Diaries*. London: Harper Collins.

Wilson, Bryan R. (1969). *Religion in Secular Society*. Harmondsworth: Penguin.

_____. (1981). "Morality and the Modern Social System." In *Religious Values and Daily Life, Acts 16, International Conference for the Sociology of Religion*. Paris: C.I.S.R.

_____. (1982). *Religion in Sociological Perspective*. Oxford: Oxford University Press.

_____. (1985). "Morality in the Evolution of the Modern Social System." *British Journal of Sociology* 36 (September): 315-332.

Wilson, George B. (1940). *Alcohol and the Nation*. London: Nicholson and Watson.

Wilson, James Q., and Richard J. Herrnstein. (1985). *Crime and Human Nature*. New York: Simon and Schuster.

Yates, A. J. (1990). "The Natural History of Heroin Addiction." In David M. Warburton (ed.), *Addiction Controversies*, 8-20. Chur Switzerland: Harwood Academic Publishers.

Yunker, J. A. (1976). "Is the Death Penalty a Deterrent to Homicide? Some Time Series Evidence." *Journal of Behavioural Economics* 5: 45-81.

Zeisel, Hans. (1983). "The Deterrent Effect of the Death Penalty: Facts and Faith." In Hugo Adam Bedau (ed.), *The Death Penalty in America* (3rd ed.), 117-137. New York: Oxford University Press.

British Official Publications

Hansard

Hansard: Official Reports of Parliamentary Debates. All references to *Hansard* except where otherwise specified refer to Hansard 5th series.

Criminal Statistics

Criminal Statistics England and Wales

Statistics Relating to Criminal Proceedings, Police, Coroners, Prisons, Reformatory and Industrial Schools and Criminal Lunatics for the year 1894, Part I Criminal Statistics. (1896). London: H.M.S.O.

Statistics Relating to Criminal Proceedings, Police, Coroners, Prisons, Reformatory and Industrial Schools and Criminal Lunatics for the year 1895, Part I Criminal Statistics. (1897). London: H.M.S.O.

Statatistics Relating to Criminal Proceedings, Police, Coroners, Prisons, Reformatory and Industrial Schools and Criminal Lunatics for the year 1898, Part I Criminal Statistics. (1900). London: H.M.S.O.

Criminal Statistics England and Wale, 1929. (1931). London: H.M.S.O.

Criminal Statistics England and Wales, 1934. (1936). London: H.M.S.O.

Criminal Statistics England and Wales, 1935. (1937). London: H.M.S.O.

Criminal Statistics England and Wales, 1999. (2000). London: H.M.S.O.

Criminal Statistics England and Wales. Crime in England and Wales 2001/2002 Supplementary Report. (2003). London: H.M.S.O.

Criminal Statistics Scotland

Criminal Statistics, Statistics Relating to Police Apprehensions, Criminal Proceedings and Reformatory and Industrial Schools for the year 1929. (1930). Edinburgh: H.M.S.O.

Criminal Statistics, Statistics Relating to Police Apprehensions, Criminal Proceedings and Reformatory and Industrial Schools for the year 1930. (1931). Edinburgh: H.M.S.O.

Criminal Statistics, Statistics Relating to Police Apprehensions, Criminal Proceedings and Reformatory and Industrial Schools for the year 1932. (1933). Edinburgh: H.M.S.O.

Criminal Statistics, Statistics Relating to Police Apprehensions, Criminal Proceedings and Reformatory and Industrial Schools for the year 1933. (1934). Edinburgh: H.M.S.O.

Reports

Law Commission. (1966). *The Reform of the Grounds of Divorce: The Field of Choice.* Cmnd. 3123 London: H.M.S.O.

Law Commission. (1990). *Family Law: The Ground for Divorce*, Law Commission, No. 192, HC 636 1989-90. London: H.M.S.O.

Law Commission. (1995). *Consent in the Criminal Law, a consultation paper.* Consultation paper 139. London: H.M.S.O.

Report of the Committee Constituted by the Army Council to Enquire into the Law and Rules of Procedure Regulating Military Courts Martial. (1919). Cmnd 428. London: H.M.S.O.

Report of the Committee on Homosexual Offence and Prostitution. (1957). (Chairman, Sir John Wolfenden), Cmnd. 247. London: H.M.S.O.

Report of the Inter-Departmental Committee on Abortion. (1939) (Chairman W. N. Birkett) Ministry of Health/Home Office. London: H.M.S.O.

Report of the Inter-Departmental Committee on Proposed Disciplinary Amendments of the Army and Air Force Acts. (1925). Cmnd. 2376 . London: H.M.S.O.

Report of the Royal Commission on Capital Punishment 1945-1953. (1953). Cmnd 8932. London: H.M.S.O.

Report of the Royal Commission on Divorce and Matrimonial Causes. (1912). Cmnd 6478. London: H.M.S.O.

Report from the Select Committee on Capital Punishment. (1931). London: H.M.S.O.

Report of the War Office Committee of Enquiry into Shell-Shock. (1922). Cmnd. 1734. London: H.M.S.O.
Royal Commission on Marriage and Divorce: Report, 1951-1955. (1956). Cmnd 9678. London: H.M.S.O.
Special Report from the Select Committee on the Armed Forces Bill (1957). [HC 143]. Cmnd 247. London: H.M.S.O.
Statistics of the Military Effort of the British Empire During the Great War 1914-20. (1922). London: War Office, H.M.S.O.

Unpublished Materials

Fuller, M. R. "Parliamentary Voting Patterns on Non-Party Issues." M. Phil thesis, University of Southampton, 1970.
Moyser, George. "Voting Patterns on 'Moral' Issues in the British House of Commons 1964-69. Conference Paper.
The papers of Geoffrey Fisher, Archbishop of Canterbury, Lambeth Palace Library.
Report of the Homosexuality Policy Assessment Team. (1996). London: Ministry of Defence. February.
Transcript of the shorthand notes of Newgate Ltd , Official Court Reporters to the Central Criminal Court. Sentencing remarks of his Honour Judge Rant Q.C. in the case of *R. v Ian Wilkinson, Peter John Grindley, Colin Laskey, Anthony Joseph Brown et al.*, Wednesday, 19 December 1990.

Law Cases

American Supreme Court Cases

Doe v Bolton (1973) 410 US 179; 93 S Ct 739; 35 L.Ed 2d 201.
Furman v Georgia (1972) 408 US 238; 92 S Ct 2726; 33 L.Ed 2d 346.
Gregg v Georgia (1976) 428 US 153; 96 S Ct 3235; 50 L.Ed 2d 30.
Griswold v Connecticut (1965) 381 US 479; 85 S Ct 1678; 14 L.Ed 2d 510.
Roe v Wade (1973) 410 US 113; 93 S Ct 705; 35 L.Ed 2d 147.

Cases England and Wales

A.C = Law Reports, Appeal Court
All E.R = All England Law Reports
Cr. App. R = Criminal Appeal Reports
K.B. = Law Reports King's Bench Division
Q.B. = Law Reports Queen's Bench Division
W.L.R = Weekly Law Reports

Ash v Ash [1972] 2 WLR 347.
R. v. Bourne [1938] 1KB, 687 [1938] 3 A E.R. 615.
Brown (Anthony) Lucas, Jaggard, Laskey, Carter, and Cadman v R [1992] 1QB 491 [1992] 2WLR 441, [1992] 2All ER 552 [1992] 94 Cr App R.
Brown (Anthony), Lucas, Jaggard, Laskey, Carter v R [1994] 1AC 212.
Livingstone-Stallard v Livingstone-Stallard [1974] 3 WLR 302.
R. v Ministry of Defence ex parte Smith, R. v Same ex parte Grady, R. v Admiralty Board of the Defence Council ex parte Beckett, R. v Same ex parte Lustig-Prean [1996] Q.B. 517.
Williams v Williams [1964] A.C. 698.

Irish Cases

I.R. = Irish Reports
The Attorney General v X and others. IR [1992]: 1.

European Court of Human Rights Cases

E.H.R.R = European Human Rights Reports
Dudgeon v United Kingdom (1982) 4 E.H.R.R. 149.
Laskey, Jaggard and Brown v United Kingdom (1997) 24 E.H.R.R. 139.
Lustig-Prean and Beckett v United Kingdom (2000) 29 E.H.R.R. 548.
Modinos v Cyprus (1993) 16 E.H.R.R. 485.
Norris v Ireland (1991) 13 E.H.R.R. 186.
Smith and Grady v United Kingdom (2000) 29 E.H.R.R. 493.
Open Door Counselling and Dublin Well Woman v Ireland (1993)14 E.H.R.R. 244.

Index